STORIES FROM
FIRST-YEAR COMPOSITION

PEDAGOGIES THAT FOSTER STUDENT
AGENCY AND WRITING IDENTITY

T0290703

Practices & Possibilities

Series Editors: Nick Carbone, Mike Palmquist, Aimee McClure, and Aleashia Walton

Series Associate Editor: Karen-Elizabeth Moroski

The Practices & Possibilities Series addresses the full range of practices within the field of Writing Studies, including teaching, learning, research, and theory. From Joseph Williams' reflections on problems to Richard E. Young's taxonomy of "small genres" to Adam Mackie's considerations of technology, the books in this series explore issues and ideas of interest to writers, teachers, researchers, and theorists who share an interest in improving existing practices and exploring new possibilities. The series includes both original and republished books. Works in the series are organized topically.

The WAC Clearinghouse, Colorado State University Open Press, and University Press of Colorado are collaborating so that these books will be widely available through free digital distribution and low-cost print editions. The publishers and the series editors are committed to the principle that knowledge should freely circulate. We see the opportunities that new technologies have for further democratizing knowledge. And we see that to share the power of writing is to share the means for all to articulate their needs, interest, and learning into the great experiment of literacy.

Other Books in the Series

Patricia Freitag Ericsson, *Sexual Harassment and Cultural Change in Writing Studies* (2020)

Ryan J. Dippre, Talk, Tools, and Texts: A Logic-in-Use for Studying Lifespan Literate Action Development (2019)

Jessie Borgman and Casey McArdle, *Personal, Accessible, Responsive, Strategic: Resources and Strategies for Online Writing Instructors* (2019)

Cheryl Geisler & Jason Swarts, Coding *Streams of Language: Techniques for the Systematic Coding of Text, Talk, and Other Verbal Data* (2019)

Ellen C. Carillo, *A Guide to Mindful Reading* (2017)

Lillian Craton, Renée Love & Sean Barnette (Eds.), *Writing Pathways to Student Success* (2017)

Charles Bazerman, *Involved: Writing for College, Writing for Your Self* (2015)

Adam Mackie, *New Literacies Dictionary: Primer for the Twenty-first Century Learner* (2011)

Patricia A. Dunn, *Learning Re-abled: The Learning Disability Controversy and Composition Studies* (2011)

STORIES FROM
FIRST-YEAR COMPOSITION

PEDAGOGIES THAT FOSTER STUDENT
AGENCY AND WRITING IDENTITY

Edited by Jo-Anne Kerr and Ann N. Amicucci

The WAC Clearinghouse
wac.colostate.edu
Fort Collins, Colorado

University Press of Colorado
upcolorado.com
Louisville, Colorado

The WAC Clearinghouse, Fort Collins, Colorado 80523

University Press of Colorado, Louisville, Colorado 80027

ISBN 978-1-64215-030-8 (PDF) | 978-1-64215-031-5 (ePub) | 978-1-60732-980-0 (pbk.)

DOI 10.37514/PRA-B.2020.0308

Printed in the United States of America

Library of Congress Cataloging-in-Publication Data

Names: Kerr, Jo-Anne, editor. | Amicucci, Ann N., editor.
Title: Stories from first-year composition : pedagogies that foster student agency and writing
    identity / edited by Jo-Anne Kerr and Ann N. Amicucci.
Description: Fort Collins, Colorado : The WAC Clearinghouse ; Louisville, Colorado : University
    Press of Colorado, [2020] | Series: Practices & possibilities | Includes bibliographical
    references.
Identifiers: LCCN 2020017328 (print) | LCCN 2020017329 (ebook) | ISBN 9781607329800
    (paperback) | ISBN 9781642150308 (pdf) | ISBN 9781642150315 (epub)
Subjects: LCSH: English language—Composition and exercises—Study and teaching (Higher)—
    United States. | Education—Study and teaching (Higher)—United States. | Report writing—
    Study and teaching (Higher)—United States. | Critical pedagogy—United States.
Classification: LCC PE1405.U6 S76 2020 (print) | LCC PE1405.U6 (ebook) | DDC 428.0071—dc23
LC record available at https://lccn.loc.gov/2020017328
LC ebook record available at https://lccn.loc.gov/2020017329

Copyeditor: Meg Vezzu
Designer: Mike Palmquist
Cover Image: Glenn J. Asakawa. Copyright © University of Colorado Colorado Springs. Used with permission.
Series Editors: Nick Carbone, Mike Palmquist, Aimee McClure, and Aleashia Walton
Series Associate Editor: Karen-Elizabeth Moroski

The WAC Clearinghouse supports teachers of writing across the disciplines. Hosted by Colorado State University, and supported by the Colorado State University Open Press, it brings together scholarly journals and book series as well as resources for teachers who use writing in their courses. This book is available in digital formats for free download at wac.colostate.edu.

Founded in 1965, the University Press of Colorado is a nonprofit cooperative publishing enterprise supported, in part, by Adams State University, Colorado State University, Fort Lewis College, Metropolitan State University of Denver, University of Colorado, University of Northern Colorado, University of Wyoming, Utah State University, and Western Colorado University. For more information, visit upcolorado.com.

Contents

Acknowledgments

We thank each author who has contributed their time, research, and teaching experience to this collection. We are deeply appreciative of our authors' enthusiasm in giving us glimpses into their first-year composition classrooms through their chapters and for their patience and support in the process of this collection's development. We are also grateful to those authors who, in addition to contributing chapters to the collection, joined in the creation of the collection's multimedia content so that readers might interact with authors' ideas in multiple forms.

We are ever grateful to Mike Palmquist, Founding Editor and Publisher, and Nick Carbone, Practices & Possibilities Series Editor, at the WAC Clearinghouse, for their excitement about this project and their innovative suggestions that led to several revisions to the collection, including the creation of its multimedia components. We are thankful, too, for the guidance and support of the anonymous reviewers who read and responded to this collection.

We owe special thanks to Helen Collins Sitler, whose idea for an NCTE panel in 2013 sparked the conversation that led to this collection, to Susan Welsh, who participated on that panel and encouraged our work, and to all the FYC teachers who attended that NCTE panel and showed us through their questions and ideas that a collection that focused on student agency and identity in FYC would be welcomed.

Jo-Anne extends gratitude to her supportive and ever-patient husband, Larry, and to her sister, Jackie, for her interest and encouragement. Ann is grateful to her parents, Edward and Rita, for their tireless support and unconditional love.

Foreword

James Paul Gee

Arizona State University

Teaching "Freshman Writing" has always been a vexed task.

Should we teach the students to write in the disciplines they intend to major in? It's hard. The students do not necessarily know what they will major in. We cannot know the ways with words of all disciplines. And, too, it may well be that today's students should not be majoring in disciplines but rather in themes or challenges.

Should we teach the students to find their "voice" (really "voices") in writing? It's hard. "Voices" are social identities formed through belonging and membership in groups outside Freshman Writing courses and not necessarily committed to the course's norms or even the university's. And such groups do not make judgments based on our grades.

Should we teach a myriad of modes of expression ("genres")? It's hard. There are way too many of them and each one requires, again, active and committed participation in a group outside the Freshman Writing class if it is to have real meaning.

Should we teach critique? It's hard. You cannot criticize what you do not know, and our students know different things and little of it deeply enough yet to engage in authentic critique. While it is true that critique often precedes understanding in some types of academic literature, the other way round is better.

Should we teach "critical thinking"? It's hard. Critical thinking requires mastery of a great deal of "content" in a domain and meta-skills, both of which serve as tools for critical thinking. Our classes cannot teach enough content—let alone enough for each student's interests—to teach critical thinking beyond some generic version.

Should we teach the basics? It's hard. If a student comes to college not knowing the basics of writing, that student has problems that go beyond Freshman Writing. Furthermore, the basics (just like cooking techniques) are pretty worthless when not embedded in the making of some authentic dish, and there are a great many types of dishes connected to a great many "cuisines" owned and operated by specific groups of people.

Should we teach the essay? Well, it is a dead form today, largely used for sorting people to assign rewards that have little actually to do with essays. Furthermore, what we teach as "essays" today has little to do with either Montaigne or Bacon, the inventors of the two major essay forms.

Of course, the problem here is just what Linda Adler-Kassner said it was in her 2017 Conference on College Composition and Communication Chair's

DOI: https://doi.org/10.37514/PRA-B.2020.0308.1.2

Address: "Because Writing is Never Just Writing." For me, writing is always and everywhere part of (Big "D") "Discourses;" that is, it is integral to participation in social groups with their own evolved histories, norms, ways with words, and practices, almost all of them not beholden to—or even very respectful of—Freshman Writing courses.

So, what is one to do? Well, the authors you are about to meet in Jo-Anne Kerr and Ann Amicucci's *Stories from First-Year Composition: FYC Pedagogies that Foster Student Agency and Writing Identity* do a wonderful job helping us think through these vexed, hard, but fascinating problems. You and I as readers of this book will have to come up with our own answers, and I am sure there are a number of good ones, not just one. As we do so, we will confront the nature of writing, and maybe even universities, anew.

Writing is the "Maker Movement" part of literacy. Writing is to literacy what game design is to gaming. We celebrate making today but have done little to solve the problem of one of our oldest and most important forms of making: writing. Universal literacy as reading, not writing, started in the West (in Sweden) as a form of enforcing religious beliefs. And, indeed, reading has often been supervised by religions, states, and institutions who want us to read (understand) in certain ways. In this context, writing has been deeply suspect, since in gaining the power to make, there is the deep risk people will break though to new understandings, forming and joining new groups with the power to question.

Today, young people are writing—in interest-driven groups ("affinity spaces") on the internet—more than ever before. Writing as making is spreading and coming into its own. In the act, writing, like all powerful technologies, is being used for both evil and good. We can say this at the very least, though: It is the job of the Freshman Writing teacher to lead young people to the good. Yes, that requires making choices and taking risks and responsibility. It's a dangerous job. Not for the timid.

Work Cited

Adler-Kassner, Linda. "2017 CCCC Chair's Address: Because Writing is Never Just Writing." *College Composition and Communication*, vol. 69, no. 2, 2017, pp. 317–40.

STORIES FROM
FIRST-YEAR COMPOSITION

PEDAGOGIES THAT FOSTER STUDENT
AGENCY AND WRITING IDENTITY

Introduction

Jo-Anne Kerr

INDIANA UNIVERSITY OF PENNSYLVANIA

Ann N. Amicucci

UNIVERSITY OF COLORADO COLORADO SPRINGS

The collection you are about to read tells a story of hope, its chapters echoing Doug Downs, who highlights in "What is First-Year Composition?" the vast possibilities that first-year composition (FYC) contains. He writes, "First-year composition can and should be *a space, a moment, and an experience*—in which students might reconsider writing apart from previous schooling and work, within the context of inquiry-based higher education" (50). Downs is hopeful for such possibilities despite a discouraging "public charter" that expects FYC to cure students of all grammatical wrongs (54). In charting the ways that composition studies has resisted FYC's positioning as a "skills" workshop, Downs celebrates the best of what FYC can and does accomplish, particularly because we focus on who students are. He writes, "We are people who take students seriously and use instruction to keep students in school rather than writing them off" and argues that "[u]sing the course to expose alternative conceptions of writing that better account for students' lived experiences is a terrifically productive use of the course" (58, 60). It is this focus on students that gives us hope for the future of FYC.

Not only are today's successful FYC pedagogies not skills-based, they are not solely writing-based either, not in the way that "writing" is conceived of in the public eye. This is because, as Linda Adler-Kassner reminds us, writing is never "just writing." She argues, "This lament, this story that students 'can't write,' [heard from faculty in other disciplines] works from the premise that writing is 'just writing.' It's a thing that writers bang out. It is constituted of words that are clear, that mean the same thing to everyone, that are easily accessible and need only to be plugged into forms" (317). We know that writing is much broader: it is the world-building of literacy acquisition (Bazerman 571–72), it is critical thinking (Pough 308-09), and it is about people, the very people in our classrooms (Johnson 527). Kristine Johnson argues that *The Framework for Success in Post-Secondary Writing*, perhaps the single most important document guiding current FYC pedagogical practice, is, indeed, about teaching people. She writes:

> [T]he Framework asks writing teachers to address the person behind writing products and processes—to consider intellectual agency and the ethical aims of writing instruction in an increasingly technocratic educational landscape. Teaching habits of mind asks who writers should become and why they should

become that way, which in turn revives difficult, enduring questions associated with the rhetorical tradition and the liberal arts: can virtue be taught, must a good speaker also be a good man, should writing instruction presume to cultivate taste and civic virtue, and should writing instruction be political? (527)

Johnson's argument embodies Adler-Kassner's point: writing is never just writing. Today's FYC pedagogies, grounded in the *Framework* and the eight habits of mind it advocates practicing, actively resist a public charter of skills-based education and actively resist the lure of prior learning assessments that devalue the place of FYC in the academy. In the chapters collected here, readers will find evidence of this resistance: evidence of pedagogies that make clear the value of FYC to students' development as writers.

However, why is it necessary to resist? Against what pressures should (and must) teachers of FYC push?

As noted above, a "public charter" exists, a charter that presupposes that FYC exists to guide first-year students to the ability to write well—that is, "correctly," on the assumption that writing is a skill, monolithic and easily gained through skill and drill. And this public charter exerts great control over FYC pedagogies, resulting in what Sharon Crowley calls a submission to others' definitions of the profession: "Throughout our history we have acquiesced to definitions of our profession, and our disciplinary goals, given us by others. . . . I wonder why we think that our professional interests are best served by continuing to speak discourses that are imposed upon us, hierarchical and exclusive as they are" (237). This public charter also plays out in policy. At one of our institutions, state mandates have required us to award credit for the institution's first required composition course when a student earns a score of 3 on the AP Language and Composition or AP Literature and Composition exam and credit for both of the institution's required composition courses when a student passes the CLEP College Composition exam. Despite state-wide resistance from writing faculty, such policies persist.

Such state mandates are only one pressure point for first-year composition today. The Conference on College Composition and Communication (CCCC), the world's largest professional organization for researching and teaching composition, hosts an annual conference, where writing teachers gather to discuss theory, pedagogy, and challenges facing the profession, among other things. At recent conferences, Chairs' Addresses have lamented additional challenges to the existence of FYC: government pressures to gauge student success through standardized tests (Glenn 421), the award of dual credit in high school (Carter 384; Valentino 371), pushes to award credit through prior learning assessment and to remove writing requirements in college (Anson 333–34; Carter 386), and encouragement to use predictive analytics uncritically in the name of student success (Adler-Kassner 326–28). Some FYC teachers may hear the annual CCCC Chair's Address in person at the conference, but many more read excerpts from it on

Twitter, watch a video of the address on YouTube, or read the address when it is published each year in the journal *College Composition and Communication*. The annual Chair's Address serves as a "state of the profession" update that guides FYC faculty to attend to the most critical aspects of our work.

In Chris Anson's CCCC Chair's Address in 2013, a fictional art history professor comes to terms with the decline of higher education, realizing he can no longer ignore the many pressures facing his profession:

> He had little idea that so many conditions inside and outside of higher education were asking for attention. Oh, it was always playing like a kind of annoying Muzak in the background—it's not as if he shut it out. But his campus preoccupations now seem so local . . . He feels strained and irritable. The Muzak has reached a full blare. And the loudest note, for him, is the zeal to speed up education—to get this odious college thing done, finished, over . . . As if learning should be a race for just enough credentials to join throngs of pedestrian, information-programmed bureaucrats, without the habits of mind to reflect on their material conditions and the political forces behind them, or to see beyond the horizon of a flat world. (333–34)

This fictional professor's realization encapsulates what so many of us in composition studies face today. We cannot ignore nation-wide erosion of the value of a well-paced two- or four-year college degree. We cannot ignore the reality that, as Joyce Locke Carter writes, "Our students are being taken away from us" (386) by efforts to award credit for FYC in so many ways other than taking a composition course in college.

Yet despite the "public charter" that devalues writing education and despite the fact that the portion of students taking FYC on a college campus continues to decline, we are filled with hope for our FYC classrooms. We hear in our students' reflective writing the desire to embrace the power that writing affords. We hear from teachers stories of how FYC courses have opened students' eyes—not only as writers but as critical thinkers. And we hear in the same CCCC Chairs' Addresses that sound so many warning calls about the current state of FYC a resounding reminder of who our students are and why it is to their benefit to be in our classrooms. When Marilyn Valentino describes the increasing numbers of "first-generation freshmen, who had no intention of going to college (or even finishing high school), [who] appear at our doors" (366), when Howard Tinberg calls for us to pay attention to all students' stories, "especially the novices, whose stories we need to hear" (339), and when Malea Powell describes the colonialist history of education and the imperative for composition studies to work against the ways our students' "bodies are marked and mobilized in dominant culture" and the ways "their language is represented in dominant culture" (411), we hear the opportunity to do important work with student writers, to demonstrate to the students who are in our classrooms the value of becoming a rhetorically sensitive listener, reader, writer.

The evidence of resistance to FYC's public charter and argument for the value of FYC we offer results, in part, from a focus in each chapter on FYC students' stories—from reflections, student writing, and interviews—shared by FYC instructors and from depictions of FYC classes and pedagogies. And while the pictures of FYC classrooms that emerge do demonstrate the value of FYC, value that extends well beyond the public charter to which Downs alludes, at the same time they offer a window into FYC that allows for a reconceptualization of the course that highlights, as stated above, the best of what FYC can and does accomplish.

In the following section, we first refer to the use of voices (students', teacher-scholars', and co-editors') to present a story of FYC that demonstrates what the chapters taken as a whole tell us about the service that this course offers to students. We next elucidate this service through a discussion of theoretical underpinnings that provide support for and understanding of the service we identify. Finally, we share an overview of the collection, preceded by a brief explanation of how *Reflect Before Reading* prompts," discussion questions, writing prompts, reading lists, and multimedia components work together to support professional development.

A Story of First-Year Composition

We include multiple voices in this collection—students', teacher-scholars', our own. Students' voices are shared, for we believe in their potential to serve as sources of knowledge about FYC. Also present are the voices of teacher-scholars who have authored chapters in this collection, as they explain their teacher-research, tell us about their FYC courses, and describe their students. Finally, our voices are implicit, as we have helped shape each chapter through our conversations with authors, as well as explicit in our introduction and chapter-connected discussion prompts and multimedia content in which we synthesize, explain, and connect to pertinent theoretical foundations.

Taken together, these voices tell a new story of FYC, one that supplants the older story, begun in the latter part of the eighteenth century, that positions FYC as a service course to meet the needs of students who didn't know how to write "correctly" and was based upon the belief that "good" writing means following the rules. Over the past fifty years, teacher-scholars and researchers, interested in learning how to teach composition more effectively, worked to generate understandings of writing and composition pedagogy, thus creating a new story of FYC, one that includes the recognition of writing as heuristic, context-dependent, and performative. Our collection adds another chapter to this story by including FYC students' voices and sharing a variety of pedagogies that depict what FYC looks like today. As editors, we have interpreted the story that emerges, our transaction with this text leading to the recognition of a new service that FYC offers. Yet we recognize, as is the case with any story, that it can be interpreted differently, with different ideas about service emerging through our readers' transactions with the story the chapters as a whole present. We encourage these different understandings and interpretations in our chapter-connected print and multimedia content where readers are asked to respond to questions, reflect on and revisit their own beliefs about FYC through reflective writing, and consider authors' conversations about the connections among their ideas.

While the collection as a whole shares a picture of FYC today, it also functions as a critical ethnography; what we share not only includes discoveries about students' development as academic writers and about FYC but also opportunities to examine the "common sense" existence of FYC in colleges and universities, an existence resulting, at least in part, from a belief in the capability of first-year composition courses to "serve" students and the academy—FYC's "public charter." But, furthermore, it offers evidence for its continued presence despite what Carter asserts—that it is "not hard to imagine a world where FYC no longer takes place in college" (384)—and the "pressure points" alluded to above.

The subtext of our story suggests that reconceptualizing the "service" of FYC will encourage us to become advocates for its existence in higher education, drawing attention to the course as a means by which first-year students can gain entrée to the academy and a way to promote ways of thinking that will serve these students not only in the academy but beyond.

Next, we identify and explain the service provided by FYC that our chapters, taken together, demonstrate. We do this by first examining the notion of dialogic pedagogy; we then tease out from this concept key ideas related to identity construction, agency, and the notion of "wide-awakeness" to explain how this service is made available to students. Finally, we ask readers to re-see and reconceptualize their identities as teachers of FYC to inform the advocacy for FYC in which they engage.

FYC and Dialogic Pedagogy

The pedagogies demonstrated by the chapters in our collection exhibit what Deborah Britzman calls "dialogic pedagogy" (54). For Britzman, dialogic pedagogy "demands and constructs complex social relationships" and "invites consideration of the social negotiation necessary for the production and interpretation of knowledge" (54).

The "complex social relations" that Britzman sees as integral to dialogic pedagogy are present in FYC environments and result from teachers' attitudes and beliefs, both of which are suggested by their interactions with students. Of particular relevance with regard to this characteristic of dialogic pedagogy is "caring," as defined by Nel Noddings. For Noddings, "caring" is "a way of being in a relation, not a specific set of behaviors" (17). This relation, if it is caring, is a "connection or encounter between two human beings—a carer and a recipient of care, or cared for" (15). The teacher must work to help students develop the capacity to care" (19) so that relational caring can occur, something that requires teachers' attention and persistence. As a result, teachers must be "vigilantly mindful"; they must listen and watch for details that suggest students' "concerns, interests, and inclinations" (Danielewicz 166), something that the pedagogies showcased in our collection clearly attend to. Given FYC instructors' concern for students' subjectivities and accompanying voices, caring of the kind that Noddings believes is essential to effective teaching is present and is promoted and sustained by the activities in which FYC teachers and students engage—peer response groups, student-teacher conferences, and reflection, to name a few. Identifying features of sound composition pedagogy, these activities also allow for knowledge and interpretation to result from engagement in discursive acts.

Dialogic Pedagogy and the Construction of Writerly Identities

The FYC class in which dialogic pedagogy is practiced is a space in which students are given occasions to construct identities as writers, the importance of which has been amply recognized in research and scholarship (see Bartholomae; Brooke; Ivanič; Yancey, *Reflection*). Here, though, we present additional thinking about identity relevant to the story that our collection shares.

In *The Gene: An Intimate History*, Siddhartha Mukherjee asserts the important role that genes have in "specifying our identities as individuals" while also noting that differences are "interposed against cultural and social constructions of the self" (355). While he is examining and elucidating gender differences here, his reminder of the role that genes play is an important one when considering identity formation and construction, as identity is a "unique and rippled landscape" (369), the construction of which is, in part, a result of "how we define, categorize, and understand [ourselves] in a cultural, social, and political sense" (351). Thus, although individuals' identities are genetically determined to a great degree, there remains the process of identity construction and understanding of self that takes place in a cultural, social, and political context, a process that results in an identity that fuses with the genetically determined identity but remains open to continual reconstruction. Germane to this understanding of identity and identity formation is what Britzman states about identity—that it is not "out there, a stability to be reached" and that it should be perceived as "infused with possibilities" (29).

FYC is, of course, a space in which discourse infuses all endeavors; thus, identity construction and discourse are interwoven, the recognition of which provides important implications for course design and teaching and evidence for the new story of FYC that we seek to highlight.

Readers are likely familiar with James Paul Gee's theory of Discourses. Discourse, for Gee, is a kind of "identity kit" ("What" 51) and so is closely linked to the construction of identities. While discourse is both written and spoken language, it is also, as he notes, the ways by which people combine language use with ways of "thinking, acting, interacting, valuing, feeling, believing." It involves, too, the use of symbols, tools, and objects in contextually appropriate ways, a process that also leads to enacting different identities (Gee, *An Introduction* 13). Gee sees individuals as active and engaged participants in discourse who bring particular partialities to any discursive act; simultaneously, though, this engagement in discourse also promotes the development of identity.

In FYC classes, students are invited to become writers—to take on a writerly identity—through engaging in discourse (speaking, writing, acting, using symbols and objects). The space in which this occurs is a kind of transitional space where their previous ways of thinking about writing and about themselves as writers represent another discourse that bumps up against new discourse and discursive acts, resulting in the use of "borderland discourse," discourse in which disparate personal subjectivities are put in contact toward a point of integration. The integration then leads to changes (cognitive, emotional, corporeal) resulting in identity growth, changes, and increased metacognitive awareness (Alsup 205). Janet Alsup's examination of borderland discourse is related to the development of teacher identity; however, her thinking can be applied to the development of a writerly identity. Alsup calls borderland discourse "an expression of an intellectual-emotional leap," and she suggests metaphor creation and visual thinking as ways to engage in borderland discourse (10). In the FYC class, engaging in borderland discourse can include metaphor creation and visual thinking related to writing as well as reflection, discussion, and producing different types and genres of writing. This process, then, permits students to bring their partialities regarding writing and themselves as writers to their work, acknowledging and accommodating these while at the same time connecting them to a nascent writerly identity.

Perceiving the development of writerly identities in FYC courses as a result of, in part, engagement in borderland discourse permits us to understand the value of students' engagement in discursive acts and the importance of fostering students' understanding of and belief in themselves as writers so that they can experience FYC as "a space, a moment, and an experience" and to "reconsider writing apart from previous schooling and work" (Downs 50). This understanding and belief will come from opportunities to engage in discourse that accommodates old and new ways of thinking, thus assisting with the acceptance of a new reality for writing and of oneself as writer while at the same time accommodating students' lived experiences

However, what value does the construction of writerly identities through discursive acts have for student writers? We now turn to the notion of agency to further explore and elucidate the service FYC courses offer to students, service implied by the story our chapters, taken together, tell about FYC, today. We begin with sharing some thinking about agency, what it is, its value, and how it relates to identity. Then we examine the FYC classroom to demonstrate how agency is promoted in this environment.

What is Agency?

Michael Oakeshott identifies agency as "the starting place of doing," a starting place that is a "state of reflective consciousness . . . the agent's own understanding of his situation, what it means to him" (37). An agent is someone who has an understanding of himself in terms of his wants and his powers and an understanding of the components of the world he inhabits. And an agent's action serves as a demonstration of this understanding (32).

Before acting, an agent deliberates, a process that Oakeshott calls "reflection" (42) so that any action that is chosen results from an intelligent response. Agents' actions may be indicative of practice—"a set of considerations, manners, uses, observances, customs, standards, canons, maxims, principles, rules, and offices specifying useful procedures or denoting obligations or duties which relate to human actions and utterances" (55). Practices can be followed but can also be "neglected or violated" (55). There is freedom in agency, then, given that the agent is in an "understandable" situation, with the "doing" an "intelligent engagement" (37).

Jane Danielewicz references Oakeshott's definition of agency, explaining that agency is a quality that allows people to believe they are capable of action (163). They must feel empowered to act but also possess efficacy. For Danielewicz, agency is not dependent upon being granted power or position. What is key is that individuals understand that they can change a situation by some action of their own. Agency is always possible; people are agents when they experience themselves as such—when they see themselves as agents, having "the power of freedom or will to act, to make decisions, to exert pressure, to participate . . . or to be strategically silent" (Danielewicz 163). Thus, identity and agency intersect.

With identity construction and agency closely aligned, it is worthwhile to reconsider FYC in light of this and to note how the environment of FYC has the potential to be conducive to the construction of writerly identities and the development of a capacity for agency through writing and engagement in other discursive acts. We now turn to the FYC classroom and the pedagogies therein to demonstrate how this space, through "a discourse of becoming" (Britzman 42) can foster agency.

Cultivating Agency in FYC

As agency is the "starting place of doing" and the will to act, it follows that students need to believe in their abilities to act and to believe that their actions have meaning and effects (Danielewicz 167). Encouraging these beliefs for students in FYC classes can result when students are given time, ownership, and response, the three fundamental components of effective practice. In providing these essentials for student writers, instructors are abrogating their own roles as dispensers of knowledge to become the guide on the side, guiding students as they construct knowledge and meaning in a community of learners and writers. The learning environment that results when best practice is in place promotes the process by which students become not only writers but also readers, critical thinkers, and responders—a process that occurs in a meaningful context, thus allowing for students to perceive themselves as writers—and writers who possess agency.

What occurs, and what promotes the development of agency, is a process by which students are representing and re-representing themselves in forms made available to them. This recursive representation in which they engage is identity-making through trying out different representations of the self. In FYC, students learn how to represent themselves as writers through engaging in authentic writerly behavior (writing, sharing their writing, responding to the writing of others, reading) as well as by representing their thoughts, ideas, beliefs, etc. in their writing, and thereby representing themselves.

These self-representations in FYC are not discrete processes; rather, they are integrated into the social interactions that occur in FYC. Recursive representations are constant, not something people do only intermittently. However, some contexts do encourage the process more than others—allowing room for more possibilities (Danielewicz 168). And, certainly, the FYC class is one of these contexts. If students see themselves as writers and thus take on identities as writers, agency follows: the will to act because of a belief and understanding that their actions as writers have meaning and effect, something that the FYC environment fosters.

Also necessary, though, as stated above, is a belief in efficacy—students' belief in their capabilities as writers; thus, the development of confidence is requisite, something that is also promoted in the FYC environment where students are treated like writers and given autonomy through choice, ownership, and response. Finally, engagement in FYC activities also allows opportunities for revision of representations through repeated acts of representation. Through engagement in discourse, students continually represent and re-represent themselves and, in doing so, construct and reconstruct identities while developing capacity for agency as writers. Interestingly, this recursive representation is mirrored by the act of writing itself—a recursive action that permits the continual opportunity to revise and thus to represent and re-represent oneself in writing.

Furthermore, through the relational caring described above, the capacity for agency is nurtured, as such a relationship necessitates teachers and students knowing one another—something that can be accomplished, to an appropriate degree and in appropriate ways, through the discursive acts in which students and teachers engage in FYC. While engagement in discourse allows for the construction of identity, it also affects the identity that is constructed and thus students' understanding of self as writer—and what they can do with the craft that they are honing. This, then, becomes the "starting place of doing" for them as writers.

Having examined identity construction and agency within a framework of dialogic pedagogy, we now examine and explain a final feature of this pedagogy to elucidate another service that FYC offers—not only to students but also to teachers of FYC.

Dialogic Pedagogy and Wide-Awakeness

Instructors who engage in dialogic pedagogy in their FYC courses encourage within their students what Maxine Greene refers to as "wide-awakeness"—the capacity of being completely attentive to life and its requirements, a kind of level of awareness or mindfulness (218). In the FYC class, teachers promote students' wide-awakeness by helping them develop the capacity to consider what they are doing and to take responsibility, often accomplished by allowing for choice and ownership of projects and by asking students to reflect on their choices and on the writing they produce. In doing so, students are also being made aware of alternatives (choosing another genre by which to construct and share understandings, for example) and of "possibilities in situations that they confront" (223). Agency and wide-awakeness are thus inextricably linked.

But teachers themselves who are committed to dialogic pedagogy must also practice wide-awakeness. As we note at the beginning of our introduction, teachers of FYC have often "acquiesced to definitions of our profession" (Crowley 237), and Downs asserts that we must "work the tension between what we're expected to teach and what we *ought* to teach" (59). While feelings of powerlessness can understandably result from repeated acquiescence and by the work demanded when we try to resolve the tension that Downs identifies, Greene reminds us that there is an antidote for feelings of disempowerment—individuals must engage in a conscious effort to consider conditions and to question "forces that appear to dominate. . . . Only then can they develop the sense of agency required for living a moral life" (219).

The very agency and wide-awakeness that dialogic pedagogy promotes in students also encourages wide-awakeness in FYC teachers, and thus agency, as it allows them to "break with the mechanical life, to overcome their own submergence in the habitual . . . " (Greene 221). Wide-awakeness keeps teachers of FYC keenly aware of the questions that all teachers face: "What shall we teach them? How can we guide them?" (221). To answer these questions, Greene asserts that teachers must be aware of their own values and commitments to do their jobs; they must gather their resources and, through what John Dewey calls "choice of action," work on the "formation of self" (221).

Greene reminds us that reality can be perceived as a given, impervious to change, and that we have learned to understand it in standard ways (219). FYC teachers may be inclined to perceive their role and FYC in familiar ways, taking for granted its existence and how it can and should be taught. However, wide-awakeness calls for ongoing reflection on and understanding of FYC—its role in the academy and its potential to assist students as they transition to college students who are fully members of the academy. This collection is designed, in part, to foster wide-awakeness as we ask readers to see and re-see FYC as it exists today and to consider what this course offers to students—its real service and, therefore, a reason for its existence. And we believe that the wide-awakeness that will result (or be strengthened) will inform and make more effective the advocacy in which we must engage.

Before we share an overview of the chapters included in our collection, we explain the use of professional development components throughout the collection and how these components serve as introductions as well as invitations to think more carefully and deeply about FYC, our practice, and our roles as FYC instructors.

Professional Development Components

In addition to offering readers a means for reconceptualizing FYC and their roles as FYC instructors to inform their work as advocates for the course, we invite engagement in professional development. These invitations take the form of *Reflect Before Reading* prompts, discussion questions, writing prompts, suggested reading, and multimedia components. *Reflect Before Reading* prompts ask readers to reflect on and articulate ideas related to the pedagogies presented in each chapter, thereby affording opportunity for reexamination of their FYC teaching identities. After the chapter has been read, we ask readers to respond to questions that encourage additional engagement with the chapter; we invite them to complete a reflective writing activity, and we include "For Further Reading," a list of suggested readings that offers additional ideas that augment and relate to the chapter. Multimedia components, accessible to readers through links within the book itself and as stand-alone resources on the book's website, include podcasts and videos that provide readers with supplemental content to enhance the theme of each part of the book and the information shared in selected chapters.

By giving readers the chance to transact with our chapters in this way, we believe that, as with our first-year students who develop writerly identities by engaging in discursive acts, our readers will develop deeper and more enriched understandings of their identities as teachers of FYC, understandings that will allow for greater agency and an accompanying willingness to reject how others define our profession. The reflective questions and writing activities that we offer to our readers may also facilitate engagement in borderland discourse and so a means for readers to integrate disparate personal subjectivities on the way toward an "intellectual emotional leap" (Alsup 16) that will promote wide-awakeness and identity growth.

An Overview of the Collection

The chapters that follow are divided into three parts, focused on complicating current notions of FYC pedagogy, fostering students' development of writing identities, and teaching FYC with a focus on student agency. In Part 1, "Problematizing Today's Notions of First-Year Composition," we hear from three authors who question current FYC practices related to teaching students how academic writing works, supporting LGBTQIA students, and incorporating technology into the classroom. Though each author in this part troubles current FYC practices, each also describes how we can remedy problematic practices in our FYC classrooms.

First, in "Double Standards and Sunshine: Exploring Expectations for Professional and Student Writing in FYC," Doug Downs asks us to acknowledge the double standards rife among the ways academics actually write and the ways we ask FYC students to engage in academic writing practices. Among other double standards, Downs examines the disconnect between professionals' collaborative writing practices and our insistence that students work alone, and the tendency for an academic working in a particular subject area to be familiar with its literature and reuse citations while expecting students to research and read through new subject areas each time they begin a project. Downs draws on his and Elizabeth Wardle's Writing about Writing pedagogy to describe a Writing about Faculty Writing focus in FYC that allows students to learn how academic professionals actually write.

Next, Howa Furrow asks readers to become aware of and question the ways we inadvertently create unsafe spaces in FYC for lesbian, gay, bisexual, transgender, questioning or queer, intersex, and asexual (LGBTQIA) individuals. In "Teacher as Ally: Supporting LGBTQ Student Writers in the Composition Classroom," Furrow addresses an important and sensitive topic in discussing how students navigate FYC and the academy as LGBTQIA individuals. She shares student perspectives on negotiating unsafe spaces on campus, including those that may arise through writing prompts and class discussion in FYC. Furrow describes steps teachers can take to create safe spaces "by disrupting the silence . . . [and] intentionally making ourselves the allies of our LGBTQ students."

Part 1 ends with Ann N. Amicucci's chapter, titled "Three Student Voices on Technology in First-Year Composition." In this chapter, we hear students' takes on how technology use is constructed and often restricted in FYC and other first-year courses. These students share how teachers' idiosyncratic choices about technology use constrain their learning. They also share several positive experiences with technology use in FYC, including use of digital technologies to listen to and analyze music, locate electronic resources for research, and maintain contact with classmates. It is the last of these that students say they want more of: opportunities to connect with each other and their teachers through social media outside of class. This chapter demonstrates how students' ideas can be taken into consideration when we make decisions about the use of technology in our FYC courses while also encouraging us to rethink the restrictions we place upon our students' use of technology in class.

To accompany Chapter 3, an author-editor video is available, in which Ann Amicucci discusses the challenges inherent in promoting student agency in classroom technology use and practical ways to overcome these challenges.

As an accompaniment to Part 1, Podcast 1 features authors Ann Amicucci and Doug Downs in a discussion of the current state of FYC and ways of disrupting the status quo. They also talk about how their pedagogies work to promote students' agency as writers and how their own identities as teachers of FYC have evolved as a result of their scholarship.

In Part 2, we move to questions of student identity. In this part of the book, titled "Fostering Students' Development of Writing Identities," four chapters explore who students are as writers in our FYC classrooms, and all four use reflective writing practices to promote students' self-identification as writers and with writing practices.

First, Helen Collins Sitler, in "Becoming a Person Who Writes," examines the ways students acquire agency as writers in a Basic Writing course. Sitler describes a pedagogy grounded in trust of students' authority to shape their futures as writers. She discusses how her students craft writerly identities that mesh with their tendencies to write only when assigned to and to doubt their abilities as writers. Yet she tells us that for these students, "Inexperience with writing is the issue, not capability." She follows two students as they gain experience and confidence in Basic Writing, then describes the paths these two take in their continued identity formation as writers beyond FYC, one majoring in criminal justice and the other in human resources management. Sitler's pedagogy is one that opens up "that larger world of writing" for students by enabling them to see themselves as actual writers.

This chapter features an author video. Helen Collins Sitler presents additional classroom practices, beyond those shared in Chapter 4, for promoting students' writing identities. In particular, she shares insights into the value of providing students with interested and authentic readers who can share response and feedback to inform revision, explaining how to do this within the environment of an FYC course.

Second, in "Encouraging Potential in Liminal Space: Student Writer Reflection," Martha Wilson Schaffer explores students' self-assessment of their writing and these students' potential as writers beyond the FYC course. Schaffer examines students' potentiallity—their "ongoing capacity for creative work" (Haswell and Haswell 20). She describes students' negotiations of FYC as a liminal space between what they have accomplished prior to college as writers and what they will go on to encounter as writers in the academy. Schaffer writes, "Whether they saw themselves as writers seemed to depend upon their negotiations between external expectations of the FYC Program . . . and their internal perceptions of what they were capable of doing." Schaffer's students describe their past and future selves as writers, with this self-assessment serving as a method for facilitating their growth as writers beyond the FYC classroom.

Next in Part 2, Jo-Anne Kerr presents an FYC pedagogy that leads students to develop writerly dispositions. In "Teaching for Transfer in the First-Year Composition Course: Fostering the Development of Dispositions," Kerr explores how FYC offers students opportunities to develop transferrable writing practices and a mindset of themselves as agentive writers. Her approach to FYC enculturates students into academic discourse by leading them to dismantle and demystify its "rules" and expectations. Kerr's students reflect on their beliefs about writing and the writing rules they have been taught, then define themselves as writers in relation to an academic discourse community.

An author-editor video is available for this chapter. Jo-Anne Kerr speaks about the importance of and rationale for uncovering FYC students' beliefs and understandings about writing and themselves as writers and how to go about doing this in a way that validates these beliefs and understandings while also providing opportunity for students to reexamine and revise them.

In the final chapter in this part of the book, "Linguistic Socialization: More Than 'regular talk,' 'paraphrase and stuff,'" Brian D. Carpenter talks with students after their completion of a Basic Writing course. He discusses students' position in Basic Writing—already fraught due to the stigma of being placed in a lower-level course—and demonstrates how teaching from a position of academic socialization can positively affect writers' progress. The writers Carpenter interviews are also multilingual, a feature that complicates their college experiences. He discusses examples of these students' work in class and their reflections in a subsequent semester on how the concept of cohesion they practiced in Basic Writing plays out in writing and communicative situations beyond the course.

In an author video available for this chapter, Brian Carpenter delves more deeply into linguistic socialization and the concept of cohesion, explaining how attending to linguistic socialization promotes students' identities as writers, especially those students labeled as "basic" writers.

Podcast 2 features Part 2 chapter authors Jo-Anne Kerr and Helen Sitler in a discussion of how their FYC pedagogies promote students' development of and reflection upon their writing identities. They also share specific assignments and teaching strategies that they have used in their FYC courses that help students rethink their writerly identities.

In Part 3 of this book, "Promoting Student Agency in FYC," we invite readers to consider two pedagogical approaches and one student perspective, all of which describe how students gain agency through FYC courses built on the principles of dialogic pedagogy. While the whole collection emphasizes FYC pedagogies that foster student choice, chapters in Part 3 place a particular emphasis on describing how we as FYC teachers can position students as agents within their writing education.

Part 3 begins with "Design Into: Reflection as a Tool for Growth," in which Angela Clark-Oates, Michelle Stuckey, Melissa Williamson, and Duane Roen examine student agency within the context of an online FYC course and electronic portfolios. The authors examine the way an FYC ePortfolio and its accompanying reflection give students the opportunity to practice metacognition, a habit of mind touted as contributing not only to students' success in writing but also to their successful participation in academic, professional, civic, and personal discourse. The authors demonstrate how their process of designing reflection into a curriculum (see Yancey, "The Social") promotes students' ability to make choices as writers, understand the efficacy of those choices, and carry these writing abilities beyond the FYC course.

Next, we hear from Kara Taczak, Liane Robertson, and Kathleen Blake Yancey in "A Framework for Transfer: Students' Development of a 'Theory of Writing.'" The authors describe a theory of writing project within their Teaching for Transfer curriculum that gives students agency to become writers able to adapt to multiple writing situations. Taczak, Robertson, and Yancey present reflections from three students on their developing theories, one of whom writes, "I am a very analytical writer. . . . When writing I always like to establish a good knowledge base by using my own ideas, but also looking at other ideas and sources that can contribute to my writing." We hear from this and other students in the chapter who describe taking ownership of their writing processes and the choices within them. The theory of writing assignment allows students to identify the writing concepts they employ and the ways they will carry these concepts into new writing situations.

Podcast 3 features Kara Taczak and Kathleen Blake Yancey in a discussion of their Teaching for Transfer curriculum. They explain how two assignments, the theory of writing assignment and mapping, help students understand and be able to meet different expectations for writing in different contexts. They also share how the curriculum can be adapted to meet the needs of students at different college and university institutions.

The collection concludes with a chapter written by one of our students. In "A Transition," Ashley M. Ritter, one of the students whose perspectives are presented in Kerr's chapter, joins us to share her story of unlearning certain writing constraints in the transition from high school English class writing to FYC, then carrying her disposition as a writer into her studies in psychology. We hear from Ritter a description of multiple turning points in her writing education as she navigates the high-school-to-college transition and, later, the transition from undergraduate to graduate study and to a career. Readers will find in Ritter's story a first-person account of gaining agency in FYC and the ways this agency as a writer carried beyond the course. We conclude the collection with Ritter's chapter because it embodies the value this collection places on listening to students' stories and attending to what they tell us about writing and our teaching of writing.

Across the collection's ten chapters and its multimedia components, readers will find many examples of successful FYC pedagogies and many descriptions of the benefits of pedagogies that promote student agency and students' development of writerly identities at the same time. Yet we cannot take these successful pedagogies as an indication that FYC can remain a static space or a given feature in the higher education landscape. Rather, we must, as FYC teachers, continue to engage critically with questions of the new service that FYC provides to students and, in turn, engage in the work of promoting the value of FYC to our students and to our many other stakeholders. We call for readers to cultivate wide-awakeness in considering FYC pedagogies and our students' needs so we can remain aware of how to best serve students in their development as writers in the FYC classroom.

Works Cited

Adler-Kassner, Linda. "2017 CCCC Chair's Address: Because Writing is Never Just Writing." *College Composition and Communication,* vol. 69, no. 2, 2017, pp. 317–40.

Alsup, Janet. *Teacher Identity Discourses: Negotiating Personal and Professional Spaces.* National Council of Teachers of English, 2006.

Anson, Chris M. "2013 CCCC Chair's Address: Climate Change." *College Composition and Communication,* vol. 65, no. 2, 2013, pp. 324–44.

Bartholomae, David. "Inventing the University." *When a Writer Can't Write,* edited by Mike Rose, Guilford, 1985, pp. 134–65.

Bazerman, Charles. "2009 CCCC Chair's Address: The Wonder of Writing." *College Composition and Communication,* vol. 61, no. 3, 2010, pp. 571–80.

Britzman, Deborah P. *Practice Makes Practice: A Critical Study of Learning to Teach.* State U of New York P, 2003.

Brooke, Robert. "Modeling a Writer's Identity: Reading and Imitation in the Writing Classroom." *College Composition and Communication,* vol. 39, no. 1, 1988, pp. 24–41.

Carter, Joyce Locke. "2016 CCCC Chair's Address: Making, Disrupting, Innovating." *College Composition and Communication,* vol. 68, no. 2, 2016, pp. 378–408.

Crowley, Sharon. "Composition's Ethic of Service, the University Requirement, and the Discourse of Student Need." *JAC,* vol. 15, no. 2, 1995, pp. 227–39.

Danielewicz, Jane. *Teaching Selves: Identity, Pedagogy, and Teacher Education.* State U of New York P, 2001.

Downs, Doug. "What is First-Year Composition?" *A Rhetoric for Writing Program Administrators,* edited by Rita Malenczyk, Parlor, 2013, pp. 50–63.

Gee, James Paul. *An Introduction to Discourse Analysis: Theory and Method.* Routledge, 1999.

Gee, James Paul. "What is Literacy?" *Negotiating Academic Literacies,* edited by Vivian Zamel and Ruth Spack, Erlbaum, 1998, pp. 51–59.

Glenn, Cheryl. "2008 CCCC Chair's Address: Representing Ourselves." *College Composition and Communication,* vol. 60, no. 2, 2008, pp. 420–39.

Greene, Maxine. "Wide-Awakeness and the Moral Life." *Exploring Education: An Introduction to the Foundations of Education*, edited by Alan R. Sadovnik et al., Routledge, 2018, pp. 218–24.

Haswell, Janis, and Richard Haswell. *Authoring: An Essay for the Profession on Potentiality and Singularity*. Utah State UP, 2010.

Ivanič, Roz. *Writing and Identity: The Discoursal Construction of Identity in Academic Writing*. John Benjamins, 1998.

Johnson, Kristine. "Beyond Standards: Disciplinary and National Perspectives on Habits of Mind." *College Composition and Communication*, vol. 64, no. 3, 2013, pp. 517–41.

Mukherjee, Siddhartha. *The Gene: An Intimate History*. Scribner, 2016.

Noddings, Nel. *The Challenge to Care in Schools: An Alternative Approach to Education*. Teachers College, 1992.

Oakeshott, Michael. *On Human Conduct*. Clarendon, 1975.

Pough, Gwendolyn D. "2011 CCCC Chair's Address: It's Bigger than Comp/Rhet: Contested and Undisciplined." *College Composition and Communication*, vol. 63, no. 2, 2011, pp. 301–13.

Powell, Malea. "2012 CCCC Chair's Address: Stories Take Place: A Performance in One Act." *College Composition and Communication*, vol. 64, no. 2, 2012, pp. 383–406.

Tinberg, Howard. "2014 CCCC Chair's Address: The Loss of the Public." *College Composition and Communication*, vol. 66, no. 2, 2014, pp. 327–41.

Valentino, Marilyn J. "2010 CCCC Chair's Address: Rethinking the Fourth C: Call to Action." *College Composition and Communication*, vol. 62, no. 2, 2010, pp. 364–78.

Yancey, Kathleen Blake. *Reflection in the Writing Classroom*. Utah State UP, 1998.

Yancey, Kathleen Blake. "The Social Life of Reflection: Notes Toward an ePortfolio-Based Model of Reflection." *Teaching Reflective Learning in Higher Education: A Systematic Approach Using Pedagogic Patterns*, edited by Mary Elizabeth Ryan, Springer International, 2015, pp. 189–202.

Part 1. Problematizing Today's Notions of First-Year Composition

The authors in the first part of the book turn a critical eye on practices we may take for granted in FYC. Doug Downs introduces us to Professor Plum, a fictional faculty member whose writing and collaborative practices demonstrate how professional academics write and highlight the double standards that exist between writing expectations we place on our students and those we place on ourselves.

Howa Furrow demonstrates for readers how seemingly innocuous features of FYC courses, such as students' lack of anonymity in a small-class setting, can create unsafe spaces for LGBTQIA individuals. Furrow describes ten ways teachers can be allies—including by actively demonstrating allyship and confronting homophobia in the classroom.

Finally, Ann N. Amicucci questions how technology can be used in FYC courses and includes how a few students report benefitting from such use in their own courses. She also draws attention to the drawbacks of constraining students' technology use and calls for readers to take student perspectives into consideration when making classroom technology decisions.

Extras

- Listen to a podcast conversation among Part 1 authors Doug Downs and Ann Amicucci and editor Jo-Anne Kerr for ideas on how to disrupt the status quo in FYC: 🎧 Listen to the Part 1 Podcast[1]
- Watch a short video of Ann Amicucci discussing how to overcome the challenges inherent in promoting student agency in classroom technology use: 🎬 View the Video

---

1. The videos and podcasts referred to on this page are available on the WAC Clearinghouse at https://wac.colostate.edu/books/practice/stories/.

Chapter 1. Double Standards and Sunshine: Exploring Expectations for Professional and Student Writing in FYC

Doug Downs
MONTANA STATE UNIVERSITY

Reflect Before Reading

Before reading Doug's chapter, think about your professional writing and the process in which you engage to produce this writing. How did you learn this process? How has this process evolved over time? Have you shared how you write with your FYC students? Or any of your writing—drafts or polished pieces? What value might be there in doing so?

~ ~ ~

It's no secret that one of first-year composition's primary roles is enculturation: for students with little idea of the workings or purpose of "academia" as an activity system, FYC is one place they begin to become acquainted with systems of scholarly inquiry and "higher education." James Paul Gee's notion of Discourses as a way of understanding literacy has been helpful in letting us understand students' encounters with academe in terms of a meeting of primary and secondary Discourses—those of university administration, major disciplines, and other disciplines encountered through general education. FYC is often center-stage for the clash or convergence of students' "saying (writing)-doing-being-valuing-believing combinations" ("Literacy" 6) with those of the institutions they're attending. We can take, for an example pertaining to FYC, Keith Hjortshoj's prediction that students holding to earlier-learned discursive values may universalize "good writing," while FYC will often teach that the features of good writing vary from one situation to another (33). Prima facie, then, there is value in comparing these "identity kits" (Gee, "Literacy" 7) brought by students and offered by institutions, and in building FYC to be a site for such reflexive encounters.

As we do so, however, it is not sufficient to explore what the academy says it values in student writing at the college level. FYC should also be a site for investigation of double standards, the inconsistencies between what new college students are told the academy values in academic writing and the academy's—that is, its faculty's—actual writing practices. In this chapter, I catalog elements of writing processes and textuality in which we can find striking distance between

DOI: https://doi.org/10.37514/PRA-B.2020.0308.2.01

23

how faculty actually write and how students are instructed to write. I derive that catalog by following an imaginary "composite" faculty member who embodies a typical range of faculty writing habits and practices, dramatizing elements of her writing processes which conflict with messages students receive about how writing works and how it should be done. I frame these elements themselves as Discourse markers and analyze the roots of double standards in the different activity systems which students and faculty are perceived to be members of. I argue that one way FYC can help students begin to acquire their chosen Discourses within academe is by presenting a critical and even resistant front to the academy's own stories about writing. Following this analysis, I show how writing-about-writing approaches to FYC—in which students read scholarship on writing and then design small-scale primary research on questions of their own—allow students to investigate firsthand the gaps between the stories this Discourse of higher education tells about writing in the academy and the actual writing practices of its members—a simultaneously subversive and supportive pedagogy. There is power for student writers not only in recognizing moments of "Do as I say, not as I do," but even more in seeing instances where some of their own struggles—which the academy's stories about writing often frame as student *deficit*—actually are simply a function of writing itself, or of unjustifiable faculty demands. In any such cases, greater awareness can translate to greater self-efficacy and improved dispositions toward writing, as well as offer key invitational moments to help students believe that they truly can be (invited to be) knowledge-makers in the academy.

I'll begin by introducing my composite faculty writer, and then divert briefly to lay out some framing theories and premises that undergird this chapter. Then I'll create a set of categories, drawing on the example of the faculty writer, that suggest what FYC students can study in terms of faculty behaviors, standards, and habits of mind. Having seen what's available for students to study, I'll briefly outline some curricular designs for such a course.

It Was Professor Plum, with a Candlestick, in the Library

To dramatize and embody a "professional academic writer" whose writing habits and circumstances can be juxtaposed with those of student writers, I've written a character who amalgamates trends demonstrated by various studies of professional academic writers, such as Susan Peck MacDonald's studies of research and writing practices in the humanities and social sciences and Dorothy Winsor's studies of engineering writing. This prototype professor-writer is built as well from anecdotal observations on two campuses where I've been employed as a professor of English and have encountered faculty-as-writers both as guest speakers in my own classes and in various offices and committees on campus, from grant-coordination to Institutional Review Board (IRB) to college and university promotion-and-tenure committees. The resulting composite professor may not reflect every reader's "typical" faculty writer (if there is such a thing), but will, I hope, be generally recognizable to readers who have a range of experiences with faculty writing across their campuses.

Meet, then, Gina Plum. She's an associate professor of Climate and Meteorology, and she has an article to write. Her small research team of three has been working on the problem of classifying local climate zones—such as "urban heat islands," the comparative warmth of a city to its surroundings.[1] Previously, the field of climate studies has only differentiated "rural" and "urban" regions, and much finer-grained differentiation is needed in *kinds* of rural and urban regions to help explore the causes of heat-island effects. Plum and her colleagues have a refined taxonomy of climate zones to propose. Their paper, targeted to a field-leading journal such as *Bulletin of the American Meteorological Society*, will be multimodal—graphics- and color-intensive, including color photographs of actual research sites, multi-color data tables, and figures such as color diagrams and charts. Unlike some articles in the natural sciences, it will also be lengthy—as long as thirty pages including appendices, which will also be highly graphical. Its reference list will number over seventy. Plum will, of course, use a "writing process" to create the piece, and while it might not involve a candlestick in the library, it will make for an interesting comparison to students' writing practices and the constraints on them.

Being tenured, Plum is hardly writing such a piece for the first time. But *how* does she know her task? Good answers to this question draw on a number of social theories of writing that serve as premises for my chapter, so I'll pause the narrative long enough to overview them. I've already broached Gee's sociolinguistics-based literacy theory centered on Discourses. These (always written with a capital D) are "ways with words, feelings, values, beliefs, emotions, people, action, things, tools, and places that allow us to display and recognize characteristic *whos* doing characteristic *whats*" (*An Introduction* 19). As such, a Discourse comprises "a sort of 'identity kit' which comes with costume and instructions on how to think, act, talk, and write, so as to take on a social role that others will recognize"—the "saying-doing-being-valuing-believing combinations" that tell people how to *be* in given situations ("Literacy" 7). People performing a Discourse, Gee says, are those we'll take to be a "real" *X* (e.g., hero, president, plumber) (*An Introduction* 18). Gee offers us a social theory of writing—understanding the rhetorical notion of *audience* as "discourse communities"—that is grounded in shared *languages* ("ways with words"). How does Professor Plum understand her writing task? In part, as conversation within her Discourse of climate studies. My discussion takes these principles as given.

This chapter is also grounded in activity theory, a lens on Professor Plum's knowledge of her writing task which looks less at language and more at the *activity* she is collaborating to accomplish. Culturo-historical activity theory, according to David Russell, "analyzes human behavior and consciousness in terms of

---

1. For an example of just such research, see Stewart and Oke.

activity systems: goal-directed, historically situated, cooperative human interactions" which are mediated by tools, including language and writing ("Activity" 53). Over time—through laboratory apprenticeships, graduate studies, postdocs, professional meetings, and reading and writing scholarly texts—Professor Plum has been enculturated into an activity system whose goal is to better understand the workings of climate and its sources and influences. She's learned the genres—"typified rhetorical actions based in recurrent situations" (Miller 27)—which are some of her activity's most common writing tools for creating, sharing, and building consensus around knowledge toward that end. As Cheryl Geisler et al. note, the nature of the activity helps shape the writing both directly and by shaping the rhetorical situation that shapes the writing. If Gee's Discourse theory gives us a much more sophisticated lens on the traditional rhetorical category of "audience," then activity theory as Russell, Dorothy Winsor, and Charles Bazerman use it provides a significantly more sophisticated lens on the traditional rhetorical categories of rhetorical situation, context, and exigence identified by Keith Grant-Davie.

A final premise to my thinking in this chapter involves the nature of the course in which Professor Plum would have gained some of her earliest academic writing experience: first-year composition. I proceed with specific understandings of the purposes and roles of FYC, which I've written about at length in a number of other collections.[2] I advocate for a radically different role for and look of FYC than Plum, as a composite *typical* faculty member 20 years out from her FYC course, would probably have encountered. As evidenced by the foci of the most popular FYC textbooks, by taxonomies of composition pedagogies such as Richard Fulkerson's and Gary Tate et al.'s, and by critiques of first-year composition including Sharon Crowley's and David Smit's, Plum's 1990s FYC course likely focused, in one way or another, on how to write researched arguments, and was designed in response to what I call college composition's *public charter* ("What" 51). This charter—our various stakeholders' agreement to make a massive public and private investment in college writing instruction because of the value it adds to a college education—is based on stakeholders' convictions that writing is the basic, transferable, grammatical skill of transcribing speech to print, and that this skill is essential to both social standing and employment prospects. FYC courses that teach these skills are therefore a wise investment. Importantly, however, this charter is neither a necessary purpose for writing instruction—there is a wide range of others—nor the most achievable purpose, because the charter contains faulty premises about the nature of writing. Because writing is *not* a basic grammatical transcriptive skill, attempting to teach it as such is likely to yield frustration. The current volume, in contrast, premises that another valuable and achievable purpose for FYC is to help student writers find their voices by developing them as members of the academy itself. This is an achievable purpose, should we choose it, and accords well with

---

2. See Downs, "What"; Downs and Robertson; Mallory and Downs; Wardle and Downs.

what I unequivocally *do* see as a central purpose of FYC instruction: creating "a space, a moment, and an experience—in which students might reconsider writing apart from previous schooling and work, within the context of inquiry-based higher education" ("What" 50). Rather than "teaching writing," we can teach students (about) the principles at the heart of our work as writing scholars: access to the resources and benefits of higher education, writing as interaction (rather than one-way transmission of information, another faulty metaphor), valuing of student and writerly voices, the nature of textual production and "how texts got that way," and the nature of rhetoric and writing as a rhetorical activity. The rest of this chapter will take these roles for FYC as a starting point.

Plum's Process, Products, and Writing Lifeworld

In the interest of brevity, my analysis of our composite faculty writer's experience will focus just on areas of most obvious divergence from what students frequently experience when writing at the college level. While much of what follows I'll assert as typical differences, not all readers will agree either with the degree or the typicality of what I identify. That's fine—my goal is to raise questions rather than support any single claim beyond dispute. Any of my claims may be treated as investigatory hypotheses that we should probe with further research, as long as they can be read as plausible areas of question. Rigorous research related to a number of questions that I'll raise is limited; I will be clear when I'm working from anecdote and acknowledge its limitations. At the same time, anecdote will often be amply sufficient for asserting the plausibility of a given question or area of inquiry.

Collaboration

Beginning at the beginning of Plum's writing process—before any writing on her article, before she even knows what to say—perhaps the most obvious observation is that Plum is involved in collaborative writing to begin with, both synchronically and diachronically. First, synchronically, Plum knows from the beginning of her project that she does not have sole responsibility for the writing she'll produce; she is not producing in isolation. Plum begins her research with a team. They've had to collaboratively generate grant proposals to fund their data collection and analysis. They've had to divide the labor of review of literature, data collection itself, and data analysis. Working in the sciences, they've understood since graduate school that these writing tasks are shared, divided, or otherwise distributed. They've had to learn their field's conventions for who is named first author and what that means. They've learned to strategize when to divide drafting by section, co-draft, or hand all first-drafting to one writer.

By contrast, students throughout their schooling are assumed to be working alone unless otherwise specifically instructed by a "special" assignment. As a result, even though collaborative writing and team projects are increasingly common features of college education across majors, these experiences are "marked" as unusual. The typical educational experience still leaves students conceptually "backward" on the fundamental nature of "writer," in comparison to how most (though perhaps not all) graduates are re-socialized by professional writing after school.[3] Most early college students are educated to believe that writers *by nature* (if not always in practice) work alone and independently. Unassigned collaboration is treated as *cheating* at many schools, including my own institution, whose student code prohibits collaboration unless explicitly assigned: "Unless otherwise specified, students may not collaborate on graded material. Instructors are encouraged to provide collaborative learning opportunities but must state, in writing or by electronic means, the limits of assistance permitted between and among students in a course assignment or academic evaluation" (*Conduct* 120.00 B). This expectation—explicit sometimes, and more often implicit—parallels the written reflection of one of my own students, Megan Evans. Evans wrote, "While faculty are expected to and encouraged to work with their peers . . . students are expected to do the exact opposite . . . produce . . . a piece of writing that is singularly their own."[4] Students like Evans perceive—and I would argue that there truly exists—a double standard: collaboration is lifeblood for professional writers but suspect and alien for students.

Diachronically, this writing of Plum's will not be independent of her other recent writing. Her article will not stand detached from the grant proposal which yielded funding for her team's work, the massive set of project-management documents that accompanied the grant and the research, the field- and lab-notes that assisted in data analysis, and the rounds of emails between researchers that guided the project to the state in which it currently stands and which will guide its drafting. The article to be written is related to various conference papers and posters that have presented other findings along the way and likely directly builds on previous publications. Just as it will never occur to Plum that she stands isolated as a writer, the piece to be written is inherently "in collaboration with" the maze of texts that precede and will stem from it. This incredibly complex network of texts and writers—even for a relatively "small" project such as Plum's—exemplifies Russell's principle of polycontextuality—multiple activity systems and complex genre systems creating the context for any single piece of writing.

---

3. See Beaufort's *Writing in the Real World: Making the Transition from School to Work* and Winsor's "Genre and Activity Systems: The Role of Documentation in Maintaining and Changing Engineering Activity Systems" in *Written Communication*.

4. Following Amy Robillard's enjoinment to use students' real names, when I quote my prior students' writing in this piece, I've obtained their permission to use their real names. Students' writing quoted from IRB-approved datasets gathered under promise of anonymity made during informed consent is quoted anonymously.

Activity and Genre

By contrast, Russell's analysis demonstrates relatively impoverished polycontextuality in the realm of student work. Many student projects begin and end with a single written assignment or several repetitions of the same assignment. Only more rarely do assignments create a "project arc" so that students work on separate but related pieces of a large project across a course. Dan Melzer's *Assignments Across the Curriculum* provides rich data on the relative rarity of such integration of multiple writing assignments into larger projects. Projects that span multiple *courses*, Melzer finds, are vanishingly rare in the typical college curriculum. One reason for this difference, of course, is that the activities in question are different. Professor Plum is engaged in ongoing professional research which runs on a clock of years rather than weeks, includes funding in six or seven figures, and spans several institutions. The richness of genres that stand in and behind her research articles exists because many kinds of very large-scale work must be mediated by different writing tools over long periods of time.

Furthermore, Plum experiences one of the oldest saws of rhetorically-savvy writing instruction—*"know your audience"*—very differently than most students. She actually *does know* her audience, literally and specifically: it's highly likely she has met professionally and even socially with the handful of readers qualified to peer review her work, in the course of professional meetings and other collaborations over the years. She might count the editor of the journal her article will go to as a colleague, or even a friend. Academic-research worlds are quite small, and Plum probably personally knows many of her individual readers. Nor is this phenomenon necessarily limited to professional writing in academic research. In many—probably most—professional writing scenes and activities, from marketing pitches to engineering proposals to land management grants to feasibility studies for city councils, writers can know their audience members individually and even actively consult with them during drafting.

Compare that to a student writing an assigned history essay, philosophy paper, lab report, or music review, where they are encouraged to write for "their peers," an "educated reader," a "general audience," or the teacher alone. "Knowing" these audiences is usually much more difficult and vague. Data I collected with a research team in my writing program in 2014 suggest that, for most of the 135 first-year students whose reflective writing we've studied, "know your audience" tends to mean "try to get a sense of the *type* of person who you mean to speak to." One representative student, for example, writes that "The audience is important. This decides the style, format, and writing style of the paper. In some cases, mainly for lay audience, any general style is acceptable. Writing must be planned for the discourse community you are writing for." There's a certain level of "audience awareness" here, but stark lack of refinement in comparison with how experienced insiders think about their audiences as, for example, seen in Ann Beaufort's and Dorothy Winsor's descriptions of professional and academic writers.

Of course, the activity system of climate research is vastly different from the activity system of college education. Unlike with expectations for collaboration, this difference in activities is not necessarily a "double standard." There are student-only genres, and limitations to what can be assigned, that the activity system of higher-education simply necessitates. Where double standards may arise, however, is when we deny students the ability to *study* professional activity systems because they're "only students," or when we ignore that these differences exist.

Sources and Research

Before Professor Plum and her colleagues can write seventy-plus references into their article, they have to find and read them. Plum's deep knowledge of her Discourse means that the research team has already read many of these references—the list might not look terribly different from that in the project's grant proposal. The important principle here is *accretion*: with time, Plum has built up a quickly accessible, deeply layered cognitive network of source texts. That first-year college students lack the same rich network is not what constitutes a double standard in the use of sources; what does is the different reasons for their use. Students are widely taught to use sources to "back up" their arguments. Frequently this translates to students as a conviction that they are not believable unless sources make their arguments for them, as I point out in *Teaching Our Own Prison*. Findings from both a 2010 dataset in which I observed 12 students searching for and reading sources online and a 2014 dataset of pre-FYC and post-FYC reflective writing from 135 students are consistent with my earlier findings: students understand sources as factual, informational, and primarily for the purpose of "backing up" arguments. A very typical "planning question" students ask in the 2014 dataset is, "Is this paper completely factually based? Or can I muse over ideas that are not proven with sources?" Many students seem to see research as a problem of transmitting stacks-of-facts to the teacher in order to "prove" whatever the student writer wanted to say to begin with. In contrast, Professor Plum and her co-writers are citing sources in order to contextualize their work in a vast network of ongoing conversation, a process noted by Carol Berkenkotter and Thomas Huckin. For them, sources are *relational*, rarely included simply to "back up" a claim. Maureen Mathison articulates this relationship with sources as more often one of *critique*: "Scholars evaluate each other's projects as they sustain and transform disciplinary information" (315). Professor Plum's claims are mostly grounded not in the "proof" offered by prior research but in her primary data—something students are often not assigned to collect or develop to begin with.

Another significant double standard around the use of sources relates to "avoiding plagiarism," a greater risk for students than for professional writers because students repeatedly quote at length from source material while professionals (in fields outside the humanities, at least) are much more likely to briefly summarize it. Put a student's paper on climate research next to a piece by Professor Plum, and one of the most significant differences in uses of references is likely to be that Plum states the work of her sources in a one-line or few-line very high-level summary, while the student writing will tend to rely much more on extensive quotation or paraphrase, as Rebecca Moore Howard, Tricia Serviss, and Tanya K. Rodrigue point out. Rebecca Moore Howard and her "Citation Project" research team have shown that this pattern in students' source use leads to frequent instances of patchwriting and plagiarism, as students tend to write "from sentences selected from sources" instead of writing globally *about* their sources (187). Plum does the latter. Because students learn from an early age that "research writing" means quoting sources, we have instructed them to do a thing that professional writers go on to learn *not* to do.

Invention and Authority

Professor Plum's inventional process as she arrives with her colleagues at a draft also probably looks significantly different than her students'. How do these faculty writers come up with what to say, and what will be understood as giving them the right to say it? To say that they draw on extensive reading to help make sense of what they see in their primary research, and to say that they build their sense of what to say *from* what those data enable them to report, seems like an obvious statement. And because this inventional ability arises directly from their Discourse and activity system, it may seem another area where no double standard exists between student and professional writing. Until we look at the messages students receive throughout schooling, which seem much different in perhaps unnecessary ways. As critiqued by Paulo Freire and now scores of others, educational settings tend to treat students as blank slates, empty minds to be "filled" with "material" that is "delivered" to them. (The national discussion of the past several years on MOOCs comes to mind.) In the eyes of many college instructors, students write from *deficit*: they are not believed to know what they're talking about unless their writing proves they do. They are presumed to have little *of their own* to say, a conviction which subtly tinges the very purpose of assigning writing to begin with: judgment about distance from *incompetence*. Readers skeptical of this point should explore standard practices for assigning lab reports at their own institutions. In our own literature, the expressivism of the 1970s was born in Mina Shaughnessy's, Ken Macrorie's, and many others' critiques of this faculty attitude. That the attitude remains with us can be seen in the testing mania which swept primary and secondary education over the past decade and now threatens higher education.

Such a presumption is clearly in the back of Emily Jo Schwaller's mind when, as one of my writing students, she reflected on how refreshing a particular FYC course had been in comparison to other college courses. "We began to challenge the [expectation] that [student] writing is meaningless writing, scripted writing," and instead created "a [primary] research method . . . designed to fit our question."

What Schwaller's reflection describes is the difference between students as *tabula rasa* learners and students as *makers of knowledge*. Professor Plum's writing, in contrast to that of students in many college classes, will be met with an initial presumption of competence and value. It may be read *very* critically and perhaps even with a presumption of inadequacy—is it "good enough" to be in X journal?—but that is much different from an opening presumption that the writers don't know what they're doing or that they have nothing to say.

At the same time that the work of student writers is frequently read from a deficit perspective, student writers are held to high standards of invention: they are nearly always expected to work alone, using only "their own" ideas except when "borrowing" those scrupulously cited from sources. (The use of sources then becomes its own admission of writerly knowledge deficit, citations becoming confessional.) This expectation of independent invention creates a strong double standard with professional researched writing, which would be seen as incompetent if it *were not* developed in intense interaction with other professional writers and readers. (For example, submitting an NSF grant without consulting with the program officer throughout drafting is *verboten*.)

Objectivity and Voicelessness

Can Professor Plum use "I" in her article? Many, probably most, students learn throughout secondary schooling that research writing may not use "I," may not be based on personal opinion, and requires objectivity, and that the writer may not be present in the writing. I assume this claim will be acceptable to any writing instructor who has faced endless raised hands about whether it is "okay to use 'I' in this paper." A truism among many FYC instructors is that this is the first belief we begin trying to break students of, but Hyland finds many bestselling college research textbooks that explicitly condemn first-person reference in research writing. Questions about whether the use of "I" is allowed, and the negative correlation in students' minds between "I" (authorly presence) and objectivity, are rife throughout student writing. My student Adam Schreuder wrote a representative comment: "Before every paper in every class I will ever have for the rest of my life, the question must be asked, 'Are we *allowed* to used "I" in our paper?'" In our 2014 dataset, the most common question that students both at the beginning and at the end of their first-year composition class believe they need to ask in new writing situations is, "Can I use 'I'?" It arises for more than 90 of 135 respondents in their post-course reflections, in one form or another. Across our dataset, the use of "I" is associated with informal, unprofessional, un-factual, un-researched writing, attending the premise that the absence of "I" renders the writing "objective."

These findings have remained consistent over two decades of my research (see *Teaching Our Own Prison*). Students are taught relentlessly in primary and secondary school that schooled (academic or researched or informational or formal)

writing must be objective and that it may not use "I," and students' college experiences more often than not reinforce that perception rather than overturning it.
High school teachers teach students to remove themselves from their research
writing because they believe that's what will be required in college: students are
given to believe they must remove themselves from their researched writing because this is what the "grownups" do. Scientific writing is famously imagined to
be so scrubbed of personality that it takes place almost entirely in passive voice
and third-person.

Yet according to genre researcher Ken Hyland, "Academic writing is not just
about conveying an ideational 'content', it is also about the representation of self.
Recent research has suggested that academic prose is not completely impersonal,
but that writers gain credibility by projecting an identity invested with individual
authority, displaying confidence in their evaluations and commitment to their
ideas" ("Authority" 1091). Hyland bases this conclusion on large-corpus analyses of research articles across a range of natural science, engineering, social science, and humanities fields, which he says demonstrate that "while impersonality
may often be institutionally sanctified, it is constantly transgressed" ("Humble"
209). First person pronouns are used with regularity in the humanities and social
sciences and increasingly in the natural sciences, Hyland shows, to explain self-
benefits, state purposes, explain procedures, elaborate arguments in ways that
emphasize what the writer believes are most important aspects, and state results
in the form of claims ("Authority" 1100-06). Examining the ways that researchers
blend claims of novelty with integration of their work into existing knowledge,
Berkenkotter and Huckin show that writers' claims often demonstrate a "highly
contingent and tentative epistemic status" (49). That is, scholarly articles typically negotiate the integration of what is essentially *personal* knowledge with more
widely established knowledge that has gained consensus within their Discourses.

In short, should Professor Plum and her coauthors wish to use first person
references, state a personal opinion, acknowledge and front the motives behind
their writing, or even crack a joke, they will be in good company. That freedom
establishes a clear double standard in comparison to the notions students' early
educational experiences leave them regarding what personal presence is permis-
sible in academic writing, and there is no evidence that college writing education
uniformly or even widely overturns this belief.

Workflow

I noted earlier that Professor Plum has different timelines for writing than do
most college students, as it would be rare for her to move from "topic" selection
to final draft in five weeks. Beyond timelines, however, Plum's collaborative writing process created with an eye toward peer review by a high-level journal will
be radically different from the typical student writing process in ways that may
constitute double standards, different expectations for students simply *because*

they are students. Primary and secondary education routinely wind up teaching students "the" writing process: prewriting, drafting, revision, editing. In schools, though, this process is rarely able to be truly implemented as professional writers experience it: genuinely iterative, recursive, developmental, and chaotic. Rather, it is usually presented as stepwise and linear: we do not draft until we have pre-written; we do not revise until we have drafted. Many college writing courses begin to chip away at such stepwise linearity conceptually, yet assignments designed to promote or require truly non-linear processes (not merely multiple revision loops) are rarely described in our literature. As writing student Kelsey Weyerbacher notes of many of her college writing experiences in which faculty *did* attend to process:

> What still bugs me, though, is the expectation of "drafts." As a peer tutor at the Writing Center at MSU, I have learned over and over again from students that everyone's writing process looks different. It made no sense to me when I would turn in my drafts, when my professors in my literature classes would comment, "This is not a draft." Umm, excuse me? Do you see my writing? Do you see my drafting? . . . Why is it the professor's idea of time management that is the deciding factor in my drafting?

Weyerbacher sees some faculty "beginning to change this ideal," but believes the older, rigid ideas about process are still dominant when teachers pay attention to drafting at the college level.

Professional writing processes, in contrast—particularly collaborative ones—are much less likely to proceed stepwise and linearly. Rather, different parts of Plum's article will be drafted at different times by different writers, and often not in order. (A methods section might be drafted weeks before an introduction or background section.) Different parts of the article may be in different "stages" of the process at the same time—and what *is* a "stage" of writing once "a" process is divided and iterated through an interactive collaboration with other writers and readers? More contemporary process language calls these *phases* of writing, and more complex models of writing process, such as Daniel Perrin and Marc Wildi's looped phase-progression model, graphically demonstrate how numerous phases of writing can be happening simultaneously or jumped into and out of repeatedly (380).

Again, if students are not assigned work that demands such complex processes, it would in one sense be unfair to label the expectation that student writing proceed stepwise and linearly (as often constrained to by assignment design and deadlines) a double standard. But there seems to be a double standard if we don't demonstrate, and invite students to participate in, writing tasks *complex enough* to require such processes. (Or to acknowledge professional publishing's fairly ubiquitous laxity with deadlines, as compared to the strict ones students are held to.)

Similarly, we may be failing to strongly enough resist a popular misconception among students that every act of writing should be a unique and inspired act of creation, and any acts that aren't result in bad writing. Students seem slow to become aware how little completely original writing happens in professional, particularly business, settings. I see little awareness among college students—and humanities professors—I encounter that good writing in most professional settings *can* in fact result from boilerplate, from patterns and templates, from *formulas*. This unawareness creates a double standard whereby professional writers identify texts, patterns, and strategies that work and endlessly reuse them, while students themselves imagine or are explicitly instructed that every individual text is to be a unique creative act.

Editorial Assistance

Suppose that Professor Plum and her co-authors have by now proceeded to a full draft, in the same way that students, in vastly less time, with vastly fewer resources, starting from scratch, enjoined not to put themselves in their writing, but to use a lot of sources to back up their ideas, have reached a draft of their own. What happens to these drafts now? Plum, as a professional writer, has a wide array of editorial resources available to her. Colleagues, mentors, journal or book editors, even freelance copyeditors to help her finalize her piece for submission. She has some assurance of having a significant number of "tries" to get the piece right. A certain level of difficulty in her piece will actually be expected for early drafts, because so few scholarly articles are accepted without substantive revisions. Plum and her colleagues could say, "I just can't get this paragraph to work right, so I'm going to leave it as is and see what my editor says about it," and "get away with" that.

Students in many college-writing circumstances have some analogous level of peer review and teacher assistance with their writing, but even at best such editorial assistance would be inconsistent across classes, and limited. Many a teacher will grade what they get on first appearance; some will not even allow revision. I've taught writing in five institutions of higher education over the past 23 years, and directed writing programs at two of those, directly overseeing the work of more than 150 fellow writing instructors over time. The majority of my colleagues in every program I've observed do not use portfolios, and they grade drafts the first time they collect them. The majority of my colleagues also have not required revision after they've read a piece, instead making revision optional if the piece is poor enough to demand it. And these are the writing instructors on campus; are faculty in other fields any more likely to do differently? We have no evidence to say so. Even campus writing centers routinely refuse certain kinds of editorial assistance to students as a principle of sound writing center theory (see every issue of *Writing Center Journal* ever), because writing centers are working to correct the misimpression that grammar is the most important part of writing. In the vernacular: "We don't edit." Well, who does edit, for students?

Professor Plum meanwhile need not fear that mildly problematic work will fail to go out for peer review so long as the potential value of the manuscript is clear to editors and the prose is clear enough to prevent misreading. Particularly in a world where increasingly large proportions of scholarship in English are written by second-language writers, and where many academic fields simply expect poor writing from their practitioners, syntactic standards are well below "perfection" or even steadily quality fluency. For any moderate difficulties Plum's work shows in this regard, she can expect either to have some editorial assistance in preparing an accepted manuscript for publication, or to be producing "camera-ready" copy which will go into print flaws and all.

Indeed, faculty writers—with their vastly greater experience with textual production, greater knowledge of the subjects they're writing on, longer timeframes for producing writing and ability to bend deadlines, their workload and agency frequently distributed through collaborative writing, and with the presence of significant editorial assistance—even with all these aids, faculty writers face no expectation of perfection in their drafting, while student writers with very limited time, subject-matter expertise, writing experience, and outside assistance will frequently receive grade-killing criticism for even minor infelicities in reasoning, research, presentation, or editorial polish. There's a reason the world's best writers have the world's best editors—but therein lies one of the greatest double standards of all for students, because for a student, to be edited is to be cheating.

Product Measures

Suffice to say, the world is not replete with instances of poorly edited reference pages keeping a scholarly paper from being accepted for publication and then professionally copyedited, but many a research paper has missed an A because a teacher noticed too many proofreading errors and violations of MLA style in a student's piece. Students are powerfully aware of this double standard, and in reflections I see from my writing students, it receives some of the most comment. Nathan Voeller, for example, noted a case where students were prohibited from using a list of "dead words" in their writing by an instructor. "I once found, to my bitter amusement, one of the infamous dead word combinations in a prompt written by the list's creator." Sadie Robertus spoke of "a couple professors [who] are sticklers for perfect syntax, perfect grammar, perfect everything. But then they pass out their syllabus, and I discover errors everywhere!" She went on to speak of a second-year FYC instructor who encouraged students to "provide plentiful details, a strong thesis, and clear, concise sentences in their papers. Yet this same professor only gave his assignments verbally"—didn't even write them out. Angie Mallory encountered a professor who promised students they would not be graded on correctness but rather on out-of-the-box thinking, and yet resulting grades were low and the vast majority of feedback on the papers related to correctness. At the time, Mallory, in preparation to be a teacher, wrote, "If you claim you aren't going to grade on something, then the focus of your feedback can't be on that thing." Even more telling regarding cultural expectations for perfection in student writing, Mallory wrote: "It takes a lot of effort for a student to believe that correctness is not the goal, and if we want students to come along with us on the semester journey we intend, then we have to safeguard that fragile trust. If we preach 'Shitty First Drafts' then we have to be prepared to receive them, and praise the messy learning." Certainly many FYC classrooms do so; but just as clearly, many more classes, in the experience of our students, are headed by faculty who hold students to higher standards than their own editors hold them. My favorite response when a faculty member on my campus complains about the quality of student writing is to ask if I might see a copy of that faculty member's most recent draft that went out for peer review. I have seen successful, high-publishing faculty literally blanch at that request—and then back down from their criticism of students.

Bob Broad and Richard Haswell have both demonstrated exhaustively just how much attention teachers continue to pay to mechanical correctness in student writing, while Joseph Williams long ago showed with chilling effectiveness how professional writers "earn" greater forgiveness for errors in their writing simply because of their professional status. It is an astounding double standard—though an understandable one—that while Professor Plum might limit most of her comments on a student's paper to pointing out its syntactic infelicities, her own article will rise or fall on the merits of its argument, methodology, data quality, and impact. Student work is frequently read in relative haste and in a surface fashion, and teachers (as Broad and as Haswell show) tend to grade on mechanical correctness both because of its high visibility and its relative objectivity. It is far easier to see, critique, and explain a comma error than it is a multi-link logical flaw. So there's a reasonably good chance that the grading of writing in a typical college course revolves on surface-level errors, so much so that as Broad found, teachers who sense but cannot explain a flaw in a paper's argument tend to mis-diagnose the problem as a grammatical error. I think it likely that the same widespread attention to and misunderstanding of surface error that Broad's and Haswell's studies find also accounts for the truism in WAC work that time will initially need to be spent getting faculty across campus to define "writing" more broadly than *grammar* and to talk about aspects of students' writing beyond correctness.

Professor Plum's paper, in contrast, will tend to be peer reviewed more patiently and deeply, with most attention focused on *the work it is meant to accomplish* within its activity system, and how it indeed accomplishes that work.

Sunshine and Access: FYC as a Space to Study Double Standards

In sum, the narrative of Plum contrasted with student voices and experiences suggests that there are significant differences in faculty and student writing experiences that would cast writing in a richly different light for FYC students, were they only aware of those differences. I advocate that we consider such awareness-building crucial for FYC courses whose purpose is understood as enculturating students into academia as practitioners of academy inquiry. And FYC can certainly be built to do so.

Take, for example, a writing-about-writing approach to FYC, where writing becomes the studied subject of a writing course by integrating the reading of composition research with small primary research projects on questions about writing and writers.[5] To study double standards, such a course would have students encounter some of the issues this chapter demonstrates by reading the same research I've cited in my discussion of these issues, and then designing their own small-scale primary research on resulting research questions of their own. A student could study, for example, recursion in "real-world" writing processes by interviewing professionals who write to get descriptions of their habits. Student research on the professional writing practices of a discipline could enact Lave and Wenger's community-of-practice social learning theory and its emphasis on apprenticeship[6] as students shadowed faculty or other professionals for a semester, observing and interviewing about their writing. Or, from a discourse-studies angle, students could collect and analyze artifacts of professional writing processes—developing, for example, a map of the various written genres that led up to or contributed to a given publication.

FYC cannot be a site where students can begin becoming true participants in academe if our teachings are rife with mischaracterizations *of* the writing practices of academe. By encouraging students to investigate faculty's writing practices, we create a kind of apprenticeship. More importantly, we could call out and hopefully reduce or eliminate the double standards that have throughout FYC's history tended not simply to go unchallenged, but be actively reified and reinscribed by FYC. Lighting up these inconsistencies between the writing practices to which education relegates students and those of actual faculty thus becomes a significant step toward the inclusion of student voices in the academy that this book advocates.

---

5. For more information about a writing-about-writing approach to FYC, see Downs' *Teaching Our Own Prison* and "Teaching First Year Writers to *Use* Texts"; Downs and Wardle's "Teaching About Writing, Righting Misconceptions: (Re)Envisioning FYC as Intro to Writing Studies" and "Reimagining the Nature of FYC: Trends in Writing About Writing Pedagogies"; Wardle and Downs' "Looking Into Writing-About-Writing Classrooms"; Wardle's "Creative Repurposing for Expansive Learning"; and Downs and Robertson's "Threshold Concepts in First-Year Composition."

6. See Artemeva's "Toward a Unified Social Theory of Genre Learning" in *Journal of Business and Technical Communication*.

Works Cited

Artemeva, Natasha. "Toward a Unified Social Theory of Genre Learning." *Journal of Business and Technical Communication,* vol. 22, no. 2, 2008, pp. 160–85.

Bazerman, Charles. "Speech Acts, Genres, and Activity Systems: How Texts Organize Activity and People." *What Writing Does and How It Does It: An Introduction to Analyzing Texts and Textual Practices,* edited by Charles Bazerman and Paul Prior, Lawrence Erlbaum, 2004, pp. 309–39.

Beaufort, Ann. *Writing in the Real World: Making the Transition from School to Work.* Teacher's College, 1999.

Berkenkotter, Carol, and Thomas N. Huckin. *Genre Knowledge in Disciplinary Communication: Cognition / Culture / Power.* Lawrence Erlbaum, 1999.

Broad, Bob. *What We Really Value: Beyond Rubrics in Teaching and Assessing Writing.* Utah State UP, 2003.

Conduct Guidelines and Grievance Procedures for Students. Montana State University, 2015, http://www.montana.edu/policy/student_conduct/.

Crowley, Sharon. *Composition in the University: Historical and Polemical Essays.* U of Pittsburgh P, 1998.

Downs, Doug. "Teaching First Year Writers to *Use* Texts: Scholarly Readings in Writing-About-Writing in First-Year Comp." *Reader: Essays in Reader-Oriented Theory, Criticism, and Pedagogy,* vol. 60, 2010, pp. 19–50.

———. *Teaching Our Own Prison: First-Year Composition Curricula and Public Conceptions of Writing.* Dissertation, University of Utah, 2004.

———. "What Is First-Year Composition?" *A Rhetoric for Writing Program Administrators,* edited by Rita Malenczyk, Parlor, 2013, pp. 50–63.

Downs, Doug, and Liane Robertson. "Threshold Concepts in First-Year Composition." *Naming What We Know: Threshold Concepts of Writing Studies,* edited by Linda Adler-Kassner and Elizabeth Wardle, Utah State UP, 2015, pp. 105–21.

Downs, Doug, and Elizabeth Wardle. "Reimagining the Nature of FYC: Trends in Writing-about-Writing Pedagogies." *Exploring Composition Studies: Sites, Issues, Perspectives,* edited by Kelly Ritter and Paul Kei Matsuda, Utah State UP, 2012, pp. 123–44.

———. "Teaching About Writing, Righting Misconceptions: (Re)Envisioning FYC as Intro to Writing Studies." *College Composition and Communication,* vol. 58, 2007, pp. 552–84.

Freire, Paulo. *Pedagogy of the Oppressed.* 30th ed., Bloomsbury, 2000.

Fulkerson, Richard. "Composition at the Turn of the Twenty-First Century." *College Composition and Communication,* vol. 56, 2005, pp. 654–87.

———. "Composition Theory in the Eighties: Axiological Consensus and Paradigmatic Diversity." *College Composition and Communication,* vol. 41, 1990, pp. 409–29.

———. "Four Philosophies of Composition." *College Composition and Communication,* vol. 30, 1979, pp. 343–48.

Gee, James Paul. *An Introduction to Discourse Analysis: Theory and Method.* Routledge, 1999.

———. "Literacy, Discourse, and Linguistics: Introduction." *Journal of Education,* vol. 171, no. 1, 1989, pp. 5–17.

Geisler, Cheryl, et al. "IText: Future Directions for Research on the Relationship between Information Technology and Writing." *Journal of Business and Technical Communication,* vol. 15, 2001, pp. 269–308.

Grant-Davie, Keith. "Rhetorical Situations and Their Constituents." *Rhetoric Review,* vol. 15, 1997, pp. 264–79.

Haswell, Richard. *Gaining Ground in College Writing: Tales of Development and Interpretation.* Southern Methodist UP, 1991.

Hjortshoj, Keith. *The Transition to College Writing.* 2nd ed., Bedford/St. Martin's, 2009.

Howard, Rebecca Moore, et al. "Writing from Sources, Writing from Sentences." *Writing and Pedagogy,* vol. 2, no. 2, 2010, pp. 177–92.

Hyland, Ken. "Authority and Invisibility: Authorial Identity in Academic Writing." *Journal of Pragmatics,* vol. 34, 2002, pp. 1091–1112.

———. "Humble Servants of the Discipline? Self-Mention in Research Articles." *English for Specific Purposes,* vol. 20, no. 3, 2001, pp. 207–26.

MacDonald, Susan Peck. "The Analysis of Academic Discourse." *Discourse Studies in Composition,* edited by Ellen Barton and Gail Stygall, Hampton, 2002, pp. 115–33.

———. *Professional Academic Writing in the Humanities and the Social Sciences.* Southern Illinois UP, 1994.

———. "Voices of Research: Methodological Choices of a Disciplinary Community." *Under Construction: Working at the Intersections of Composition Theory, Research, and Practice,* edited by Christine Farris and Chris Anson, Utah State UP, 1998, pp. 111–23.

Macrorie, Ken. *Telling Writing.* 3rd ed., Hayden, 1980.

Mallory, Angie, and Doug Downs. "Uniform Meets Rhetoric: Excellence through Interaction." *Generation Vet: Composition, Student Veterans, and the Post-9/11 University,* edited by Sue Doe and Lisa Langstraat, Utah State UP, 2014, pp. 51–72.

Mathison, Maureen. "Writing the Critique, a Text about a Text." *Written Communication,* vol. 13, 1996, pp. 314–54.

Melzer, Dan. *Assignments Across the Curriculum: A National Study of College Writing.* Utah State UP, 2014.

Miller, Carolyn R. "Genre as Social Action." *Genre and the New Rhetoric,* edited by Aviva Freedman and Peter Medway, Taylor & Francis, 1994, pp. 20–36.

Perrin, Daniel, and Marc Wildi. "Statistical Modeling of Writing Processes." *Traditions of Writing Research,* edited by Charles Bazerman et al., Routledge, 2010, pp. 378–93.

Robillard, Amy. "Young Scholars Affecting Composition: A Challenge to Disciplinary Citation Practices." *College English,* vol. 68, 2006, pp. 253–70.

Russell, David. "Activity Theory and its Implications for Writing Instruction." *Reconceiving Writing, Rethinking Writing Instruction,* edited by Joseph Petraglia, Erlbaum, 1995, pp. 51–77.

———. "Writing in Multiple Contexts: Vygotskian CHAT Meets the Phenomenology of Genre." *Traditions of Writing Research,* edited by Charles Bazerman et al., Routledge, 2010, pp. 353–64.

Shaughnessy, Mina P. "Diving in: An Introduction to Basic Writing." *College Composition and Communication*, vol. 27, no. 3, 1976, pp. 234–39.

Smit, David. *The End of Composition Studies*. Southern Illinois UP, 2004.

Stewart, I. D., and T. R. Oke. "Local Climate Zones for Urban Temperature Studies." *Bulletin of the American Meteorological Society*, vol. 93, no. 12, 2012, pp. 1879–1900.

Tate, Gary, et al. *A Guide to Composition Pedagogies*. 2nd ed., Oxford UP, 2013.

Wardle, Elizabeth. "Creative Repurposing for Expansive Learning: Considering 'Problem-Exploring' and 'Answer-Getting' Dispositions in Individuals and Fields." *Composition Forum*, vol. 26, 2012, http://compositionforum.com/issue/26/creative-repurposing.php.

Wardle, Elizabeth, and Doug Downs. "Looking into Writing-about-Writing Classrooms." *First-Year Composition: From Theory to Practice*, edited by Deborah Coxwell-Teague and Ronald F. Lunsford, Parlor, 2014, pp. 276–321.

Williams, Joseph. "The Phenomenology of Error." *College Composition and Communication*, vol. 32, no. 2, 1981, pp. 152–68.

Winsor, Dorothy. "Genre and Activity Systems: The Role of Documentation in Maintaining and Changing Engineering Activity Systems." *Written Communication*, vol. 16, no. 2, 1999, pp. 200–24.

———. "Rhetorical Practices in Technical Work." *Journal of Business and Technical Communication*, vol. 12, 1998, pp. 343–70.

———. *Writing Like an Engineer: A Rhetorical Education*. Lawrence Erlbaum, 1996.

———. *Writing Power: Communication in an Engineering Center*. State U of New York P, 2003.

Questions for Discussion and Reflection After Chapter 1

1. Doug's chapter demonstrates that he has carefully considered the questions that Maxine Greene identifies as being essential for teachers to ask as they enact their professional identities: What shall we teach them? How shall we guide them? In light of what Doug shares in his chapter about the disconnect that can exist between what we tell students about writing and what we actually do as writers, along with what you have learned from reading this chapter, how might you answer these questions?

2. Doug maintains that "FYC should . . . be a site for investigation of double standards . . . " and he goes on to note the inconsistences that are present between what students in FYC are told about academic writing and how it is actually practiced, using a story that relates how Professor Plum plans and drafts a scholarly piece. What double standard related to writing might you ask your students to investigate and reflect on? For example, is there a writing "rule" that they have been taught that is often broken in real-world writing that they could investigate?

Writing Activity After Chapter 1

Doug states that the "awareness building" that he describes is "crucial" to the
FYC course "whose purpose is . . . enculturating students into academia as practitioners of academic inquiry." He goes on to suggest ways that this "awareness
building" can be accomplished. Choose one of the ideas for awareness building
that he shares that you believe would work well for your FYC course. Write a draft
of this assignment for your students. What are some objectives that you believe
students would meet through their engagement in this project? How might the
assignment lead to wide-awakeness and agency?

Further Reading

Downs, Doug. "What is First-Year Composition?" *A Rhetoric for Writing Program
Administrators*, edited by Rita Malenczyk, Parlor, 2013, pp. 50–63.
Greene, Maxine. "Wide-Awakeness and the Moral Life." *Exploring Education: An
Introduction*. 5th ed., edited by Alan R. Sadovnik, Peter W. Cookson, Jr., Susan F.
Semel, Ryan W. Coughlan, Routledge, 2018, pp. 218–24.
Noddings, Nel. *The Challenge to Caring in Schools: An Alternative Approach to Edu-
cation*. Teachers College, 1992.

Chapter 2. Teacher as Ally: Supporting LGBTQ Student Writers in the First-Year Composition Classroom

Howa Furrow

PERIMETER COLLEGE AT GEORGIA STATE UNIVERSITY

Reflect Before Reading

Consider the ways that your class activities and writing assignments ask students to share personal information. Students may be asked to write about personal matters in narratives of significant or challenging life experiences or in essays where they put their own histories into conversation with those of authors read in class. In designing these activities and assignments, what thought do you give to how such work challenges LGBTQIA students who are asked to reveal private information in their writing? What options do you provide for students who may not want to write about personal matters?

~ ~ ~

> I believe all LGBT writers confront [inhibition] in their writing and in writing workshops, and at times compromise. However, it is the act of compromising that is lethal to the writer. It stunts our growth and maturity as writers.
>
> —*student (qtd. in Malinowitz 3)*

As James Paul Gee describes "Discourses," he distinguishes between primary Discourses, those we use in our everyday being, and specialist Discourses, those we use as we move among different settings (56–57). The college writing classroom requires students to develop a new specialist Discourse, that of college student writer, leading composition classrooms to be unsettling places for many students. This is especially true for students who are juggling multiple specialist discourses, such as those who are not only new college students entering the academic discourse community but also those who are trying to come into their own as lesbian, gay, bisexual, transgender, or questioning (LGBTQ) individuals in an academic setting that may be only marginally safe for them.

As educators, we know the importance of students feeling safe, confident, and competent as learners. Thus, creating a safe environment for student learning and

DOI: https://doi.org/10.37514/PRA-B.2020.0308.2.02

success is a significant part of our charge as instructors. Susan Rankin et al. found that LGBTQ students frequently feel uncomfortable in the college classroom, particularly in courses where personal information is frequently exchanged, as it is in many first-year composition classes (12). Whether straight or LGBTQ, ally teachers can play an important role in creating safer FYC classrooms.

In my own qualitative study of 30 LGBTQ college students, conducted through interviews and focus groups, participants describe concerns about their safety and identity in their campus experiences in general and their specific concerns as LGBTQ student writers in composition courses.[1] They also express worry about classroom dynamics, including interactions with both classmates and faculty; curriculum and course materials; assignments; and assessment. Equally important, however, these students also provide strategies for ally faculty to use in their classrooms to create an optimal learning environment for all student writers.

This chapter describes these students' concerns and their strategies for ensuring LGBTQ students' safety on campus and in FYC courses, including ideas about inclusive and equitable curricula and required texts. First, though, it's important to understand the threat to safety that many LGBTQ college students face and to understand the FYC course as a site of power.

Identity and Safety on Campus

Identifying as any element of LGBTQ can be difficult, even emotionally and physically unsafe, for students on college campuses. Kristen A. Renn writes that "policies and practices to protect the rights and safety of LGBT people in higher education have emerged" (132), but it is clear that much work remains in this area. Further, Renn notes that while LGBTQ students now have more protections on campus than they used to, colleges and universities have generally avoided "queering" higher education in ways that continue to leave LGBTQ students feeling that they are outsiders (132).

As Andrew J. Rihn and Jay D. Sloan write, while some may see LGBTQ campus concerns as mere marginalization, suicides of gay students show that bullying on campuses is truly a life and death issue for some students. Indeed, the National Coalition of Anti-Violence Programs has stated that the traditional college years are the time of greatest homophobic violence, as approximately 35 percent of physical homophobic attacks are carried out by adults 19 to 29 years old, and a similar percentage of the victims of this violence are that age as well (*Hate* 35–36). Rankin et al. report that LGBTQ students are more likely than other students to fear for their physical safety and to feel the need to avoid disclosing their sexual identity because of intimidation and possible negative consequences (37).

---

1. See Furrow for full study results. The present chapter presents a selection of results that are of most interest to FYC teachers aiming to support LGBTQ students.

These campus-wide concerns may seem separate from the composition class-room, but students are clear that what occurs in classrooms may have an impact on their safety on the broader campus. One student, Lincoln (all student names are pseudonyms), shared in an interview that he was physically threatened in a campus parking lot after his gender identity was exposed in class.

Another student said that he wrote about "the bathroom issue" that transgender students are likely to face:

> After writing about the bathroom issue and making myself vul-nerable in my paper about the issue that all FTMs [female-to-male transgendered individuals] face in the men's room, and my prof doing that, it sort of felt uneasy as well as unsafe more so for the bathroom, not so much for the classroom itself. For me personally, safety is as simple as acknowledging my gender cor-rectly. (Jared)

In Jared's case, his composition teacher asking him about this issue in class made him feel even more unsafe using the campus restrooms.

Writing Classrooms as Sites of Power

Beyond the intimidation and threats of physical violence that our LGBTQ stu-dents experience on campus, they may also experience the classroom as a place that reinforces the heteronormative power structure they witness outside the classroom. Lisa Delpit writes that power is always at work in classrooms, that there is a "culture of power," whose rules reflect those of the culture that has the power, that being told explicitly those rules makes acquiring power easier, and that the power is least recognized by those who have it and most recognized by those who lack it (568).

LGBTQ students recognize the rules about power because they are the same rules they see and experience in their daily lives on and off campus. They know that they can more easily acquire or maintain power by "passing" as heterosexual, either by disguising their gender or sexual identity and relationships or by remaining si-lent. They recognize that this power is also afforded their professors and classmates who may be LGBTQ but choose not to disclose this facet of their identity.

The anonymity, or lack thereof, provided in different sizes and styles of class-rooms also relates directly to one's ability to pass and, therefore, to have power comparable to others in the classroom. A large lecture hall class, in which stu-dents are rarely required to interact with each other or with the instructor, pro-vides a haven that is not afforded in a small class where students regularly interact with each other and the instructor.

FYC classes are traditionally limited in size, and instructors tend to encourage interaction, including the sharing of written pieces. In this environment, LGBTQ students must decide how much they are willing to share, and they must exercise caution if they do not want to come out. For example, three of my study participants said they had chosen to "pass" in their college composition classes, but they would have come out if there had been a good reason to do so. Another student, Jared, regretted that the choice to be out was largely out of his control because his transition from female to male was not physically and legally complete:

> I had to be [out]. Since my insurance is under my dad's, I can't legally change my name yet. So I have to email every professor before the class starts so they don't use my current legal name. In addition to that, many teachers refer to me as female anyway, because I still don't look completely male yet. So, I find myself having to correct them. One Linguistics teacher knew my name was Jared, but continually (without apologizing) referred to me as female. I basically have to come out to each and every professor, just because of the [legal] name problem I have. As for the class students, part of the problem comes up with not passing as male, so I have to come out that way again.

These power inequities that manifest themselves in the FYC classroom may marginalize LGBTQ students, resulting in silencing, more colloquially known as "being in the closet." As William Leap notes, "If the closet is part of gay culture, then the closet, too, has a language—a language that privileges silence over speech, restraint over expression, concealment over cooperation, safety over risk" (268).

Safety in the classroom, both psychological and physical, is clearly necessary for our LGBTQ students to even begin the process of learning. Hilda F. Besner and Charlotte I. Spungin note that any expression of homophobia in the classroom, whether by faculty or by classmates, can frighten LGBTQ students and make them feel "rejected and unsafe" (104). Sondra, one of my student respondents, had this experience: "One professor told me, 'You're not special because you're gay,' and I never really knew what to think about that."

Further, students who feel they must be silent, or otherwise conceal their identities, in the classroom to be physically and emotionally safe have to expend effort that could otherwise be dedicated to learning. Also, their learning may be compromised or undermined; for example, Lila shared this about her feelings of success in her composition classes:

> Often the things that made me uncomfortable as a woman also made me feel uncomfortable as an LGBT student. I did not feel comfortable in most of my classes. I am an excellent writer, and in many of my writing classes I was 'successful' in academic terms [received A grades]. However, I did not feel successful in terms of having my thoughts respected in the same way as other students.

Clearly, a classroom setting where students feel accepted and safe sets a better stage for the learning we want to see take place.

Classroom Dynamics: Interactions
with Faculty and Students

Concerns for LGBTQ students in the FYC classroom begin with the fact that they may be the only LGBTQ student, or one of only a few, in the class. Even if other students, or the instructor, are LGBTQ, they may not "come out" in the classroom, or they may have different relationships with this identity. For example, a lesbian professor may not fully understand the physical vulnerability of a transgender male student. This can be a concern for three reasons: the student may feel alone, without support; he may find that his perspectives are not represented by others or by the curriculum; and he may find himself called upon to represent "the LGBTQ perspective." One student in Neil Simpkins' research said, "When I chose to write on queer or trans topics, I was often called upon by professors in the classroom space to 'explain' how transgender identity worked, perhaps because I had opened myself as willing to discuss my identity in my writing." This additional responsibility placed on the student may be taken by some as a challenge and opportunity; for others, though, it may seem a burden. To be seen as a token capable of, and expected to, represent a population greater than oneself, especially a population as broad as the various identities that make up the LGBTQ community, adds a significant responsibility beyond that of most students in the classroom. Further, it demonstrates how power works in this type of classroom, in which an instructor, even with good intentions, has the power to ask a student to do something that might be uncomfortable for him or her, something that is not expected of other students. Another student, Michael, describes the responsibility he felt to be out in the classroom as "a little burdensome." Others describe the risk of feeling "tokenized," while some feel that they were able to be clear in the classroom and in their writing that their experiences were theirs alone and could not be generalized to a singular "gay experience."

Clearly, sharing identity and understanding the potential for negative repercussions are also concerns for LGBTQ students. In a heteronormative environment, it is a risk for a student to come out in the classroom. Yet, if they do not, they silence themselves in ways that can be detrimental to their self-esteem and to their academic success.

Lincoln and Michael, for example, found themselves wanting to confront "the straight assumption" in the classroom to correct the perception that anyone who did not come out as LGBTQ must be heterosexual. Lincoln wrote about sexual identity. He stated that his teacher graded only the grammar and made no comments on the content. He remarked that he felt the instructor "intentionally overlooked" the content, choosing to act as though it didn't exist. Michael wrote a paper about whether sexuality is genetic. In peer review, his peer editor didn't understand the topic. Michael's instructor and classmates both said his essay felt too forced, and Michael's response was, "Maybe this was true, but fighting against the status quo does take more." While both students tried to use their writing to educate others about LGBTQ issues, neither felt successful in his attempt.

Some students see their composition classroom as an opportunity to educate their instructors and classmates about LGBTQ issues. This may happen even if the instructor and some classmates do come out as LGBTQ, but it seems even more likely to occur when a student feels that he or she is the singular voice for such concerns. Lila says that her comfort level as well as her sense of responsibility led her to come out in a class: "I had a writing instructor . . . come to a one-on-one meeting and tell me, 'I can't believe I just wasted a whole day at work in diversity training.' He was not high on my list of instructors to be open with. But when HIV+ people were attacked (as a generic group) in a class, I felt compelled to speak up." For Lila, it seems that a sense of social responsibility played a significant role in choosing to come out. She didn't feel that speaking to the instructor individually would make a difference since he did not seem interested in diversity. However, with the verbal attack on HIV+ people (often associated with gay men), she felt she could not stay silent in the classroom.

Curriculum and Course Materials

The curriculum and course materials, of course, play an important role in student success in the classroom. Often, though, LGBTQ students do not see themselves represented in these essential elements. In one study, LGBTQ students were less likely than other students to agree that their institution's general education requirements and curriculum represented the contributions of LGBTQ people (Rankin et al. 155). This omission of LGBTQ role models in the curriculum results in a silence, possible feelings of exclusion, and damage to self-esteem (Hudson 2).

Textbooks, for example, send important messages through what they do and do not contain. As Michael Apple notes, both textbooks and curriculum represent not "neutral knowledge" but what society sees as "legitimate" or "official" knowledge (4). They demonstrate to students what academe sees as content worthy of study.

Martha Marinara et al. examined 290 composition textbooks for their inclusion of LGBTQ content. They found specific LGBTQ content in only 73 of these textbooks, and they noted that much of this content was focused arguments for and against gay marriage (276–77). Because of this lack of complete and authentic LGBTQ representation in composition readers, LGBTQ individuals find the textual representation in their composition classes to be focused on a singular experience that does not accurately represent the complexity and individuality of their lives. Hudson writes, "This reliance on gay marriage as a vehicle for LGBTQ inclusion in readers can actually be dehumanizing" because, as Marinara et al. note, individuals are positioned "not as full citizens in a democracy and members of families with rich and diverse experiences, but primarily as a minority group that the majority can consider only in arguments about 'rights,' a minority group that must be rescued by the straight majority to succeed" (279).

While the students I interviewed did not share their concerns about textbooks and other required readings, they did describe a lack of inclusion of LGBTQ perspectives in the overall curriculum. Helen said, "My freshman writing teacher didn't seem to think of LGBT students at all. She never included it in issues of diversity." Bruce had a similar experience: "I don't remember LGBT issues ever coming up in the classroom. I don't remember anyone ever talking about it." For these two students, then, an important aspect of their identity was never addressed, even though, for Helen, other elements relating to diversity were included in the curriculum.

Assignments and Assessment

As in curriculum and in classroom interactions, LGBTQ students also often find themselves under-represented in composition assignments. One student noted, "LGBTQ topics were rarely listed on my writing assignments" (Simpkins). Alternatively, though, they may feel pressured to disclose information about themselves for assignments. Composition instructors often tell students to "write about what they know," but Marinara et al. remind us that this directive may not feel entirely safe or comfortable for LGBTQ students:

> For LGBT/queer students, putting the responsibility on them to
> articulate themselves in classroom spaces may be the act of pre-
> venting such articulations from emerging. Indeed, at least for
> this group of students, writing about their experiences of differ-
> ence, where their difference is still taboo and circumscribed by
> fear and discourses of legality, potentially puts LGBT students
> in a difficult position. (273)

Students are very aware of the interactions between their identities as individuals and their identities as student writers. Choosing whether to write about LGBT issues may be an easy decision for some; for others, it may be much more difficult.

LGBTQ students often struggle with how much to disclose, not only in the classroom, but also in their writing. This is particularly significant because instructors often encourage them to write about personal experiences, often in the genres of description and narration. Harriet Malinowitz describes writing prompts that require students "to do such things as to reflect upon the 'self,' to narrate personal events, to interpret texts in ways that reveal the subjectivity of the writer, and to write research papers on topics that are 'of interest to them'" (24). Each of these seems to call upon students to write about topics that disclose aspects of their identity they might otherwise not choose to share.

The students I interviewed shared their feelings about being directed or asked to write about personal experiences, and some of these responses do indicate feelings of discomfiture that this type of assignment can elicit. While Jared asserted that "speaking about being lesbian and transgender since I was 16" resulted in feeling "comfortable" with this kind of writing, other students conveyed feelings of nervousness and even fear. Referring to an autobiographical writing assignment, Erica stated: "I started with two major struggles—sexuality and religion. I was a little nervous . . . because of the content." Lila said that "I generally did not feel comfortable sharing my personal experiences." Finally, Sophia remarked, "I was afraid to write too close, too deep down. I didn't want to expose myself. Straight students don't expose themselves. . . . It shouldn't be a problem, but it is." These responses to writing expectations suggest a need for caution when requiring students to write about personal experiences that may lead to more self-disclosure than the student is comfortable with.

Often, the instructor is not the only one reading the assignment, as students frequently participate in peer review or take their papers to a writing center. One student expressed an interesting concern with peer review: "In my undergraduate classes, peer review was sometimes a challenge, too, since other students would have trouble criticizing my work because they thought they would be criticizing my identity" (Simpkins).

As challenging as sharing one's writing with a classmate in peer review or in a writing center can be, many students find reading their writing aloud in class to be the most difficult type of sharing. In my study, several students shared concerns about reading a paper aloud in class.

David said that he would not write a paper about his LGBT identity because "I wouldn't have felt comfortable sharing it with strangers. I wait to share new things." Referring to being required to read drafts aloud, Lincoln noted that he had to be "careful" about what he wrote about. Sophia focused on her peers in her composition course, stating that they are "sometimes squeamish if you write about LGBT issues. . . . They only want to hear about gay people in a theoretical way, not gay people actually doing anything."

Beyond the concerns expressed by students in general, LGBTQ students find they have to be careful about how much, and with what tone, they write about LGBTQ issues if they are going to be required to read these papers aloud in class. It is apparent that not only topic choice, but also audience, which isn't always revealed ahead of time, plays a role in LGBTQ students' feelings of safety regarding writing in the first-year writing classroom.

With the concerns of LGBTQ writing students in mind, it makes sense now to turn to the role of the FYC instructor. My study participants shared many ideas for ways that composition instructors can work to address their concerns. The overarching element of this work is that of considering oneself an ally to one's LGBTQ students.

Being an Ally

The field of composition has often worked proactively to create equity for students. How can we, as composition instructors, whether straight or LGBTQ ourselves, best do this to meet the needs of our LGBTQ students? We can do this by disrupting the silence, using our own voices to speak up for those who may feel they cannot speak up for themselves, and by intentionally making ourselves the allies of our LGBTQ students. I share ten ways to begin this work.

Begin by Understanding the Importance of LGBTQ Issues for All Our Students.

In a class of 20 to 25 students, it is safe to assume that one or more students identify as LGBTQ or eventually will, one or more students have a parent or parents who are LGBTQ, and many others have close family members or friends who are LGBTQ. For these students, LGBTQ issues are everyday issues. For other students, they will likely find themselves in personal and professional relationships with people who identify as LGBTQ, and thus they will benefit from a greater awareness of LGBTQ realities, interests, and concerns.

Learn About the Current Situation for LGBTQ Individuals, Especially Those in Our Classrooms.

We must consider and re-consider what we think, know, and believe about LGBTQ individuals. Nancy J. Evans writes, "Individuals must also come to an awareness of the myths and stereotypes they themselves hold about lesbian, gay, and bisexual people" (84), and Vernon A. Wall and Evans elaborate on ways to do this:

> First, gather as much information as you can. Increase your knowledge about the topic of homosexuality. Second, examine your values and beliefs. Knowing where you stand on specific issues and having a willingness to be "stretched" can be extremely beneficial. Third, remember that each gay and lesbian student is an individual, each with different experiences and each at his or her own level of development. (35)

Some schools have resources such as diversity workshops to help teachers learn more about the academic needs of LGBTQ students.

Consider Learning More and Trying to Eliminate any Internalized Homophobia.

All teachers, and even teachers who identify as lesbian, gay, bisexual, or transgender, may want to consider learning more and trying to eliminate any internalized homophobia. For example, being a gay man does not necessarily mean that one understands the unique situations and experiences of lesbian, bisexual, transgender, or questioning individuals. These teachers may also want to learn more about LGBTQ student concerns on campus and in the classroom.

It is also important to remember that every act of personal writing is potentially an act of self-disclosure and of risk for LGBTQ students. These students
"must constantly assess the consequences of being out and negotiate the terms
of disclosure, often necessitating elaborate monitoring of what is said and even
thought, a particular complication is woven into their processes of construing
and constructing knowledge" (Malinowitz 22). Students want to know what is
expected of them in terms of topic choice and self-disclosure. They want to know
who will be reading their assignment and how it will be graded.

Teachers must also stay aware of the school and community environment
for LGBTQ students. As adults working on campus in a professional capacity,
we may not be entirely aware of what is happening for LGBTQ students in caf-
eterias and dormitories, for example. Conversing with students and reading the
campus newspaper can demonstrate how students are regarding the campus
climate. Furthermore, when a state legislature is having a vote regarding gay
rights, or considering the possibility of gay marriage or civil union legislation,
LGBTQ students and students with LGBTQ family members are likely to be
emotionally affected.

Actively Demonstrate that You Are an Ally.

The Gay, Lesbian & Straight Education Network's most recent study shows that
high school teachers who identify as allies of their LGBTQ students create safe
academic environments and demonstrate understanding of the concerns of their
LGBTQ students. One can also provide visual cues. Wear an ally logo, carry an
ally pin, or display something else that identifies you as an ally, such as a "Safe
Space" sticker, at your desk or elsewhere in your classroom. Finally, if you are
LGBTQ yourself, choosing to be "out" in the classroom is a personal decision that
you may wish to consider.

Use Inclusive Language.

Show a sensitivity to gender issues in general by using and encouraging the use
of gender-neutral language. When discussing LGBTQ issues, do so without es-
sentializing LGBTQ people. Include sexual orientation and gender identity in
broader conversations without making them seem marginalized as "other."

Set Up the Classroom as a Safe Environment.

Students need to know their instructor is on their side, and they need to hear
that what they say and experience is valid. If your curriculum requires personal
sharing, either in small groups, workshops, peer review groups, or large-group
discussions, teach students to participate equitably within these settings. Establish guidelines, such as "Everyone must be listened to; we can disagree but stay

respectful." In this way, students know that an expectation has been set for what they say to be respected.

Confront Homophobia in the Classroom.

LGBTQ students need to know that the teacher will intervene quickly and constructively if the environment begins to become less safe. Negative comments should be addressed, and the teacher should be clear that such comments should not be used to silence others. It may help to remind students that we all have different backgrounds and experiences, even if the classroom looks homogenous. Topics being discussed should be kept separate from individuals, so that controversial topics can be discussed without being perceived as a personal attack. Planning ahead and directing discussion carefully can also minimize conflict. Know ahead of time what you will say if a student makes a general comment like "That's so gay!" or if a student confronts another student about what is being shared.

Include LGBTQ Issues in the Curriculum as Appropriate.

In the composition curriculum, it is feasible for many of us to include LGBTQ issues in a variety of ways. Normalcy of LGBTQ identities can be modeled by including them on a regular basis in curriculum and discussions. It is important that students have the opportunity to see LGBTQ people living normal, successful day-to-day lives. If you want to use your classroom to begin to create social change, you can consider ways to do this that support marginalized students without jeopardizing the safety of the non-marginalized students. For example, don't introduce LGBTQ issues as topics of controversy. If you say, "This might be controversial," you add to the air of controversy, not of normalcy. Textbooks should be chosen with these concerns in mind as well.

Create, Use, and Assess Writing Assignments with LGBTQ Students in Mind.

Some students may feel additional pressure because of the subjective nature of evaluating writing. That is, they may be concerned that if they write something with which the teacher does not agree, particularly about their LGBTQ identity, they may be penalized in the grading process. Malinowitz describes an approach one may consider:

> Think of how [LGBT writers] are told to be aware of issues of audience, subject, and purpose, and to claim textual authority. Then consider the convoluted dimensions these rhetorical issues take on when lesbian and gay writers inevitably have to choose between risking a stance from an outlaw discourse or

entering into the familiarly dominant discourse of heterosex-
uality. (24)

Assignments should be explained clearly and should include how the writing
will be evaluated so that students can make an informed decision to choose a
topic that does or does not require disclosure of their sexual identities. Broadly
interpretable prompts allow all students to write about a topic they feel they can
write well about or wish to explore in writing. Multiple drafts allow students to
revise if they discover they have not written appropriately to the assignment. In
terms of evaluation, students want to know that teachers will read their paper
with an open mind. Some students may be concerned because of the subjective
nature of evaluating writing and fear that if the teacher's beliefs are different from
their own, they will be penalized.

Some assignments may make students uncomfortable if they require students
to put part of themselves aside, or if students have to struggle with whether or not
they must put part of themselves aside. For example, an assignment might ask
students to write about success. This topic may seem innocuous, but an LGBTQ
student, particularly one struggling with coming out issues, may have difficulty as they consider all the ramifications of what it means to be successful and
LGBTQ-identified in a largely heterosexist society.

Be Proactive in Educating Others and Broadening Perspectives for Colleagues and Students.

There are many ways to demonstrate one's support for LGBTQ students and colleagues outside the classroom. Take the initiative to share your own experiences
in addressing these issues with others. Ask your school to provide professional
development about LGBTQ issues. Support Safe Space Training for teachers and
staff. Help students form a Gay Straight Alliance. Read relevant articles in professional journals, and attend relevant sessions at professional conferences.

Works Cited

Apple, Michael W. "The Text and Cultural Politics." *Educational Researcher*, vol. 21,
no. 7, 1992, pp. 4–19.

Besner, Hilda F., and Charlotte I. Spungin. *Gay and Lesbian Students: Understanding
Their Needs*. Taylor & Francis, 2000.

Delpit, Lisa. "The Silenced Dialogue: Power and Pedagogy in Educating Other People's Children." *Cross-Talk in Comp Theory: A Reader*, edited by Victor
Villanueva, National Council of Teachers of English, 1997, pp. 565–88.

Evans, Nancy J. "Creating a Positive Learning Environment for Gay, Lesbian, and
Bisexual Students." *Teaching to Promote Intellectual and Personal Maturity: Incor-
porating Students' Worldviews and Identities into the Learning Process*, edited by
Marcia B. Baxter, Jossey-Bass, 2000, pp. 81–87.

Furrow, Hannah. "LGBT Students in the College Composition Classroom." *Journal of Ethnographic & Qualitative Research*, vol. 6, 2012, pp. 145–59.

Gee, James Paul. "Discourses in and Out of School: Looking Back." *Framing Language and Literacies: Socially Situated Views and Perspectives*, edited by Margaret R. Hawkins, Routledge, 2013, pp. 51–82.

Hate Violence Against Lesbian, Gay, Bisexual, Transgender, Queer, and HIV-Affected Communities in the United States in 2010. National Coalition of Anti-Violence Programs, 2011, https://avp.org/wp-content/uploads/2017/04/2011_NCAVP_HV_Reports.pdf.

Hudson, John. "Breaking the Silence: Toward Improving LGBTQ Representation in Composition Readers." *Composition Forum*, vol. 29, 2014, compositionforum.com/issue/29/breaking-the-silence.php.

Kosciw, Joseph G., et al. *The 2013 National School Climate Survey: The Experiences of Lesbian, Gay, Bisexual and Transgender Youth in Our Nation's Schools*. Gay, Lesbian & Straight Education Network (GLSEN), 2014, https://files.eric.ed.gov/fulltext/ED570433.pdf.

Leap, William. "Language, Socialization, and Silence in Gay Adolescence." *Reinventing Identities: The Gendered Self in Discourse*, edited by Mary Bucholtz, A. C. Liang, and Lauren A. Sutton, Oxford UP, 1999, pp. 259–72.

Malinowitz, Harriet. *Textual Orientations: Lesbian and Gay Students and the Making of Discourse Communities*. Heinemann, 1995.

Marinara, Martha, et al. "Cruising Composition Texts: Negotiating Sexual Difference in First-Year Readers." *College Composition and Communication*, vol. 61, no. 2, 2009, pp. 269–96.

Rankin, Susan, et al. *2010 State of Higher Education for Lesbian, Gay, Bisexual & Transgender People*. Q Research Institute for Higher Education, 2010, www.campuspride.org/wp-content/uploads/campuspride2010lgbtreportssummary.pdf.

Renn, Kristen A. "LGBT and Queer Research in Higher Education: The State and Status of the Field." *Educational Researcher*, vol. 39, no. 2, 2010, pp. 132–41.

Rihn, Andrew J., and Jay D. Sloan. "Rainbows in the Past Were Gay: LGBTQIA in the WC." *Praxis: A Writing Center Journal*, vol. 10, no. 2, 2013, http://www.praxisuwc.com/rihn-sloan–102.

Simpkins, Neil. "Meeting the Needs of LGBTQ Students in the Writing Center." *Another Word from the Writing Center at the University of Wisconsin-Madison*, 18 Nov. 2013,https://dept.writing.wisc.edu/blog/meeting-the-needs-of-lgbtq-students-in-the-writing-center/.

Wall, Vernon A., and Nancy J. Evans. "Using Psychosocial Development Theories to Understand and Work with Gay and Lesbian Persons." *Beyond Tolerance: Gays, Lesbians and Bisexuals on Campus*, edited by Vernon A. Wall and Nancy J. Evans, American College Personnel Association, 1991, pp. 25–38.

Questions for Reflection and Discussion After Chapter 2

1. How might you incorporate LGBTQIA-related content into reading material or options for writing assignments in your courses?

2. Where and how is safety for LGBTQIA students a topic of discussion on your campus and in your department? What resources exist on your campus to support students and educate faculty? Have you taken advantage of any of these available resources? If so, how have they helped you understand and support your LGBTQIA students?

Writing Activity After Chapter 2

Choose one of the following lines of dialogue and imagine a student has just said it in the middle of class. Write the scene that follows, describing your response to the comment and the dialogue that follows among you, the speaker, and other students. Student comments:

"That's so gay." (Said in a derogatory manner.)

"The story doesn't say if the spouse is a woman, but she has to be a woman, because the narrator is a man."

"I want to do my research project on transgender bathroom legislation."

"Are you a guy?" (Upon meeting a classmate with a gender-neutral name.)

"It's stupid that the college lets us list preferred pronouns in our accounts now. Why would anyone care about that?"

Further Reading

Fox, Catherine. "From Transaction to Transformation: (En)Countering White Heteronormativity in 'Safe Spaces.'" *College English*, vol. 69, no. 5, 2007, pp. 496–511.

Hurlbert, Claude. *National Healing: Race, State, and the Teaching of Composition.* Utah State UP, 2012.

Mitchell, Danielle. "I Thought Composition Was About Commas and Quotes, Not Queers: Diversity and Campus Change at a Rural Two-Year College." *Composition Studies*, vol. 26, no. 2, 2008, pp. 23–50.

Pruitt, John. "Heterosexual Readers in Search of Queer Authenticity through Self-Selected LGBT Novels." *Teaching English in the Two-Year College*, vol. 42, no. 4, 2015, pp. 359–374.

Chapter 3. Three Student Voices on Technology in First-Year Composition

Ann N. Amicucci
University of Colorado Colorado Springs

Reflect Before Reading

How do you elicit students' thoughts and opinions about your FYC course? Have you ever asked students their opinions about assignments or asked if the course and/ or assignments should be altered in some way? Finally, what policy do you have in place that concerns the use of cell phones and other electronic devices during class? How did you arrive at this policy?

~ ~ ~

Meet Rachel, Bethany, and Zachary, three first-year college students who are avid users of digital technologies. Each uses a mobile device to text daily, and each engages with and creates content on Facebook frequently. Rachel, an English education major, reads posts on Facebook daily and creates her own, looks through people's pictures, and uses the site to stay in touch with long-distance friends and family who are just some of her roughly 900 friend connections on the site. Bethany, an international business major, also reads and writes material on Facebook daily, and she uses an instant messenger online every day to chat with family and friends. She has roughly 300 friends on Facebook and often switches back and forth between texting and instant messaging within a continued conversation with the same person. Zachary, an English education major like Rachel, also writes on Facebook daily and looks at photographs on the site just as often.

As teachers, we know that many of our students have daily digital writing habits that look like Rachel's, Bethany's, and Zachary's, and we often talk with each other about the role such technologies can play in FYC. Yet in professional scholarship on the uses of technology in FYC, student voices are largely missing. As Susan Kirtley questions, "How can we know if our theories and practices are relevant and appropriate when developed without student input?" (210). In inviting you to consider the perspectives of three first-year college students on technology use in the FYC classroom, my aim is to prompt ideas for innovative technology use in FYC while simultaneously arguing for the inclusion of student perspectives in research on this subject.

At the time I interviewed them, Rachel, Bethany, and Zachary (all pseudonyms) were first-year students at a mid-sized public university who had completed their

DOI: https://doi.org/10.37514/PRA-B.2020.0308.2.03

required FYC course; none was a student of mine, though Bethany and Zachary happened to have had the same FYC teacher. Each student completed a survey of his or her frequency of use of a range of digital technologies, then met with me for an individual conversation. Through these surveys and interviews, I gathered information about these students' non-academic digital literacy practices—the ways they use digital technologies to read and write for non-academic purposes—and their perceptions of the value or lack thereof in utilizing such literacies in FYC courses. Rachel, Bethany, and Zachary did not, to my knowledge, know one another, and my conversation with each was separate and confidential from those with the others. Yet commonalities emerged in how each of these students described possibilities for bringing their existing digital literacy practices into FYC: each argues that because technology facilitates ease in achieving course learning objectives, students should be encouraged to use digital tools in the classroom. Each calls for social media to be used to facilitate connections among students in a class. And each makes the case for why students, not teachers, should decide when and how students may use digital technologies in FYC.

In published scholarship on this subject, teachers report using digital technologies in FYC in two primary ways: by assigning multimodal, digital composition projects and by utilizing digital, social tools for FYC activities. The former, to my surprise, did not come up in my conversations with students. Though our field has experimented successfully with numerous ways of composing with and through digital technologies, these first-year students did not readily envision moving away from traditional composing methods in FYC. However, the latter subject addressed in published scholarship, that of utilizing digital, social tools for FYC activities, was echoed in each student interview. It is here—the use of digital social technologies, particularly to facilitate connections with others—that Rachel, Bethany, and Zachary see the greatest potential for technology use in FYC.

Multimodal, Digital Composition and Social Media in FYC

While teachers' use of digital technologies in FYC varies widely, there are, as I have noted, two primary ways that teacher-scholars report using technology in the FYC classroom that are relevant to my discussion here: by designing writing projects that employ digital, multimodal composing methods and by facilitating community and connection among students through the use of digital, social tools. In two authors' work on this subject, we find rich descriptions of what digital composition projects can look like in FYC.[1] Daniel Anderson describes a digital project that gives

---

1. By "digital composition projects," I mean any course projects that include the use of digital technologies in meaning making; creating websites, digital videos, or audio essays would all be considered forms of digital composition, as would writing a blog entry or preparing a set of PowerPoint slides.

students a great deal of freedom to select the technologies they use. Jody Shipka, similarly, defines a multimodal, digital project in which students choose not only their medium of composition but also their audience and purpose for composing.

In "The Low Bridge to High Benefits: Entry-Level Multimedia, Literacies, and Motivation," Anderson discusses a pedagogical approach that gives students freedom to shape an assignment for their own purposes within a multimodal framework. Anderson assigns students to compose playlists: "Students create either a profile or a short narrative by identifying a set of songs that represents the identity of a person or tells a story" (47). This assignment provides a low-stakes introduction to multimodal composing for FYC students by drawing on familiar literacies of text-based composing and sorting music, while also pushing students to develop expertise in skills such as creating HTML links and understanding fair use of song excerpts (47–48). By providing a "low-bridge integration of media," Anderson's assignment gives students "an entrée into informational and remix literacies and can also open avenues that bridge audio literacies with composition" (56–57). In this way, Anderson uses FYC projects to expose students to composing possibilities beyond alphabetic, linear text.

In a similar vein of affording students choice in a digital composition project, Shipka discusses in "A Multimodal Task-Based Framework for Composing" the "rhetorical events" her first-year writers compose, termed as such because they do not fit the strictures of "linear, argumentative, thesis-driven print texts" (282). In one such project, for example, a student interviews her classmates about their hometowns, researches features of those hometowns online, then recreates the websites she finds to incorporate images of her classmates (281–82). In this particular FYC assignment, Shipka's students have the freedom to define the aim, audience, and media of their compositions rather than compose in ways that are confined by traditional expectations of academic writing. One student records a video, another compiles electronic sounds and images to accompany a paper, and still others choose to compose multimodal projects that do not incorporate digital technologies, such as a student who creates a quiz taken by reading a piece of paper held up to a mirror. Shipka demonstrates how her students still achieve common FYC learning outcomes while completing such widely varied assignments; for example, all students' work involves incorporating voices from other texts into their own (286). Her discussion highlights the fact that FYC teachers can widen the possibilities for students' use of technology greatly while still ensuring that students accomplish what they need to in a course.

Many other scholars report ways of using digital, social tools—often tools that are already part of students' digital literacy practices—in FYC activities; I will highlight two such scholars' work here: Nicole Emmelhainz's work with a multimodal class blog and Abigail A. Grant's use of texting for class activities. In "Status Update to Term Paper: Social Network Sites as a Medium for Collaboration," Emmelhainz describes a class blog on which students compose with images and links in addition to traditional text and use the blog's features to engage with each other's ideas (100). She writes that her goal in introducing FYC students to blogging was to help them "understand that the ways in which the technology supported the presentation of their ideas actually *enhanced* their ability to communicate, to make connections with their peers" (101). In a manner similar to Anderson's approach with low-bridge technologies, Emmelhainz gives her students the opportunity to learn a new form of composing that does not differ too drastically from the traditional forms of composition with which they are familiar.

Grant also draws specifically on a digital literacy her students already practice by suggesting in "Textperts: Utilizing Students' Skills in the Teaching of Writing" that FYC teachers capitalize on students' predilection for communicating in writing through text messages. Grant argues that students frequently practice many writing process activities through text messaging. She writes, "Students want to write and enjoy doing it every day. They just do not seem to be very keen on writing in the genres that their instructors typically require. They text message, Tweet, Facebook, note, email, list, save, and edit" (250). Grant says her students think carefully about how to compose their text messages, even going as far as to write collaboratively with the assistance of their peers. Because students already consider written language closely within the genre of texting, Grant suggests that teachers use text messaging as a genre for in-class writing practice by having students write poetry that is confined to the 160-character limit of a text message, using this character limit to focus students' attention on "editing skills," and using texting as a starting point for a conversation about genre limitations and audience expectations, both in regards to the genre of text messages and other written genres with which texting can be contrasted (253). By drawing on one of students' existing writing literacies, Grant posits that teachers can give students more agency in the FYC classroom, making students the experts—or "textperts" (248)—in a genre of writing.

The praxis described by Anderson, Shipka, Emmelhainz, and Grant only scratches the surface of scholarship in this area, as numerous teacher-scholars are bringing digital literacies into the FYC classroom, and many are linking specific course activities to students' existing digital literacy practices. What the four pieces of published literature discussed here have in common is attention to who students are: to what technologies they are comfortable with, to the technologies they already use and may desire to use in the classroom, and to the value of giving students agency in choosing which digital technologies to use and how to use them. As teacher-scholars investigating effective uses of digital technologies in FYC, we can deepen such scholarship by acknowledging students' perspectives on this topic. In what follows, I discuss Rachel's, Bethany's, and Zachary's takes on what effective technology use can look like in FYC.

The Convenience of Technology in Education

Rachel, Bethany, and Zachary had varying experiences with technology in FYC, though each had been guided by an FYC teacher to use digital technologies to aid in class work. In Rachel's FYC course, digital technologies were positioned as a research resource. Rachel's teacher assigned readings in a digital format and taught the class how to use the university library's research databases to locate outside sources for a literature review, and Rachel also completed a project that required students to evaluate the credibility of several websites. She explains that the teacher "gave us an evaluation rubric and then you had to [figure out] what's the sponsor of this site, who wrote it, what's the copyright, is this credible, you know, making us start to question what we're looking at online, more than just trusting the average person." Rachel says that having to formally evaluate websites was new to her, but explains, "I know that you should always question what you read online, just because it's online." She explains that her preference is to work with print rather than digital sources but that she did see the value in learning to turn a critical eye on digital source material rather than "just trusting" that it contained credible information. Rachel doesn't mention cell phone use in her FYC class, though we will hear from Bethany and Zachary that phones were used frequently in theirs. In Rachel's FYC class, computers were only used when students were working on course projects, and given Rachel's penchant toward print texts, she was satisfied with computer use being somewhat limited in the course; she finds this to be "a good balance of technology and other things in the class."

Bethany and Zachary, who had the same teacher for FYC, used digital technologies in class in less formal ways. Their FYC course was thematically focused on music, and students in the course were frequently asked to watch and analyze music videos and compose song lyrics. Zachary explains that the course employed digital technologies in relation to these assignments: students used YouTube to watch music videos and iPods and Windows Media Player to listen to music related to class projects. Whereas Rachel's class involved technology use only within the academic realm—that is, Rachel's teacher taught students to use digital tools and gave them the opportunity to use such tools only in ways that academic writers typically use them—Bethany and Zachary's teacher reached beyond traditional technology use within the academy and prompted students to use digital tools they already use but to now use them for academic purposes.

Bethany relates that the FYC teacher also encouraged students to use any digital devices they had to connect to the internet as a resource during class. She says that the teacher "let us for sometimes if we needed to look stuff up, he's like, you know, I don't care, you can get out your phone, search, you know, look it up, and it's faster than, okay, I'm going to write this down, remember to go home and look it up." Bethany's description is one of a classroom without figurative walls. She notes that because many students have phones with internet access, the teacher often geared students to see that access as a resource that can enhance the work they do in the classroom. Both Bethany and Zachary describe their FYC classroom environment as one in which digital devices were often in play, with students using cell phones and computers frequently in class.

Talking with Bethany and Zachary about the role that cell phone use plays in their FYC classroom led me to reflect on how phones were positioned in my own FYC courses. Whereas these students' teacher encouraged phone use—and in doing so, demonstrated to students how the digital tools they already had access to could be used as academic resources—my own students at the time encountered a "Classroom Courtesy" policy on the syllabus that read, "Cell phones and other electronic devices should be turned to silent and put away during class time." Talking with Bethany and Zachary got me thinking that perhaps my own impulse to curtail any digital device use in the classroom, in order to maintain students' focus and prevent distractions, was in fact denying students the opportunity to enhance their classroom learning by using these very devices. I will return to these questions shortly, to illustrate how these students' perspectives shaped my approach to cell phone use in the FYC classroom.

Making Connections through Social Media

Because all three students text and use Facebook often, it is unsurprising that each looks to the connections afforded by these forms of digital communication for ideas of how to utilize technology in FYC. Bethany says that her instructor's policy of allowing students to use their phones to look up information could be taken a step further in FYC by encouraging students to text during class, which she has found to be useful in other courses. "My business class is like 200 people," she says, "and sometimes you can't hear the teachers so you know, if you just text the person you know, without talking it, [you can ask] *What did he say?*" She suggests that when a class discussion or in-class activity is taking place—not a test or other assessment, she stresses—students could text people they know outside of class for input and answers or even text others in the same room. Doing so might even give more students opportunities to participate in class; students who may be reluctant to speak aloud in class or join in a lively discussion may be more comfortable contributing via their phones, either by starting conversations with others outside of class on the class topic or connecting with others in the room to share their perspectives.

All three students say they make connections through texting with classmates outside of the classroom. In her business course, Bethany and a group of other students exchanged numbers for this purpose. She says, "We don't talk, you know, we don't hang out outside of class but . . . we'll text each other, be like *Hey, what was the assignment in class today?* or *How did you submit your paper?*" Bethany has made specific connections with peers in her business course to facilitate her success in college; these are different than her social connections with friends, and she describes texting as the vehicle for making these connections possible. Rachel explains that she uses Facebook for similar reasons. She says, "[I]t's good for college in the sense that if you have a class with somebody and you need something, you can send them a message, and you're like *Hey, do you have this?*" For Rachel, too, these are academic rather than social connections. Rachel describes getting a Facebook message from someone in her math class who she doesn't know, asking her for information about announcements made in class that this other student missed. Rachel explains that Facebook is "a very good tool" for purposes such as this one—she says, "[I]t is nice in the sense academically that if you need help, you can outreach to people in your college."

Rachel argues that the way she uses Facebook to connect with classmates to ask questions or talk about homework could benefit students in an FYC class. She suggests that teachers can use Facebook groups to bring FYC students together outside of the classroom:

> [I]f classes formed groups on Facebook and then you can write stuff right on the group page, and share things, you could prob-ably like share links or share this and that. . . . That would be really cool. That way, you know, outside of class, everyone's con-nected, because everyone has Facebook. . . . It'd be nice if any-body needed help with something, they could go on the Face-book page and say, *Does anybody know . . . this?*

In such a scenario, Rachel explains, classmates could answer each other's questions. In the same way that the student in her math class reached out to Ra-chel for help, Rachel sees the potential for students to help each other in FYC by connecting on Facebook, but her perspective suggests that many students don't readily facilitate these connections on their own and that FYC teachers could play a role in facilitating them.

Zachary also sees potential for his use of Facebook to enhance an FYC course. Students in his FYC course only used email to connect with one another outside of class, primarily to circulate work on a group project. But, Zachary explains, the group project may have been easier if students had had other ways to communi-cate. He says:

> Say like in my writing class this last semester, we had one proj-ect where we did a CD mix where we, we had a group of people, we each picked songs and wrote up analyses for them. But if we were sitting in class and one of the people didn't send in their part of our paper and wasn't there that day . . . if one of us had had their Facebooks, we could have just pulled out our laptops real quick and gone on, see if they were on. . . . and say, *Are you coming? What's going on here?*

We can hear a similar value in Zachary's and Bethany's ways of describing a classroom without figurative walls, a classroom in which conversation is not limited to those who are present in the classroom during class time. As a teacher, I perceive a student who is absent from a class meeting as being wholly absent from participating in class for that day. Zachary sees things differently. For him, a student's absence from the physical classroom doesn't preclude the student from participating in class, and Zachary shows how encouraging students to connect via a tool like Facebook would be one way to keep students present in the conversation when they are absent from the room. In further explaining the CD mix project, Zachary says that email was the only digital tool students used to keep in touch and that it was useful for combining parts of the project, but "other technologies could be helpful for like, *Hey, when do you want to meet up for this?* or like in class, *Where are you? We need you."* Like Rachel and Bethany, Zachary points out the communicative potential that digital technologies could offer students in FYC. Zachary and his classmates could certainly have initiated their own connections via Facebook or texting, but they didn't, and similar to what the two other students have indicated, Zachary sees an opportunity here for FYC teachers to aid students in facilitating these connections.

These students' descriptions of Facebook and texting as ways to connect members of an FYC class highlight their desires to make connections with classmates that otherwise might not be present. Depending on class size, FYC students may not have the opportunity to get to know every other person in the room; but, if these students were encouraged to connect with each other via texting or in an online social space such as Facebook, they may take the opportunity to contact each other for class-related questions in ways they would not pursue otherwise. Rachel's perspective, in particular, demonstrates that she is interested in more than just individual connections with other students—she is interested in creating a digital community where all students in a class can connect with one another. As I will discuss shortly, listening to these students' perspectives led me to start creating Facebook group pages for my FYC courses, as I found that a class Facebook page enabled me to achieve the values that each student here hoped to gain through the use of digital connections among FYC students.

Students Should Choose When to Use Technology

Underlying all of Rachel's, Bethany's, and Zachary's perspectives on technology in FYC is a strong desire to have some degree of autonomy in choosing what digital technologies to use during class. Bethany explains that although she would text during her classes, she didn't bring her laptop to any courses in her first semester of college because doing so wasn't encouraged by her teachers. She says that she would prefer to use a laptop for her classes because "it'd make things [easier], do your notes on the computer . . . so you can just take it, you don't have to worry about having ten different notebooks." It's not that Bethany's teachers said she couldn't use a laptop in class; they simply didn't say she could. Because her teachers weren't encouraging this technology use, she didn't initiate it on her own. In reflecting on my own classroom policies in light of Bethany's experience, I found that I took a similar approach as her teachers, typically telling my students what technologies they *couldn't* use in the classroom but not highlighting those that they could. Bethany's behavior suggests that while students benefit from having the choice of what technologies to use in the classroom, we need to make these choices visible and explicit.

Zachary also sees potential for more technology to be used across all his college courses. In a Nutrition and Wellness course he took, for example, students were required to use the course management system Desire2Learn (D2L) for assignments but were not permitted to use laptops during class. Zachary found this combination of course requirements to be incongruous and argues that students should have been able to use D2L during class meetings since use of the platform was required for the course. Conversely, he had other courses in which he was permitted to use a laptop to take notes and chose not to, saying that "if I'm writing it down . . . I'll remember the information better." Zachary had thought closely about when and where the use of his laptop would benefit his learning, but he was limited in the agency he had to employ that laptop use to his benefit.

Zachary's overall opinion on the use of technology in college courses centers on student choice: he wants to be able to choose when and how to use digital technologies based on how they will help his learning in a course. But, Zachary says, he understands why some teachers are hesitant to allow students to use laptops during class time. Zachary says that his teacher who did not permit computer use during class "had the normal teacher fear [that] instead of us paying attention to the lecture, we'd be on Facebook." He says this fear is warranted: "I've . . . seen it with a couple of kids who have brought their laptops to [class]. As much as they're taking notes, they're also switching over to Facebook, talking to one of their friends." Zachary says he prefers to have the choice to use a laptop so he can determine when having one in class will be useful to him.

Rachel points out a similar concern, that encouraging cell phone and computer use in FYC might create opportunities for students to use digital technologies in ways that would detract from their learning in the course. When her class met in a computer lab, for example, she noticed that a number of students became distracted with social media online. "I think it's just a . . . force of habit," Rachel says. "You get on the computer and you just immediately log on Facebook for no reason at all . . . it's not like anything really important happened from the time you left your room to the time you got there but, just for some reason, we do that." Rachel says that using social media for class purposes "could be beneficial if kids used it in the right way and didn't abuse it." Both Rachel's and Zachary's experiences with students using digital tools for personal purposes—and in ways that pulled their attention away from the class—highlight the challenges we face as teachers in deciding how to construct digital tool use in the classroom. Do we ban the use of cell phones during class time, knowing that doing so limits students' use of valuable resources? Do we let students decide whether to use phones, knowing that doing so opens the door for digital distractions? Or is there some way for us to do both, to teach students to use digital tools to enhance their learning while making effective choices to avoid distractions? Though Zachary and Rachel acknowledge ways that digital technologies can become a distraction in the classroom, all three students say that technology use can aid learning, primarily due to the ability students have to access class-related information online or in conversation with each other via digital communication. These students see the choice to use technology—and to hopefully use it wisely—as one that should be theirs, not their teachers'.

Drawing on Student Expertise

As we consider how to best utilize digital technologies in FYC, we can turn to students for insight into what uses of technology and what particular technology tools will inform their learning in the course. Bethany's, Rachel's, and Zachary's perspectives show that they are already reflecting on the role of technology in their courses in thoughtful ways—their opinions, along with those of other students, can help shape technology-enhanced pedagogies.

Speaking with these students has not only led me to revise my own practices of technology use in FYC, it has deepened my understanding of the wealth of knowledge students bring to the FYC classroom about their own learning processes, specifically how these learning processes are informed or augmented by technology use. As Angela Clark-Oates, Michelle Stuckey, Melissa Williamson, and Duane Roen demonstrate in their chapter in this collection, the practice of reflection, specifically on writing practices and processes, holds deep value for students' learning in FYC. I see value, too, in the fact that students' reflections can inform our teaching practices, as these reflections give us insights into how we can best create courses and classrooms that facilitate student learning.

One way I have drawn on these students' reflections on technology use is by creating Facebook pages for each of my FYC course sections. My students post low-stakes writing assignments, such as reading responses, to our Facebook page rather than turning these assignments in in hard copy, and part of these low-stakes assignments involves responding to each other's posts. Students and I also use the page for course announcements—students will remind each other when class is meeting in a different location for the day, and I'll post information about majors fairs and other events on campus. The page also opens up possibilities for sharing and commenting on multimodal texts. In a class activity that asks students to explore campus and collect examples of graffiti, for example, students now post pictures of the examples they find to the class Facebook page, and we view them there for discussion when students return to the classroom. Some students have shared with me that they appreciate the convenience of writing and responding to each other's work in this format, and others have said that receiving a Facebook notification each time a classmate posts something is a good reminder to keep up with their work for the course.

The Facebook page serves to connect students in others ways, too. When students in my research-based FYC courses create surveys as part of their research projects, they post survey links to the page and request classmate participation. Students also use the page to ask each other questions about class. More than once, I've logged into the page on the morning an assignment is due and have discovered that late the night before, someone posted a question about the assignment and someone else shared an answer—peer-to-peer support that happens at hours when the writing center is closed and students know I won't be checking my email. In utilizing Facebook for my courses, I don't require any student to create an account. Those students who prefer not to use Facebook complete required assignments via email, though this does mean they miss out on the community-building aspects of the course page.

I've put Rachel's, Bethany's, and Zachary's ideas into practice in another way as well, by giving my FYC students autonomy to define how digital technologies will be used during class meetings. Rather than provide the class with a policy on cell phone and computer use, I now ask my classes to engage in small-to-large group discussion on the first day of class to define the parameters of this policy themselves. Across several sections of FYC, my students have arrived at a nearly identical policy: that each individual should police his or her own use of electronic devices, and that this use should never be a distraction to others in the room. Students have said in these discussions that they appreciate the opportunity to craft a classroom policy, and while I have still had to occasionally ask someone to stop texting and pay attention to what the rest of the class is doing, students have largely respected my and each other's boundaries in using electronic devices in class.

I encourage teachers to speak with their students, to find out how students perceive their uses of technology within education and how they might prefer to use technology in FYC. This conversation with students can take multiple forms. Teachers might ask students early in the term to discuss classroom technology policies or have students complete a low-stakes written reflection on the digital tools they use in everyday life and how they'd like to use those tools to enhance their learning in a course. What is most important here is that we do not make assumptions about the digital tools students use and their preferences for these tools. In creating class Facebook pages, for example, I've encountered a small number of students who are adamant about not using social media at all and a few others who have needed assistance in learning to use this digital tool for class purposes. Readers who speak with their students will certainly encounter additional perspectives different from those presented here. By continually asking our students to reflect on and discuss the ways technology is and can be present in their daily lives and their lives within an educational setting, we can develop FYC pedagogies that account for and validate students' perspectives on their learning.

Works Cited

Anderson, Daniel. "The Low Bridge to High Benefits: Entry-Level Multimedia, Literacies, and Motivation." *Computers and Composition*, vol. 25, 2008, pp. 40–60.

Bethany. Interview. Conducted by Ann N. Amicucci, 14 Dec. 2011.

Emmelhainz, Nicole. "Status Update to Term Paper: Social Network Sites as a Medium for Collaboration." *The CEA Forum*, vol. 42, no. 2, 2013, pp. 97–108.

Grant, Abigail A. "Textperts: Utilizing Students' Skills in the Teaching of Writing." *Social Software and the Evolution of User Expertise: Future Trends in Knowledge Creation and Dissemination*, edited by Tatjana Takseva, Information Science Reference, 2013, pp. 247–58.

Kirtley, Susan. "Students' Views on Technology and Writing: The Power of Personal History." *Computers and Composition*, vol. 22, no. 2, 2005, pp. 209–30.

Rachel. Interview. Conducted by Ann N. Amicucci, 9 Dec. 2011.

Shipka, Jody. "A Multimodal Task-Based Framework for Composing." *College Composition and Communication*, vol. 57, no. 2, 2005, pp. 277–306.

Zachary. Interview. Conducted by Ann N. Amicucci, 15 Dec. 2011.

Questions for Discussion and Reflection After Chapter 3

1. How do you use digital technologies in your FYC course? For example, do your students compose multimodal projects or other digital composition projects? What is your rationale for including these projects? What challenges, if any, have they presented for you in terms of design, assessment, student interest?

2. Have you tapped into students' expertise with nonacademic digital technologies in any way? If so, how did doing so inform your course design and pedagogy?

Writing Activity After Chapter 3

Identify a wobble moment that you experienced as an FYC teacher. Perhaps it was a moment related to the use of digital technologies in your FYC course or a moment caused by your attempts to "work the tension" between what you are expected to teach (FYC's public charter) and what you believe you ought to teach. Reflect on this wobble moment and consider these questions: How did you contend with this moment? Did engaging with the cause of the wobble open up possibilities for you? Explain. Or were you unable to engage with this moment? If so, why was this the case?

Further Reading

Fecho, Bob. *Teaching Outside the Box but Inside the Standards: Making Room for Dialogue*. Teachers College P, 2016.

Hermans, Hubert, and Agnieszka Hermans-Konopka. *Dialogical Self Theory: Positioning and Counter-Positioning in a Globalizing Society*. Cambridge UP, 2010.

Noddings, Nel. *The Challenge to Care in Schools: An Alternative Approach to Education*. 2nd ed., Teachers College P, 2005.

Part 2. Fostering Students' Development of Writing Identities

In Part 2, authors focus on students' own development as agentive writers, in and because of FYC. Helen Collins Sitler showcases her Basic Writing course, where students are given the task of writing in public campus spaces and proclaiming "I am a writer!" if anyone asks what they're doing. Sitler shares perspectives from two former students and describes how specific class activities led students to conceptualize their own writing identities.

Martha Wilson Schaffer focuses her attention on students' abilities to assess their own writing potential. Her conversations with student interviewees show how self-assessment within the liminal space of FYC can enable students to tell their own stories of where they've been and where they might go as writers.

Jo-Anne Kerr discusses an approach to FYC that fosters students' writerly dispositions. Kerr's FYC course demystifies academic writing expectations and prompts students to define their writing selves so they might transfer their writing abilities beyond the FYC course.

Finally, Brian D. Carpenter describes how teaching cohesion as a writing strategy and socializing students into academic writing expectations empowered students in Basic Writing and in communicative contexts outside the course. Carpenter shares experiences from multilingual writers developing academic writing identities.

Extras

- Listen to a podcast conversation among Part 2 authors Helen Collins Sitler and Jo-Anne Kerr and editor Ann Amicucci for ideas on how to challenge students' preconceived notions of what writing should be: ⏺ Listen to the Part 2 Podcast[1]
- Watch short videos of:
  - Helen Collins Sitler sharing classroom practices for promoting students' writing identities: ▰ View the Video
  - Jo-Anne Kerr discussing how to validate students' beliefs about writing while offering opportunities to revise these beliefs: ▰ View the Video
  - Brian Carpenter describing classroom practices for facilitating students' academic socialization in FYC: ▰ View the Video

---

1 The videos and podcasts referred to on this page are available on the WAC Clearinghouse at https://wac.colostate.edu/books/practice/stories/.

Chapter 4. Becoming a Person Who Writes

Helen Collins Sitler

INDIANA UNIVERSITY OF PENNSYLVANIA

Reflect Before Reading

Think about your current or former students who struggle with writing. When a student calls herself a "bad writer" or another says he "hates writing," how do you respond? What activities in your course allow students to build their confidence as writers?

~ ~ ~

The Writing Marathon was always my favorite day in Basic Writing. Usually on a portfolio turn-in day, a day when students' energy would be low from working to finish a major project, we left the classroom just to go somewhere new and write. Students' charge: Go with a couple classmates wherever you want. Take your notebooks. Write about what you see, hear, smell, taste—coffeehouses and fast food are often a part of a Writing Marathon. Let the place you're in trigger your writing. If anyone asks what you're doing, you have to reply "We're writers. We're writing."

Before anyone left the room, we all rehearsed that line. Students had to repeat loudly and with enthusiasm: "I am a writer!" Students giggled, then dutifully chorused that sentence. Then off we went to write until time to return to the classroom to tell the stories of the day's writing and for each student to share at least a small piece of what they had written. We rejoiced when sometimes students had had the chance to announce "I am a writer!" to curious passersby.

Students generally enjoyed Writing Marathon days as much as I did, but I doubt they took the "I am a writer!" routine seriously. It is serious, though, the idea of considering oneself a writer. For students in Basic Writing it is an especially serious issue. So much of a student's success in college depends on skill with words, as does much of a person's success in a career. And here they were in Basic Writing, marked in their first semester of college as individuals whose words were somehow inadequate. It raises questions: Can a Basic Writing student become someone who says and *believes* that "I am a writer"?

Writing is tied to identity. Numerous composition scholars speak to this, articulating that students' taking on a writer's identity is an essential part of any composition course. Tom Romano argues that adolescents and college students need "to have opportunities to create their identities on the page" (175). Roz Ivanič argues for the teaching of writing to be focused above all else on "helping students to take an identity as a person who writes" (85). Taking this idea one step further, Robert Brooke insists that successful teaching of a composition course is marked by students' "com[ing] to see that being a writer in their own way is a valid and exciting way of acting in the world" (40).

James Paul Gee discusses the identity-building process in terms of adopting a discourse: "Think of discourse as an 'identity kit' which comes complete with the appropriate costume and instructions on how to act and talk so as to take on a particular role that others will recognize" (51). The role of someone who writes would entail ways of talking about writing and the ability to think of oneself as having something to say. This identity, however, would be just one of many. Both Gee and Ivanič discuss the multiple identities any individual simultaneously maintains (Gee 56; Ivanič 11). Take, for example, Frankie, whom readers will meet in these pages. She arrived in Basic Writing with multiple identities that she made apparent in class and surely had others in addition. Her classmates and I knew that she was a business major, that she had been a student government leader in her high school, and that she was a multi-sport athlete. Each of these roles in her life demanded its own discourse, its own identity kit.

My course would challenge Frankie to add another identity, that of a person who writes. Given her life history including multiple identity kits already, adding this new one could create some clashes. Ivanič recognizes that taking on a writerly identity is a potentially tension-filled process (65). Further, Frankie and her peers were entering the world of higher education which would, according to Ivanič, "require [them] to extend their repertoire of literacy practices: to build and adapt existing ones and to engage in new ones" (70).

What conflicts of experience and expectation would emerge? Could being a writer sit comfortably beside being a new college student, a business major, an athlete? And so, I return to this question: Can a Basic Writing student become someone who says and *believes* that "I am a writer"?

Two Basic Writing students, Spike and Frankie, show that this process can occur. Both were part of an IRB-approved study of literacy development. Participants were volunteers who had taken my own Basic Writing classes during a four-year period designated for the study. Data used here come from students' final exams and other papers they provided and from interviews conducted by my colleague Dr. Gloria Park and her graduate assistant, Ravyn McKee.

Spike and Frankie were among nine study participants. At the time my former students were invited to participate, they were the only two who were seniors, thus the two with the most experience to share. Their experiences with Basic Writing, with writing in courses for their majors, and their planning for jobs after graduation provide an interesting picture of coming to consider oneself a writer during and after their first college composition course.

Spike and Frankie: Literacy Experiences
before Basic Writing

Spike arrived at college with his criminology major firmly in mind. During his interview, he said: "It was probably around fourth grade. . . . One of my good friends that I went to elementary school with . . . his dad was a state trooper, and I always went over to his house and communicated with him on a regular basis and it kinda influenced me to want to grow up and be a state trooper." Spike's older sister was the first in the family to hold a bachelor's degree; Spike would be the second.

Graduating in a class of 150, Spike described reading and writing as something he needed to do for school. He was diligent, but not enthused: "I always did my schoolwork and I always kept up with readings. If I had a paper, I . . . completed the paper, but I never went above and beyond schoolwork to satisfy a reading habit or anything like that." His writing experiences in school had consisted of reflections on readings for English classes, daily writes (which he did not further explain, but which I take to be short journal entries or responses to readings), and his senior paper, about the charity golf event he had helped to organize. Essay writing adhered to "the five-paragraph stance," meaning "the fundamental introduction, body, and conclusion." When asked about more writing in his classes, Spike responded that "I was never able to participate" in "classes that were for higher up students, above the normal average student." In other words, he had not taken advanced or AP courses.

While he knew his writing skills were not especially strong—"I was a pretty weak writer before coming to college"—his placement into Basic Writing was "kinda like a bummer feeling . . . it's not good." However, Spike's high school habits of diligence and persistence—"I always did my schoolwork"—carried him through the new learning curve.

Frankie arrived in college with 15 credits she had earned through joint high school/college credit classes offered through her high school. None of those courses, however, must have been in English, as she completed all of my university's required English courses. Like Spike, she had already decided on her major: business. After a few courses, she refined that major to human resources management. Interestingly, college was not her original plan: "I didn't want to come to college; I didn't want to at all. I wanted to join the military." Her parents' fears about, at that time, an active war in Afghanistan changed her mind. Their agreement was that if Frankie finished college and then still wanted to join the military, they would not object. At the point of her interview, one summer course away from graduating, she was no longer planning military enlistment. Frankie's older sister had already graduated college. Her parents' college experience is unclear; but her father owned his own business and her mother worked part-time while Frankie and her sister were growing up.

Frankie described her literacy background with positives and negatives. "I love to read." Her extensive reading, in fact, created barriers for her writing. "I strongly disliked writing. . . . I think I had read so much and so many types of things, I couldn't make my writing sound like something I would want to read. So like why do it?" Her placement in Basic Writing was not a great surprise to her: "I've never been a good test taker and when we did placement testing I probably just didn't do very well." Her high school experience, even with all those college credits, prepared her for college-level writing in limited ways. "In high school we didn't write a lot. . . . We only wrote two papers my entire high school career." For these two papers, the possibilities seem to have been minimal. When asked how she knew what to write, she said, "Normally, I was answering . . . a writing prompt or something like that. We had specific things we have to have in papers." The key guideline was the standard five-paragraph theme: "Most of our writing base was based on what you had to know for PSSAs [the Pennsylvania Department of Education mandated testing] to write those essays, like, brainstorm first, like have an introductory paragraph and something and filler stuff in middle and conclusion."

Despite limited writing experience in high school, Frankie flourished in Basic Writing. Her work was so strong that near the end of the semester I approached her about submitting a portfolio to ask for exemption from College Writing, an option my department allowed. Frankie did submit a portfolio and was approved for exemption, her work in Basic Writing considered equivalent to what any student completing College Writing would have been able to produce. Frankie's high expectations for herself allowed her to blossom when given assignments she could dig into and tools for making her writing sound like something she and others would want to read.

The Basic Writing Course as Spike and Frankie Experienced It

"I have to give you a little background because you won't understand if I don't give it to you," Frankie said, in discussing her narrative essay with her interviewer. In that spirit, we will leave Spike and Frankie for a short time and look at the Basic Writing course they experienced. This course design is reflected in the writing that Spike and Frankie did and in their development of identities as writers.

During the semesters when Spike and Frankie were in my courses, students completed three formal writing assignments. Each assignment was submitted as a portfolio; a reflection on writing decisions made from drafts to final copy was part of each portfolio. Embedded within the three major assignments were numerous smaller ones, what Frankie called "annoying little exercises." We used a writing workshop model. Students did a lot of writing in class; I used that time to provide individual feedback through conferences. I wrote scant notes on papers. Most teacher feedback came through conversation. Feedback also came from peers; writing groups, in which talk also superseded writing on papers, met at least twice for each paper. Mentor texts, i.e., writing that offers models for writing techniques that students themselves might adopt, were an important course element. The assignment sequence worked as a spiral. Each new assignment built on skills practiced and honed in the previous assignment. New learning was layered in; students could always circle back to writing techniques they had already rehearsed.

The course design reflects elements that others in this collection have advocated for. Jo-Anne Kerr speaks to the development of a discourse important for transferring writerly habits to future contexts: reading in a writerly way, feedback from readers, moving beyond one format for writing. Kara Taczak, Liane Robertson, and Kathleen Blake Yancey show that deliberate reflection on one's work and active uptake of language to describe it are essential for transfer. All of these features were part of the course that Spike and Frankie experienced.

Table 4.1 presents the major assignments for the course, accompanying in-class exercises, and the mentor texts that Spike and Frankie reference.

As is apparent in biographical information for both Spike and Frankie, each entered his/her first university semester with limited writing experience. They resemble the students that Mina Shaughnessy, the first composition scholar whose work was dedicated to basic writing, described as "have been writing infrequently" and "in such artificial and strained situations that the communicative purpose of writing has rarely if ever seemed real" (14). Today's testing culture in K–12 schools has, for many students, reduced writing to a formula in order to earn an acceptable test score. Ritter, in this collection, testifies to the pervasiveness of this practice. Thus, it is not surprising that university placement testing might reveal a limited writing repertoire among some incoming students if they do not engage in self-sponsored writing and if their writing for school has primarily focused on test preparation. Ivanič notes that "writers bring to any act of writing the literacy practices into which they have been acculturated through their past experience" (184). Test prep is the writing practice many high school students have become accustomed to. This had been the experience of both Spike and Frankie.

However, over many years of teaching Basic Writing, I have found that students assigned to my classes are capable, competent learners. Inexperience with writing is the issue, not capability. Given opportunities to write and to craft their writing, inexperienced student writers can accomplish things that surprise them.

Spike: Breaking Away from the Five-Paragraph Theme

When interviewed, Spike said, "I was expecting to come in[to his first writing course in college] with my basic writing skills as the five-paragraph essay as that's how you write." Lorna Collier addresses this kind of mismatch between what high school seniors think college writing will be about and what actually occurs, noting that students "expect to *do* writing rather than *engage* in writing, both as a way of thinking and as a way of demonstrating knowledge" (11). Very quickly, Spike realized that writing would not be simply filling in a formula: "My professor she kinda told me that's [the five-paragraph theme] not the way to go about the papers."

Table 4.1. Assignment sequence

	First third of semester	Second third of semester	Final third of semester	End of semester
Assignment:	Narrative	Researched Essay	Radical Revision	Final Exam
In-class exercises:	-quick writes -guided imagery	-collaborative topic development -quick write prompts -color coding to balance research, personal writing -bookless draft -Post-it organizing and thesis	-write from a new point of view -found poem -rework previous writing	
Skills learned:	-1st person -narrow focus -strong lead -develop evidence: anecdote, description -dialogue -organize for readability, interest -variations in paragraph length -aware of audience -revise -monitor patterns of error	-research question -find sources -gain content expertise -develop evidence: sources -recognize multiple views -integrate others' words -strong topic sentences -organize for reader needs -transitions -transition markers -monitor patterns of error	-re-envision topic -global revision -try out new form -provide reader adequate information -maintain reader interest	-provide evidence of learning -identify practices, behaviors that helped during semester -identify how to reproduce practices and behaviors in future courses
Techniques that carry over from previous assignment:		-new view of topic -strong lead -nonlinear organization -anecdote, description -dialogue -1st person -variations in paragraph length	-any skills from previous papers -writing or projects outside the course	-any skills from previous papers -writing or projects outside the course

The mentor texts the class read and discussed played a significant role in showing him new possibilities. "We started off by reading various stories . . . and we picked out the similar techniques they were using. . . . We were going to be able to try these techniques in our own writings." While this shift felt somewhat uncomfortable to Spike, like learning "there's actually another way to tie your shoe," he did what he had always done in high school. He relied on his sense of responsibility to do the assignments. By the time he submitted his narrative portfolio, the first assignment of the semester, he was recognizing the benefits of trying out some new writing techniques.

One new technique that Spike used to his advantage was writing dialogue. In his final exam, in answer to a question about which mentor authors influenced him, he named Jimmy Baca: "Baca gave me the idea to use dialog" for "not just the words coming out of the characters [sic] mouth but the feeling being expressed as well." Dialogue comprises much of his narrative and does, in fact, move the action forward more effectively than his expository sections. In the following segment he has found a credit card that someone has dropped in a busy convenience store/gas station; as he ponders what to do with the card, he notices the car parked beside his:

> The man was saying, "I do not know where it went. I had it in my hand and I went up to pay and it was gone." I walked over to the man.
>
> "Did you lose something?"
>
> The man turned around and his face was as read [*sic*] as a tomato. He looked like he was about to hit someone.
>
> "Yeah, I had it and now it is gone."
>
> "What are you looking for?" I asked.
>
> "I lost my credit card. I don't have any money on me. Some punk ass kid probably has it now and is running my bill sky high!" stated the man.

The dialogue continues until Spike establishes that the credit card he found and is still holding onto belongs to this upset man. He hands the man the card.

Spike also worked to make his speakers' language more realistic, the way talking actually sounds. From draft to final copy, *shopping* becomes *shoppin'*. *You cannot trust anyone anymore* becomes *You can't trust no one anymore*. These are tiny shifts, but they reflect a writer who has begun to understand that writers craft their work and that he, too, can craft his writing. This is a far cry from simply filling in a five paragraph template.

Spike also tested out Baca's single-sentence paragraphs. The following is a short excerpt in which he attempts to draw attention to important lines by creating them as stand-alone paragraphs. The action occurs at a local mall where Spike has gone with his friend, Nick. Nick is the first speaker:

> "Yeah I will go along." As I looked into his eyes I could tell that what he was really thinking was no way, not after what we just went through in Pac Sun.
>
> We walked over to Lids.
>
> After purchasing a hat, we were done shopping at the mall. Therefore, I asked Nick if he wanted to go get something to eat before we headed [home]. With a firm yes to my question, we then began to decide on a place to eat.
>
> We went to the Ponderosa Steak House.

Spike's use of the single-sentence paragraph is not particularly successful. Baca's single-sentence paragraphs convey vital information. Spike just uses them to shift scenes. Still the attempt again shows a writer's willingness to experiment with something new.

Spike's final foray into new techniques in his narrative is something we decided to call sidetracking. We used the term to describe a digression he added in order to stretch and slow down time within the action of the piece. It serves the additional purpose of addressing a common issue with basic writers, lack of elaboration of ideas (Shaughnessy 227–32). In his cover letter, Spike identified sidetracking as a risk he took in the writing. It looked like this:

> On my way into the store, I looked down and I saw a credit card lying between the two automatic doors.
>
> *"Should I keep it? How would I feel if this happened to me?"* These questions raced through my head.
>
> I was brought up by my mom and my dad. We live on the outskirts of town and I have been there for as long as I can remember. My dad, abandoned by his true father, is self-employed. He does concrete work, brick masonry, and his favorite, stone masonry. My mom, on the other hand, works in an office for [name of her workplace]. I was raised with the idea that stealing was not acceptable. If an item was free and I wanted it my dad would push me to ask if it would be alright if I had it. If I would take something without asking and my dad would find out he made me take it back to where I got it and ask if it was alright to have it. Stealing, in my dad's eyes, is for two types of people, people who are too lazy to get a job and those who are too lazy to pay.
>
> I finished my business and walked out to my car.

From here the essay continues with the dialogue about the upset man in the car nearby.

Nested between internal dialogue, marked by the italic font, and the actual dialogue noted earlier, the sidetrack, as noted by Spike in his portfolio reflection "really worked." I agree. It added some depth to his paper, adding a deep motivation for returning the credit card to the man who had lost it. Spike wrote, "I have seen this technique before, but I have never really given it the thought to add it in one of my own writings. This most definitely changed the way I usually write."

Unfortunately, Spike did not provide his researched essay or his radical revision for this study. His final exam, however, provides an excerpt and some commentary from the researched essay.

Spike identifies Deborah Tannen, writer of a mentor text for this assignment, as key to the progress of his researched piece. True to the creative nonfiction mentor texts we used, like Tannen's, Spike "learned how to incorporate my own story into a research paper." The following excerpt shows how he did this:

> Criminals of identity theft are very seldom caught. . . . However the government has passed a law in 2004. . . . The government has also added the Identity Theft Penalty Enhancement Act, this Act states "IN GENERAL.—Whoever, during and in relation to any felony violation . . . imprisonment of 5 years."

> When I walked out of the gas station, and the credit card was still in my hand, I walked over to my car. . . . I asked him a few brief questions about the card in my possession and I handed the card over to the young man.

While the transition between researched and personal text is bumpy, Spike has again been willing to try something new. With growing audience awareness, he articulates why he has done this: "Instead of using strictly information this technique allowed me to add a personally [sic] experience that relates to the topic to make it sound more real."

He attributed this awareness of how a writer might mix research and personal information to a color-coding exercise (based on ideas drawn from Harry Noden's *Image Grammar*) that we did with the Tannen essay. After using a highlighter, each of a different color, to mark 1) exposition; 2) narration/description; 3) quotation (quotes from sources as well as use of dialogue), students discovered that Tannen's integration of multiple writing techniques made the research she presented highly readable. Students then color-coded their own drafts, evaluated what the colors revealed to them, and revised accordingly.

Where do these examples of Spike's writing lead us? In what ways do they demonstrate his developing an identity as a writer? As noted earlier, taking on this identity means acting and talking like a writer.

As a writer new to the college classroom, Spike's incoming assumptions about writing, particularly about one-size-fits-all writing, were challenged. He responded by trying new techniques. He developed vocabulary for articulating what he was doing and why he was making particular writerly choices. Perhaps the best example is his noting that he had seen writers do sidetracking before but never considered doing it himself. Now he was doing it. His final exam includes these lines, indicative of someone who has taken on some aspects of being a writer. Basic Writing, he writes, has "busted [boosted] my confidence to be able to write with integrity for my future writing courses." Later in the same document he notes, "I am no longer afraid to try new things in my writing." He was no longer filling in a predetermined template. He was crafting his writing with a reader in mind. In baby steps, his thinking about "I am a writer" was emerging.

Frankie: Shifting an Attitude About Writing

Frankie arrived in Basic Writing having "dreaded everything I ever had to write." Her strong reading background and high school/college courses gave her an advantage. Her attitude about writing, however, was a challenge to her progress. Frankie needed to be convinced that she had some skill and that every writing experience was not dreadful.

In his study of basic writers, Josh Lederman found that teacher expectations played a key role in student performance: "The two clear success stories [students] in this study . . . both had teachers who truly believed in them, and in some deep ways, these teachers helped the students believe in themselves too" (199). Lederman's finding echoes other research on the effects of teacher expectations on student performance. Susan McLeod cautions that a teacher's negative expectations are particularly powerful; however, she also confirms that positive teacher expectations can lead to improved student performance (108-09). While Spike's writing improved mostly through adopting new techniques from mentor texts, Frankie's writing improved more in response to topic choice, in-class exercises, and supportive reader feedback.

Frankie's first paper, her narrative, focused on a school consolidation that occurred during her senior year. Two high schools in her district were merged into one. She was from the smaller school that closed. She worked her way through this self-selected topic, one she cared about, as if she were constructing an intricate jigsaw puzzle. Her writing moves were sophisticated and intentional.

Her early draft began this way:

> Senior year of high school, the year to remember, the year where you rule the school, the year you have waited for your entire life. The year for me that was turned upside down. . . . I went from a senior class of forty-six to a senior class of one hundred thirty-seven of which I knew no one but my original classmates.

She wrote of bullying, name-calling, eating lunch surrounded by strangers. Midway through the essay she briefly mentioned her Spanish teacher, Mrs. S., who had moved with the students to the larger high school:

> I had her for eighth period everyday for Spanish IV. The end of
> the day which I had with eight other kids that I had been with
> since freshman year. Some days that class took years to get to,
> those seven periods before it were the longest ever experienced
> until I finally got to what I was used to, until I finally was famil-
> iar with everything around me.

Then she moved on to describe how "I wanted to be the one to change things; I wanted to make new friends, I wanted to say I was the first consolidated class and I benefited from it."

That first draft provided much information but not much focus. The essay was moving in two opposing directions: 1) I'm an outsider; 2) I want to change things. Each idea was functioning without connection to the other. We conferenced about this, and Frankie understood the disconnect but puzzled over how to resolve it.

Before students submitted their second draft, we did one of those "annoying little exercises," an extended guided imagery prompt. Students made a quick list of snapshot moments, i.e., vivid individual scenes from the writing they were drafting. Then they selected one scene and responded to a series of sensory prompts, as if they were playing a movie in their minds: What did you hear? What did you see? What was the temperature?, etc.

Frankie's completed guided imagery described Mrs. S: "never be one to need a microphone," "always wore a skirt," "hair never out of place." It described her classroom: "vocab posters, the Spanish alphabet pictures of her and students from years past . . . maracas . . . spectacular bulletin boards. You could learn just from being in her room." This short piece was filled with detail about how important this teacher and her classroom were to Frankie.

Through this in-class exercise, Frankie's focal point emerged—her beloved Spanish teacher. In her portfolio reflective cover letter, Frankie wrote that completing the guided imagery was significant for her writing "because after doing this exercise I realized what the main focus of my paper should be as well as what direction from that point on my paper needed to head. . . . It made my paper go from several separate pieces to one flowing work of writing." She wanted to "focus more on my 'safe haven' . . . and not so much on the negative." That safe haven was her Spanish teacher's classroom.

The final copy of her essay began with some text that had been midway through her earlier draft, a nod to Mrs. S. and added new material:

> Some days that class took years to get to, those seven periods
> before it were the longest ever experienced until I got what I

was used to, until I finally was familiar with everything around me. Walking into that classroom seeing Mrs. S's familiar face and all those familiar students around me, learning like I had been learning for the last three years was in a sense for me like going home.

The new draft and later the final copy included pages about Mrs. S., her methods of teaching, and her ability to personally connect with students. In thinking about this teacher, Frankie also found the rhetorical link she needed in order to connect being an outsider with wanting to change that status. This sentence from her second draft bridged the competing ideas: "I wanted to change things, and when I began to try it started right back there in Spanish IV, with Ms. S. leading the way." It was Mrs. S' response to consolidation, Mrs. S' "courageous lead," that pushed Frankie to ask "students sitting alone in the cafeteria to come and eat with my friends and me. On the volleyball team we made a point to have one team-bonding event a week. I quickly made new friends 'from the other side.'"

In Frankie's jigsaw of revision, each draft rearranged or layered in new information. In her interview, Frankie described herself as being "really big on organization." In high school, she had been an honor student while on multiple sports teams and active in student government. In college, she was "involved in like 4–5 organizations" while carrying 18 credits. "I've always like had a lot on my plate." Her approach to revising her paper was the same as her general approach to life: How do all these pieces fit together? How can I manage them so they all make sense? For her paper, she "needed to decide what direction it needed to take . . . Mrs. S. or Consolidation. I chose Mrs. S." This decision allowed Frankie to "focus . . . on her as a person and what she did for me during the consolidation." With this as her goal, Frankie found ways for the parts of her essay to intersect, rather than cast parts off. In Frankie's words, the paper "was a lot different than what I planned on as my original topic," which had been a much more negative reporting on the consolidation.

One thing she was willing to cast off was the five-paragraph format she was familiar with. Brief nods to it appear in individual sentences in drafts. For instance, in one late draft, this appeared: "She has high standards, an amazing story and the drive to make you a better human being." In no cases, though, did she follow up by addressing each of the items in the sequence. Mentor texts appear to have had minimal effect. The one noticeable technique that was borrowed from the course readings appeared in her final copy of the paper. It came from Annie Dillard, an extra-large space between paragraphs at a place where the topic shifts. Frankie did this only once in her four-page essay.

Frankie's portfolio cover letter for her narrative spoke to the attitude noted at the beginning: "Something I have learned about myself as a writer would be that I can write. . . . I was dreading this project but with much surprise it came easily to me. I felt confident reading my work to my writing group and to you [the instructor]. . . . I liked what I was doing."

Frankie's researched essay, her second assignment of the semester, focused on another topic of great personal significance, the experiences of her sister and her mother with skin cancer. It mattered to Frankie that in Basic Writing she was asked "to write about something that we were passionate about." "She [instructor] didn't give us a prompt I didn't care about and was like blah blah blah write something on this. It was like whatever we wanted to write about so that really helped." The topic for this second piece had actually emerged many weeks before she began the paper. It had been on the list of snapshot moments she had generated for the guided composing exercise.

The creative nonfiction approach we used to writing this essay allowed Frankie to personalize the writing. She bookended two researched pages with the story of her mother and sister. In her portfolio reflection she noted that now she is "able to more comfortably write. Not every sentence is a struggle. Also I feel much more confident as a writer." She was no longer writing "because I had to for a grade."

As with the narrative, Frankie identified an in-class exercise as most helpful for her writing. Before their second draft, students used Post-it notes, one idea per note, to list key points they wanted to make in their essays. Then, in one sentence, they were to write their "So what?"—what is it that you want a reader to understand when they finish your essay? Finally, they arranged the Post-its in the order in which they thought they needed to write; thus, they left class with an outline for a revised draft. Frankie's Post-it page included seven notes, arranged in this order:

-Does artificial tanning cause skin cancer

-Mom and Angela having skin cancer

-Why they got it

-The real truth from studies

-Vitamin D

-How it affected Angela

-Would tan again?

Frankie noted that this exercise was significant because "I knew . . . where I wanted my paper to go and what things I was going to make my most important points. It also made me realize that I was going to need at least two more topics to meet the length requirement for this paper."

Indeed, she adjusted her text in her final copy. She had had some trouble with a researched section about Vitamin D. The writing was awkward and didn't fit well with surrounding text. For the final copy, she abandoned that information. Then she added segments on additional causes of skin cancer—beyond tanning beds, the specific focus of this writing—and on advancements in knowledge of how to treat skin cancer.

Her portfolio cover letter indicated that Frankie understood what she was executing well in this writing: "the detail I use to explain things" and "putting feeling into my paper." The detail she mentions arose from two factors: her ability as a researcher and her ability to make that research readable. Frankie was a skilled researcher, something she must have been taught in high school. Her bibliography included recent issues of *Gerontology, British Journal of Dermatology*, and *Dermatologic Therapy* along with several consumer editions of the more readable *Health Source*. She made this heavy material readable while carefully acknowledging each source and prepping readers with strong topic sentences. One paragraph shows how she included research throughout the essay:

> Multiple tanning regulars would argue that some people just get skin cancer. They would say it is not caused specifically from tanning. That is only because it never happened to them. Denise K. Woo and Melody J. Eide from the Department of Dermatology and Biostatistics Research Epidemiology, out of The Henry Ford Hospital in Detroit, Michigan would disagree. Their most recent study provides the most extensive evidence to date of the risk of melanoma associated with tanning beds. They recommend discouraging teenagers from using tanning beds and other tanning equipment.

We had talked about strong topic sentences, looking at Tannen's essay and some student essays as models. Frankie understood quickly how to manage her topic sentences. We also talked about selecting credible sources and about acknowledging them. Her scientific articles generally included multiple authors. She was unhappy with the lengthy, sometimes awkward method of naming them, but diligently did so. In later years, with her permission, I used her paper as a mentor text to help newer writers understand how they, too, could acknowledge the resources they had tapped.

Frankie's final paper for the semester was her radical revision. Toby Fulwiler's essay "A Lesson in Revision" provides the basis for this assignment. It asks students to play with form and language. Shaughnessy identifies absence of "play" with ideas as an issue with basic writers (236). I, too, find that my students have rarely been invited to play with language in the ways the radical revision asks of them. The assignment requires students to rethink an earlier completed essay by radically changing its form, its purpose, or its audience.

Frankie returned to her tanning bed essay for this project. She revised the researched essay into a children's story in two forms: a printed and bound copy and the Power Point presentation she had done in order to create the printed pages of the bound copy. Slides were illustrated with colorful clip art drawings. Text from the first three slides gives a feel for how her children's story proceeded:

Slide 1: One day my Mommy my big sister and I all went to the doctor. Mommy told me it wasn't the doctor for when you're sick. It was the doctor for your skin. She said he was called a Dermatologist.

Slide 2: The doctor ran lots and lots of tests on my Mommy. Then he ran lots and lots more tests on my sister. The doctor was really nice and told me I could ask as many questions as I wanted.

Slide 3: After waiting for forever the doctor came out to see us. He told us that there was something wrong with my Mommy's back and something really wrong with the back of my Sister's leg.

Frankie noted in her portfolio reflection that in order to make her radical revision effective, "I needed to keep [different elements of the essay] in order and keep the detail in them, but still take out a lot of my writing"; this time the illustrations would carry meaning as well. Her awareness of her audience was a key factor in this decision; children's books need "an easier reading level." She was also purposeful in her decision about why to revise this essay in this way: "I think this [skin cancer] is something kids should be educated about even at a young age." She was so determined to assure that her writing reached her intended audience that "I tried it out on a first grader and he paid attention the whole time."

As with Spike, readers might now ask what this shows us about Frankie's development of an identity as a writer. Like Spike, Frankie easily adopted the discourse of a writer. She was able to articulate what she changed from draft to final copy and, more important, why she made those changes. Primary to those changes was Frankie's knowing she needed to focus her writing for a particular audience. This, in turn, gave her writing purpose; it was not just for a grade. Also, like Spike, she distanced herself from formula writing, opting instead to craft writing to her own purposes.

In the cover letter for her portfolio asking for exemption from College Writing, she wrote this: "After learning multiple writing techniques I know so much more and am able to more comfortably write. I feel that what I produce is worth reading." Her key reason for dreading writing had disappeared. A surprise surfaced in her interview. When asked if she had any advice for incoming first-year students, she said, "You're not gonna get better [as a writer] unless you're writing. After I took [Basic Writing], I had a journal that I wrote in religiously every single night no matter what until about last winter break. I didn't do that before." Sometimes the journal recorded events of the day, sometimes personal things. Still, this student who had dreaded any kind of writing began and continued self-sponsored writing for several years after her first college composition course. She had not only adopted the discourse of a writer, she was, as writers do, regularly writing.

We know that students' progress in writing is idiosyncratic; thus, course design needs to reach students in multiple ways. Mentor texts and the in class exercises we did mattered in general to writers in my classes, but Spike and Frankie show how that work mattered differently to each. Conversations with them about their writing were important. The course focus on process, including draft after draft and supported challenges to try new things, was important. Spike noted in his narrative portfolio reflection that "no copy that u [sic] make is your final copy. . . . A paper is always a work in progress." Three years later in his interview, he maintained that process still mattered: "I feel that even for a final draft I feel that there is always something that you can add or change and just you can always take a different view on a paper." All of this leads me to conclude that course design needs to be deliberate. Nothing can happen by accident.

Composition courses are often thought of as service courses. The question becomes this: Service to whom? To the institution and its various constituents? To the student? To both? In her work on identity and writing, Ivanič references Lev Vygotsky's and Mikhail Bakhtin's theories of the social and dialogic nature of learning and of language use. Ivanič points to the necessity of teaching writing as a social act, through authentic tasks in which writers have a sense of purpose and of audience (339). She argues that in order for students to take on an identity of someone who writes, tasks, assignments, and outcomes need first to serve the writer (338–39).

In her discussion of teaching English language learners, Gloria Park argues for "the importance of writing in constructing identity," (336) in and outside of academic settings, and raises another issue about teaching writing as well, the need for student writers to benefit in personal ways from their experiences in writing courses. She outlines how she accomplished this in a course. One course goal was "to remind my students as well as myself of how academic writing was, and could be, seen as a form of writing to understand the world around us and not just as a conduit to mastering the linguistic code of the US educational context" (338). While my Basic Writers were not English language learners, I subscribe to the same philosophy as Park. Students should not write only traditional academic prose in Basic Writing. It is just as effective to expand writing opportunities so that students can discover themselves as people who can write and who can, in addition, write in an academic setting.

Of course, these students-becoming-writers who have had opportunities to write about subjects that matter to them in ways that challenge and stretch them leave our classrooms where their writing has been nurtured. They move into courses where we can only hope they will continue the habits and behaviors they have developed in our classes. What happens to them as writers outside the confines of a carefully crafted writing setting?

Spike and Frankie: Writing in Future Careers

Helping our students to apply ways of thinking used by the professionals they will become needs to be a goal of all writing instruction (Taczak, Robertson, and

Yancey, this collection). Indeed, Spike and Frankie found some footing with a writing identity in Basic Writing and, as their college experiences continued, grew that identity into a more professional view of themselves as writers.

Spike majored in criminology, intending even from his first college semester, to become a state trooper. His major required him to write frequently, for instance "look[ing] at a report of a crime or a study" then writing a personal reflection or applying criminological theories. By the "beginning of junior year," Spike was recognizing "how powerful writing can be and how important it is in current and future society." By that time, he had written papers for various classes, including one about racial overtones in laws guiding sentencing for cocaine users. He recognized that someone had written those laws and that, indeed, words had life-altering effects. He recognized, too, that his own words on the job would matter, especially in offering a point of view: "If I'm working with a fellow officer and he's on the same crime or something . . . and he says something but I believe another, I . . . want my part to be heard. I don't want the judge to go solely off his [the other officer's] things."

Spike expected that his future writing would be comprised largely of accident reports and investigation reports, "like first-hand accounts." He was aware of the weight his own words would carry: "If an arrest happens and you're there, you're a first-hand account, and it's important because that's what judges are gonna read . . . [in order to decide] if he's guilty or not guilty." Essentially, Spike will spend much of his career writing detail-filled narratives so that authorities beyond himself can make appropriate decisions. As a senior, Spike no longer spoke about trying new things in his writing. He spoke of writing not as a separate thing he would do but as an element at the very heart of his professional life. His words would have the heft of affecting individuals' futures.

Frankie, a human resources management major, had also expanded her identity as a writer. When asked how important writing was in her life, she answered, "Way more important than I thought it would be. I do a ton of writing." As with Spike, Frankie's major required significant writing. Her management courses demanded that she write case studies and short essays of two to five pages.

Her future in human resources management, she said, would involve writing emails, memos, letters related to hiring and firing, and reports. The sense of audience Frankie had expressed in Basic Writing three years earlier was further honed. She recognized that her written words needed to be succinct and meaningful if she wanted employees to read them. It was her job as writer, not the employees', to assure that messages were read: "If I'm writing an email or memo . . . if you make the first five or six lines about stupid things that don't matter . . . they'll stop reading."

Five to ten years in her future, Frankie expected to continue her workplace writing. By that time, she hoped to have expanded her audience, saying she wanted to be "comfortable with writing things that people higher up in the organization would be okay with reading, okay with presenting to executives. . . . I never want my writing to just stick with emails." The first-semester student who dreaded any writing foresaw a future in which her words would be "worthwhile, like making a difference."

Closing Thoughts

James Paul Gee (in this collection) argues that FYC, if it is to be continued at all, must attend to students' subject positions and social engagement with literacy in the world beyond academic disciplines and certainly beyond the classroom. Intentionality of course design, as shown by numerous writers in this collection, can usher student writers into that larger world of writing. It can foster not only transfer of skills but of dispositions and of one's view of oneself as a writer. Students who emerge from such classrooms can discover what Jane, a first-year participant in the study with Spike and Frankie discovered: "It [her Basic Writing course] . . . made me realize that there are many different ways you can write a paper and different techniques you can use when writing and not to stick to just one thing. . . . Everyone can be a writer; they just have to find it."

Works Cited

Baca, Jimmy Santiago. "Sign Language, Convict Style." *Adolescents on the Edge*, edited by Jimmy Santiago Baca and ReLeah Cossett Lent, Heinemann, 2010, pp. 113–18.

Brooke, Robert. "Modeling a Writer's Identity: Reading and Imitation in the Writing Classroom." *College Composition and Communication*, vol. 39, no. 1, 1988, pp. 24–41.

Collier, Lorna. "Listening to Students: New Insights on Their College-Writing Expectations." *Council Chronicle*, March 2014, pp. 10–12.

Dillard, Annie. *An American Childhood*. Harper Collins, 1987.

Frankie. Interview. Conducted by Gloria Park and Ravyn McKee, 24 Feb. 2014.

Fulwiler, Toby. "A Lesson in Revision." *The Subject is Writing*, 2nd ed., edited by Wendy Bishop, Boynton/Cook, 1999, pp. 73–88.

Gee, James Paul. (this collection). "Foreword."

Gee, James Paul. "What is Literacy?" *Negotiating Academic Literacies*, edited by Vivian Zamel and Ruth Spack, Erlbaum, 1998, pp. 51–59.

Ivanič, Roz. *Writing and Identity: The Discoursal Construction of Identity in Academic Writing*. John Benjamins, 1998.

Kerr, Jo-Anne. (this collection). "Teaching for Transfer in the First-year Composition Course: Fostering the Development of Dispositions."

Lederman, Josh. *Critical, Third-Space Phenomenology as a Framework for Validating College Composition Placement*. 2011. Indiana U of Pennsylvania, PhD dissertation.

McLeod, Susan H. *Notes on the Heart: Affective Issues in the Writing Classroom*. Southern Illinois UP, 1997.

Noden, Harry. *Image Grammar*. Heinemann, 1999.

Park, Gloria. "'Writing *is* a Way of Knowing': Writing and Identity." *ELT Journal*, vol. 67, 2013, pp. 336–45.

Ritter, Ashley M. (this collection). "A Transition."

Romano, Tom. "Teaching Writing from the Inside." *Adolescent Literacy*, edited by Kylene Beers et al., Heinemann, 2007, pp. 167–78.

Shaughnessy, Mina P. *Errors & Expectations: A Guide for the Teacher of Basic Writing*. Oxford UP, 1977.

Spike. Interview. Conducted by Ravyn McKee, 13 March 2014.

Taczak, Kara, et al. (this collection). "A Framework for Transfer: Students' Development of a 'Theory of Writing.'"

Tannen, Deborah. "Sex, Lies, and Conversation." *The Thomson Reader: Conversations in Context*, edited by Robert P. Yagelski and Thomson Wadsworth, 2007, pp. 306–10.

Questions for Reflection and Discussion After Chapter 4

1. During the Writing Marathon activity Helen describes, students write on campus and respond "I am a writer" if someone asks what they are doing. In what other ways can you prompt students to enact the role of "writer" during class, outside of the classroom? In what other ways can you prompt students to own the label of "writer" in the process?

2. What are the mentor texts you have in mind when writing? You might consider the "mentor texts" that you borrow discourse from in any type of writing that you do, including writing course materials.

3. How can you implement the writing activities Helen describes to foster your students' building of confidence as writers? Consider how you may adapt these activities to fit your students' levels of academic preparedness and their language and cultural backgrounds.

Writing Activity After Chapter 4

Choose a current student who you know of who struggles as a writer, or imagine a hypothetical student in FYC. Write a few sentences to describe this student's struggles with writing. Now, dream big: If this student could become a highly confident, highly skilled writer, what would that look like? Dreaming big, write a description of this student in the future that includes what he or she can do as a writer and what attitude he or she has toward writing. Now, dream a little smaller: In what reasonable ways can this student grow as a writer within a one semester course? Dreaming smaller, write a description of this student at the end of an FYC course that includes the few new (or newly refined) abilities he or she has acquired as a writer and the attitude he or she now has toward writing.

Further Reading

Corkery, Caleb. "Literacy Narratives and Confidence Building in the Writing Class-room." *Journal of Basic Writing*, vol. 24, no. 1, 2005, pp. 48–67.

Rose, Mike. *Lives on the Boundary: A Moving Account of the Struggles and Achieve-ments of America's Educationally Underprepared*. Penguin, 2005.

Williams, Bonnie J. "Students' 'Write' to Their Own Language: Teaching the African American Verbal Tradition as a Rhetorically Effective Writing Skill." *Equity & Excellence in Education*, vol. 46, no. 3, 2013, pp. 411–29.

Chapter 5. Encouraging Potential in Liminal Space: Student Writer Reflection

Martha Wilson Schaffer

CASE WESTERN RESERVE UNIVERSITY

Reflect Before Reading

Think about the ways you gain knowledge about your students, such as about their past educational experiences, interests, or goals in college. In what ways do you gain knowledge of how your students fit into certain categories? In what ways do you gain knowledge of who your students are in the process of becoming college writers? How do these varied types of knowledge enhance and inform your teaching in FYC?

~ ~ ~

I came back to graduate school after a 15-year hiatus. It started as a personal intellectual journal with forays into ancient rhetoric and cultural-historical activity theory, but then I became a graduate teaching assistant in the first-year composition (FYC) program at my university. In what seemed like no time at all, I went from being an expert to a novice. I did not know how to write a paper for my own classes, let alone teach someone else how to write a paper. Stripped of my familiar practices and routines, left adrift with a sea of knowledge that had seemingly no relevance in my new space, I was completely disoriented. I did not know *what to do*, but, worse yet, I did not know *who I was*. I felt that I was becoming someone, but I did not necessarily know who that was or what that person would do. I felt in-between most of the time—not still a lawyer and not yet a teacher, not still a student and not yet a professional, but I had a sense of excitement and wonder about my own potential to become someone else and that kept me working. As graduate students, we shared our frustrations and fears about the job market, our teaching personas, our plans and goals in formal seminar spaces and hallways, but most of my time was spent with first-year college students and I never talked to them about their experiences of being new, being un-moored from their past lives, being part of a re-orienting process. My interactions with them were shaping who I was, and, yet, I knew almost nothing about their personal experience of *becoming*. If I felt lost in spite of my years of life professional experience, how did first-year students negotiate this liminal space? How did my students conceive of their liminality? Were they similarly aware of their potentiality to be better writers, to produce better writing? And if they were, did it enhance their process of becoming a writer? So I decided to ask

DOI: https://doi.org/10.37514/PRA-B.2020.0308.2.05

How to get at someone's sense of their own potentiality? I supposed that if students did think about it, it might be in moments of reflection—on their writing projects, on the feedback they received from teachers and peers, and on their goals for the future. Reflective practice is common in FYC classrooms for the powerful learning opportunities offered by encouraging students to analyze what they have learned through a review of their writing projects as well as the assembly of print and digital portfolios (see O'Neill; Smith and Yancey; White; Yancey, "Electronic" and Reflection). In writing instruction, reflection is employed both to teach students to develop useful writing strategies and to "ask students to participate with us, not as objects of our study, but as agents of their own learning" (Yancey, Reflection 5). Through the process of reflection, Kathleen Blake Yancey asserts that "[s]tudents can theorize about their own writing in powerful ways" and that "[w]hen treated as a rhetorical act, when practiced, [reflection] becomes a discipline, a habit of mind" (Reflection 19).

Thus, I decided to use a series of interviews that would ask students about their writing projects, prompt them to reflect on those projects, and then look forward to future writing projects and future writing selves. The interviews would be acts of reflective self-assessment in which students were prompted to look back, but also to look forward, along a trajectory of their own becoming. Over the course of one semester, I studied four first-year writers and their self-assessment through processes of reflection during their enrollment in their university's required FYC course. I sought to engage students in ongoing conversation about the possibilities of looking not just reflectively at what a writer has accomplished but in looking forward to future incarnations of writing and writers through the concept of potentiality. The voices of these students describe their experience of FYC as a liminal space, in which they could explore what they were capable of as writers through reflection as well as anticipation that empowered them with an awareness of their own potentiality.

Interviews: Revelations with Limitations

I interviewed students regularly while they were enrolled in a required first-year composition class. As a novice researcher and teacher, I began with a set of questions and a plan to run the interview. But I soon discovered that students had their own plans, their own things to say, even their own questions for me. And as I let loose the formality and structure of the interviews, what they had to say—what I was ultimately trying to discover—revealed that they not only thought about their writing and themselves but that they were actively engaged in a process of creating their position within the larger structure of the writing program and the university. As my analysis and coding of the interviews uncovered, students performed a complex process of assessment through (1) reflections on past writing experiences, (2) contemporaneous assessments of present writing projects, and (3) future-looking plans and expectations for themselves as writers and community members (of academia and then, the working world). But the most exciting aspect of these conversations was that the complexity of self-assessment performed by the participants was performed not through my prompting of them to self-assess but through their own processes of negotiating their own goals with those of the writing teacher and writing program, their own sense of a writing self that included a categorization of themselves as novice writers, and their own ability to work with or against expectations set forth around them in the liminal space of first-year writing.

The liminal space of the FYC program is a rich but dense space in which to explore potentiality as a concept for self-assessment practices of FYC students because it is active and dynamic, a space where students are becoming—through unseen psychological and social changes, but also through conscious and reflective thought. Each student's experience of FYC is unique, and this small study can only tell us about the reflective practices of these four students, in this university, at this particular moment in their education. While this limits replicability, it reinforces a basic tenet of writing assessment scholarship: that assessment practices must be local and contextual so that they attend to the needs and serve the purposes of a particular program and a particular group of individuals (see Adler-Kassner and O'Neill; Broad; Huot; O'Neill). Furthermore, the students and I each bear our own subject positions within this space, intersecting within a hierarchy that constrains our interactions. I was their teacher and then their interviewer. We met in my office, in our FYC program office. Even as I write this, I am aware of an impulse to call them my students. Even though we ethically promoted each other's agency, shared, and expressed care and concern for one another throughout the process, I was always the researcher and they were the researched. While I am acutely aware of these limits, my hope (and that of the larger collection) is that this work encourages others to appreciate the value of engaging students in the overall project of FYC programming. Writing research that is grounded in the real expressions of student writers offers a messy but realistic and dynamic picture of the work that student writers do and the work that FYC programs might do to support them.

Participants and Their FYC Courses

The students with whom I worked come from a large public university located in a small town in northwest Ohio where the FYC program is the cornerstone of the university's learning outcomes with regard to written communication. The program focuses on college-level academic writing and consists of a sequence of three different courses: an intensive introductory writing course which introduces students to academic writing (required only of the most underprepared students); an introductory course in academic writing (required of most incoming first-year students); and a required academic writing course in which students develop writing skills that focus on inquiry-based essays. Typically, first-year students take one of the introductory courses and then the required course. Writing is taught as process, with opportunities for drafting, reviewing, revising, and editing. At the end of the course, students submit a portfolio containing all of their written work for the semester along with a "Narrative Self-Reflective Essay" written from a program-designed prompt that instructs students to develop a narrative essay addressing how they have developed writing skills and processes that attend to the major categories on the program's common writing rubric, which include audience awareness, organization/theme/structure, development, syntax, and word choice. This is the only formal self-assessment built into the program.

The participants successfully completed "Intensive Introduction to Academic Writing" with me as their instructor and had begun "Academic Writing," the required FYC course, when our interviews began in January 2013. They were all in the second semester of their first year of college, each enrolled in different courses with different instructors. These students were familiar with the FYC program's learning outcomes and terminology through their exposure to these in the introductory course. They were new to various elements of academic writing, and their developing understanding of these elements is reflected in our conversations over time. At the end of the spring semester, all but one of the four student participants passed the course.

Elizabeth is a white female in-state student from a rural area. She was conscientious about her writing assignments when I taught her the semester before the study. She was insightful and reflective about her writing without much prompting, and she even articulated a new writing process that she had developed for herself over the course of the semester. Susan is a white female student from a suburban area in-state. She did not demonstrate grammatical or mechanical difficulties in the introductory course, and her essays were well-developed and organized throughout the semester. Though she did not seem interested in writing for its own sake, she used writing as a tool in her education and viewed it as a way of learning. Walter is a black male student from a large city in-state. In the first week of class, he told me he was a creative writer and shared rap lyrics that he had written, but by the time we began interviews in January, he had changed his major to communications with a focus in promotions and advertising. During our interviews, he argued that writing in required FYC courses could not be interesting or entertaining—the hallmarks of good writing according to Walter. And he denied that anything he had written in FYC was of any interest to him. Julie, a black female dancer from an in-state metropolitan area, struggled with the conventions of the FYC program. Julie acknowledged that she would need to be able to write not only clearly but also persuasively in order to have others accept and follow her advice when she became a social worker. She expressed frustration with the FYC course, and toward the end of the semester explained to me that her friends had told her to "just write what the teacher wants" and she hadn't taken their advice, but now she knew they were right. This process of writing what the teacher wants, she said, was what she learned from the FYC program. Julie did not pass the required FYC course and would have to take it again.

Reflection and Negotiation in Liminal Space

The students whom I interviewed shared their self-assessments with me during their interviews, revealing a process of negotiation among a variety of aspects of their experience in FYC: between old writing lessons and new, between writer and reader, between their own goals and desires and those of the larger FYC program. Their negotiations reveal FYC as a liminal space in which they were suspended between who they were as high school students and who they are to become as college students and members of the academy. First-year writing classrooms are a site where students can mediate and negotiate their own sense of self through their contemplation of goals.

In "Betwixt and Between: The Liminal Period in Rites of Passage," anthropologist Victor Turner describes rites of passage as transformations between social, physical, mental and emotional states, ranging from graduations to wars. In the liminal state, individuals are "disengaged from social structures, [and] neophytes are alternately forced and encouraged to think about their society, their cosmos, and the powers that generate and sustain them. Liminality may be partly described as a stage of reflection" (14). It is not a far stretch to think of the first-year writer in a liminal space, both in terms of the inner processes of composing and in terms of her presence in the writing classroom, which makes this a rich location for a study of agency and practices of reflection.

In fact, some scholars have described FYC as a liminal space between noviceship and expertise. In their survey of the experience of Harvard's first-year writers, Nancy Sommers and Laura Saltz discover the "novice-as-expert paradox," in which students develop their writing skills while performing assignments beyond their skill level—in other words, "writing into expertise" (134). Sommers and Saltz assert that "those freshmen who cling to their old habits and formulas and who resent the uncertainty and humility of being a novice have a more difficult time adjusting to the demands of college writing" (134). The four students whom I worked with reveal that "clinging" and "resenting" are part of an involved process of becoming, a negotiation that goes on largely invisible to their FYC teachers.

Throughout the interview process, these four FYC student writers revealed their experience of FYC as a liminal space in their descriptions of the various kinds of negotiations they were engaged in during the semester. As Yancey explains in Reflection in the Writing Classroom,

> [W]hen writers are treated as writers, they will need to be awarded the authority that comes with writing. They may make decisions that run counter to our recommendations, and if they do so for reasons that are rhetorically sound, then we need to

> defer. Through reflection-in-action, we begin to negotiate; our
> practice changes in fundamental ways. (41)

The four students demonstrated these kinds of negotiations, and then some, in the conversations that developed around and beyond the scripted interview questions that began our monthly meetings. Elizabeth was eager to incorporate FYC lessons into her own developing sense of "good writing" and herself as a "good writer." She made connections between her FYC lessons and the larger concept of "good writing." In her first interview, she declared, "Writing is a form of communication, and communication is like essential to everyday life. So I feel it not only would it be helpful to the rest of my college experience, but for a job." A month later, with her first FYC paper completed and graded and with instruction underway on a new kind of essay that would involve integration of multiple sources, Elizabeth described activities her teacher facilitated in class to build essays in a series of steps. In reflecting on these activities, Elizabeth says, "It was interesting the way of learning something. I never really thought of doing it that way." This assessment of the teacher and her classroom activities continued throughout Elizabeth's interviews, and her description of her own work was often intertwined with her observations about the context of the assignment, its purpose, and its relation to larger educational and personal development. She was negotiating among old and new techniques, between her own sense of good writing and her new experiences with writing. Elizabeth received good grades on her FYC writing projects at the same time that she was developing and demonstrating a confidence in her own ability to make writing choices. She also received the reinforcement of a non-FYC teacher, who had praised her for employing the FYC-taught process of "synthesizing" sources into an essay for another class. Through her negotiations, she described a process of assimilation and a developing sense of agency as a developing writer in the liminal space of FYC.

Walter's interviews offer a demonstration of negotiations between self and teacher, as well as between self and writing program. Walter combines the terminology of the writing program community with his own interpretation of the purposes and effects of different rhetorical strategies. Walter's interviews are notable for his concern about whether his writing was interesting or entertaining (as opposed to "forced"). His interviews are also notable for his perception of the interview as an opportunity for him to share his criticisms of the FYC program and his suggestions for its improvement. Walter was not just assessing his own work in the course of attending FYC courses and our interviews; he was assessing the FYC program as well. Walter projected confidence in his writing in his introductory FYC class before we began our interviews, and he continually challenged my feedback on his essays. His questioning and his resistance continued through his interviews, with him explaining to me in his second interview that he knew how to write a paper and found FYC "boring." He found validation in his interpretation of a comment that his teacher had made about the expectations of the course. Walter describes his FYC teacher writing on the board, "This is not cre-ative writing, this is um [FYC] and you are writing to an academic audience." He objected to FYC courses being "so structured" and being "different than writing papers like in other classes" where "it's just like write four pages and then that's the paper." As reinforcement of the significance of Walter's distaste for boring, formulaic writing taught in FYC, Walter's general lack of interest in talking about his FYC papers contrasted sharply with his enthusiastic and detailed conversation about papers that were "interesting" to him in other classes. His short answers morphed into more energetic, detailed descriptions of writing that he was doing in other classes, such as this description of a project in one course for his major:

> I get to write about how instructor of a physical activity um just
> pretty much runs their class such as a gym teacher or some-
> thing and I get to watch how they, like the tone of their voice,
> just how they get the participation, the respect and then I have
> to critique that and I also get to write another paper about um,
> about a game. I gotta pick a game to um show a whole class how
> to play and I have make like, to have like all the details in case
> someone's never played it.

This writing was an opportunity—"I get to write"—not a requirement, or a "forced" FYC assignment for Walter.

While Elizabeth seemed to willingly incorporate instructor feedback into her own bank of knowledge about revision and preparing a final draft of a paper, Walter struggled against what he disagreed with in the instructor's commentary (in so far as it contrasted with his own knowledge and purposes in writing) and in the program's teaching. Walter maintained his own sense of what he believed was effective in his writing abilities while acknowledging the need to conform to the instructor's beliefs about what was needed for a final draft to pass the criteria set out for the course. Elizabeth, in some ways, saw herself as a novice and was open to changing her writing strategies, believing that doing so would enhance her writing ability. That belief was an awareness of her own potentiality to be a different kind of writer than she was.

Walter, in contrast, did not see himself as a novice writer, and seemed to resent what he thought was "boring" writing. With non-FYC projects, though, Walter saw an opportunity to develop his writing ability in ways that were connected to his sense of becoming a communications professional. In a similar inquiry into the student experience of becoming a writer, Anne Herrington and Marcia Curtis ob-serve a "writing into" process in their interviews of four students, finding that "they actively use writing . . . for the ongoing development of their personal identities, in-cluding their sense of themselves in relation to others" (1). In interviews, I observed what Herrington and Curtis explain: "for some students, more than for others, learning was not a passive acculturation process, but a negotiation where they were actively considering how they would position themselves in relation to teacher and disciplinary expectations" (34). This negotiation can be seen very clearly in Walter's interviews, marked by his resistance to give up his beliefs and confidence in what he believes to be good writing in the face of the requirements and demands of the FYC program and its writing instructors. As Walter explains, "I feel they like, it's set up to where you like can write about what you want to write about but then it's not really like that." Walter did not see himself as a novice, but he did not completely reject the lessons of FYC. Instead, he made negotiations in his mind and in our conversations between his idea of the writer whom he was and the program's idea of the writer he should be. Through negotiations that were possible because of the liminal space of FYC, Walter was developing a sense of his own identity and of who he might become. Elizabeth and Walter experienced the liminal space of FYC in their own unique way, but they did not experience it passively. They engaged actively in negotiations about their acceptance and integration of writing processes to come to a cohesive notion of what constitutes successful writing—a notion that they could call their own, and their negotiations happened largely with themselves, through unprompted self-assessment, reflection, and anticipation.

Reflection and Anticipation: Recognizing One's Potentiality

In addition to reflecting on what they had learned and how their writing processes had changed from one writing project to the next, these four writers were also assessing the value of changes that they had made incrementally and in terms of a larger trajectory of becoming a certain type of writer or producing a certain type of writing moving forward. They did not describe themselves as being any specific kind of writer in the moment without describing a future writing self. This movement back and forth through reflection and imagination of selves and texts in the future demonstrates that these students assessed their own capacity for being changed and changing themselves as well as their potentiality. When asked what kind of writer she might be two years from now, Julie said, "[S]omebody will read [my writing] and say, 'She is a smart writer. She's a smart person. She's very intelligent.'" Julie expressed confidence in her writing skills from the beginning. She was particularly proud of her ability to "reel" readers in and demonstrated a rather sophisticated awareness of audience. But she struggled to really understand her teacher's comments as the course progressed, and concepts such as synthesizing sources and using an academic tone escaped her even at the end of the semester. She initially told me that she felt FYC was a useful course, that she had learned a lot from the introductory FYC course that she had taken in the fall—"I learned about myself, and how I write, the good and the challenges of writing." But at the end of the semester, after the second, required FYC course, she was upset with receiving and processing feedback:

> I understand that [the teacher] told me that this is wrong, but like she told me, not help me all the way but she didn't really say

how she wanted me to change it. Since I write it for her, I change it to the way I think is right, she says it is still wrong. Okay, what is your definition of right and wrong? I know she can't do it for me, but like, what's your right? To your liking? I kept revising to the best of my ability and it still wasn't right.

One specific example of a divergence between her teacher's instructions and her own rhetorical purposes arose when Julie was writing a paper about marriage equality, in which she had written about how her own sister's homosexuality had affected her family. The teacher's feedback was that the essay was too informal, which Julie interpreted to mean "to stop putting my own personal, I guess." Julie went on to explain that "when you used to write papers you always had to put in a personal experience and that's why I'm probably like used to it so that's why I am probably like—I don't know." Julie purposefully and rhetorically used a writing technique that she had learned and successfully used before college and was now being told not to. In the end, she explained that she replaced the personal experience with source material from "like psychologists or whatever." Her frustration with her teacher's assessments of her FYC papers mounted over the course of the semester, and in the end she did not pass the required FYC course, but in her final interview, she reflected on and shared with me what she had learned from the experience:

Me at the beginning trying to do it for myself wasn't working, then I know what she wants. She said this is great, this is what I am looking for. That's the smart way—just do what they want. Not settling! You still have a mind of your own, but it's just [pause] . . . you are not settling. . . . That's how good you are; you can just write whatever they want to hear.

Remarkably, in spite of her FYC experience, Julie refused to completely give up her authority as a writer and her vision of being an effective writer one day. And even though she did not succeed in the course in the way that Elizabeth, Susan, and Walter did, Julie engaged in dynamic and rich processes of reflection on past writing experiences, contemplation on current writing processes, and anticipation of a future writer that she might become.

Susan's trajectory of interviews also revealed active processes of reflection and anticipation. When asked what writing projects she was looking forward to, Susan explained, "I don't really know what is next. I mean I know the research paper but I don't know the topics or anything. But I usually enjoy research papers if we have like an option of what to write on." She connected her past enjoyment of writing research papers to an expectation that she would enjoy an upcoming research paper assignment, even though she did not know the topic or details of the assignment yet. When I asked her what she enjoyed about research papers specifically, she answered, "Like learning new things that I didn't know before . . .

especially if it's a topic you think you are familiar on and then you learn more stuff like you're like, oh, okay." Not only did Susan's assessment of her writing projects demonstrate reflection and anticipation, but it also revealed her perception of writing as a way of learning.

Susan spoke with confidence about this writing project and about other writing projects, on several occasions noting that she "just" had the writing of the paper left to do. Susan was able to articulate things that she had learned to do differently in her writing preparations and things that she still felt that she needed to work on in her writing. At one point, she described the differences in how she was writing her current project compared to her last project as "doing a lot more organizing and like when I am finding sources, I like write down the key points. And like I research more, like I try to find the best site instead of finding, using the one I find first." She also explained that she needed to take more time with her writing because she would look back over a paper and wonder what she was trying to say, but that she was good at organizing. Her self-assessment of her writing skills and processes involved reflection and review as well as an acknowledgement of the utility of certain skills going forward into developing writing projects. Susan described her FYC papers in terms of her opportunities to revise drafts. She was able to identify what was successful in a first draft, along with what she needed to do in a second or final draft to "pass" the paper, even without instructor feedback. This awareness of her own capacity to assess and revise one paper for the better translated into an awareness of her capacity to develop further in her overall writing skills—an awareness of her potentiality, as demonstrated earlier in the excerpt from her final interview.

These students experienced the liminality of being a novice in their own unique ways, but they all described acts of agency in their process of becoming writers. Recognizing the connections between expertise and agency, Janis Haswell and Richard Haswell argue for student rights of authorship in their 2010 book, *Authoring: An Essay for the Profession on Potentiality and Singularity*. To define these rights of authorship, Haswell and Haswell interview and gather data from "real" authors (as opposed to student writers) on what they call the "phenomenology of authoring," or the inner life of authors (13). Among the traits of authoring that they discover is potentiality, which Haswell and Haswell define as "an ongoing capacity for creative work that needs to be constantly protected and nurtured" (20). This concept of potentiality becomes integral to Haswell and Haswell's call for teachers of writing to imbue student writers with a sense of authorship. They assert, "[S]tudent writers are not allowed the full rights of authorship, which include respect for the work they have not yet produced" (33). In their own unique ways, all four of the student writers in this chapter assessed their potentiality—their capacity to do "better" or different work in the future, their ability to learn, and their ability to be a writer at some later time. Whether they saw themselves as writers seemed to depend upon their negotiations between external expectations of the FYC program (through rubrics, teacher feedback, and portfolio assessment) and their internal perceptions of what they were capable of doing. The ability and willingness to negotiate these matters arose, in part, from the self-assessments that the students performed in the course of our interviews as they had the opportunity to analyze what they were experiencing. In a sense, these interviews functioned as a method of developing, or sustaining, a sense of authorship—the right to write and the right to evaluate that writing as successful or not in accomplishing individual goals as well as FYC program goals.

Implications for FYC Students, Teachers, and Programs

The narratives that these four students constructed to describe their own growth and development are narratives of negotiations between high school writing lessons and college writing instruction, between their own goals and the objectives of the FYC program, between noviceship and authorship. Their stories of negotiation reveal their experience of FYC as a liminal space in which they occupy a complicated and shifting subject position. And they are not just aware of that positionality, they are actively engaged in its shifting, in part, through processes of reflection on past work and past writing habits combined with anticipation of future work and a future self revealed through and by the writing that they perform. They are in-between in various significant ways, particularly where they are between noviceship, as Yancey, Liane Robertson, and Kara Taczak describe the state of being a new college writer (18–19), and authorship, a state described by Haswell and Haswell as being knowledgeable but also confident in one's capacity and competence as a writer (33). In this liminal space, these four student writers have the leeway to challenge internal and external limitations, to reflect on what has come to pass, and to anticipate what is yet to come. But what enables all of their negotiations is their awareness of their own capacity to grow and develop from moment to moment. These trajectories grew not just from reflection on past work and past versions of their writerly selves, but also from the companion process of looking forward, anticipating the work that they might do in the future and the writers that they might become. These student writers are not yet the writers they might be in the future, nor are they the writers that they were in the past. This process of reflecting and anticipating might be a key element of the pedagogy of potentiality that Haswell and Haswell urge writing teachers to employ.

How might we develop a pedagogy of potentiality? In *Writing Across Contexts: Transfer, Composition, and Sites of Writing*, Yancey, Robertson, and Taczak propose a "teaching for transfer" model of writing instruction that employs reflection to help students enact and achieve "a unique set of resources . . . to call upon as they encounter new writing tasks" (5). Yancey, Robertson, and Taczak describe student writers as being in a liminal state of "noviceship," from which they "write [their] way into expertise" (39). In the process of doing so, students develop a sense of their own agency, rooted in knowledge and a set of skills that they can deploy to effectively address new writing problems (43). But in using reflection to help students carry forward their skills and build their expertise, writing instructors must foster a sense of agency, the sense of agency that Yancey finds inherent in the practice of reflection (*Reflection* 5, 19). These students reveal that reflection is part of a larger process of negotiation that involves both looking back and looking forward. This is what enables them to see themselves as becoming and to derive momentum from the awareness of having potentiality to produce a better essay and to be a better writer at some point in the future.

This study is a small, initial exploration into the potential of self-assessment to empower student writers and to provide valuable information to teachers of writing and writing programs about dynamic processes that are occurring within writing classrooms almost without our knowing. It arose from my own exigence, constructed by my own abstract desire to become something new, and it formed the very concrete foundation upon which I became a teacher and scholar. What did I learn? I learned that negotiating liminal spaces is both intensely personal and invariably social, that we cannot be unaware of what our students are experiencing in the process of becoming, and that the in-between-ness of our collective experience of teaching and administrating in FYC spaces demands that we listen to our students' voices. It is impossible to extrapolate from this short time with these few students any general claim about student writer potentiality and personal methods of self-assessment. Even among these four students, not all of them succeeded in their FYC class, and not all of them engaged critically with their assessment practices in a conscious way. But these brief moments of asking and listening do suggest we might encourage students to not only reflect on the past, but to envision plans for the future and to think about their potentiality, while we foster and engage in negotiations with them in the liminal space of FYC. Reflection as well as anticipation might be part of our conversations with students in which we can ask them how they see themselves as writers and who they want to become as writers. And through these conversations, we might also engage students in powerful acts of agency by taking into account their assessments of the policies and procedures of the FYC programs in which we work together.

Works Cited

Adler-Kassner, Linda, and Peggy O'Neill. *Reframing Writing Assessment to Improve Teaching and Learning.* Utah State UP, 2010.

Broad, Bob. *What We Really Value: Beyond Rubrics in Teaching and Assessing Writing.* Utah State UP, 1987.

Elizabeth. Interviews. Conducted by Martha Wilson Schaffer, 15 Jan., 12 Feb., 2 and 19 Apr. 2013.

Haswell, Janis, and Richard Haswell. *Authoring: An Essay for the Profession on Potentiality and Singularity.* Utah State UP, 2010.

Herrington, Anne, and Marcia Curtis. *Persons in Process: Four Stories of Writing and Personal Development in College*. National Council of Teachers of English, 2000.

Huot, Brian. *(Re)articulating Writing Assessment for Teaching and Learning*. Utah State UP, 2002.

Julie. Interviews. Conducted by Martha Wilson Schaffer, 30 Jan., 28 Feb., 12, 24, and 30 Apr. 2013.

O'Neill, Peggy. "Reflection and Self-Assessment: Resisting Ritualistic Discourse." *The Writing Instructor*, vol. 2, no. 1, 2002, www.writinginstructor.org/oneill-2002-04.

Smith, JoAnne Bowman, and Kathleen Blake Yancey. *Self-Assessment and Development in Writing: A Collaborative Inquiry*. Hampton, 2000.

Sommers, Nancy, and Laura Saltz. "The Novice as Expert: Writing the Freshman Year." *College Composition and Communication*, vol. 56, no. 1, Sept. 2004, pp. 124–49.

Susan. Interviews. Conducted by Martha Wilson Schaffer, 23 Jan. and 3 Apr. 2013.

Turner, Victor. "Betwixt and Between: The Liminal Period in Rites of Passage." *Betwixt and Between: Patterns of Masculine and Feminine Initiation*, edited by Louise Carus Mahdi et al., Open Court, 1987, pp. 3–19.

Walter. Interviews. Conducted by Martha Wilson Schaffer, 25 Jan., 27 Feb., and 24 Apr. 2013.

White, Edward M. *Assigning, Responding, Evaluating: A Writing Teacher's Guide*. 4th ed., Bedford/St. Martin's, 2007.

Yancey, Kathleen Blake. "Electronic Portfolios a Decade into the Twenty-First Century: What We Know, What We Need to Know." *Peer Review*, Winter 2009, pp. 28–32.

———. *Reflection in the Writing Classroom*. Utah State UP, 1998.

Yancey, Kathleen Blake, et al. *Writing Across Contexts: Transfer, Composition, and Sites of Writing*. Utah State UP, 2014.

Questions for Discussion and Reflection After Chapter 5

1. Chapter 5 demonstrates a range of knowledge teachers can gain about students. What aspects of Martha's interview conversations could be adapted for conferences with your students or reflective writing activities?

2. How can you create space in FYC to give students agency by inviting discussion or critique of an FYC program? What challenges might you encounter in doing so?

Writing Activity After Chapter 5

Martha's reflection on her own potentiality as a new teacher led her to explore her students' self-assessments of their positions as writers in the academy. Using the introduction to Chapter 5 for inspiration, write a paragraph or two exploring your own potentiality in your current professional position. In conducting this self-assessment, you might ask: Who am I as a writer in this exact moment? Who am I as a reader today? Who am I as a teacher at my current institution or institutions? In what ways do I occupy liminal spaces in my professional work, and what strategies am I engaging in to navigate these spaces?

Further Reading

Gibson, Michelle, et al. "Bi, Butch, and Bar Dyke: Pedagogical Performances of Class, Gender, and Sexuality." *College Composition and Communication,* vol. 52, no. 1, 2000, pp. 69–95.

Skorczewski, Dawn. "From Playing the Role to Being Yourself: Becoming the Teacher in the Writing Classroom." *Teaching One Moment at a Time: Disruption and Repair in the Classroom,* by Dawn Skorczewski, U of Massachusetts P, 2005, pp. 15–37.

Chapter 6. Teaching for Transfer in the First-Year Composition Course: Fostering the Development of Dispositions

Jo-Anne Kerr
INDIANA UNIVERSITY OF PENNSYLVANIA

Reflect Before Reading

Before reading Chapter 6, think about your own FYC course. What mindsets about writing do students bring into your course from their prior writing education? What beliefs do your students hold about writing when they come to your class, and where do these beliefs come from? In what ways does your course reinforce, or ignore, or attempt to change students' incoming beliefs and mindsets?

~ ~ ~

"Writing is power."

—*Ashley, first-year composition student*

One mid-August, a few weeks before the start of the fall semester, I received an email from a student who would be in my ENGL 101 Composition I course during the upcoming semester. Ashley introduced herself and expressed interest in discovering what the course would entail. I was impressed and intrigued; I had never before heard from a prospective first-year student. I replied to Ashley's email, letting her know that I looked forward to meeting her and attached the course syllabus for her to read through. It was later that I learned from Ashley that she had been both nervous and hopeful about her ENGL 101 course—nervous about what would be expected of her as a writer and hopeful that writing assignments would be anything but five-paragraph essays.

Shortly before receiving Ashley's email, I had finished redesigning my ENGL 101 as a result of my interest in encouraging the development of ways of thinking about writing (dispositions) in first-year composition (FYC). My interest in the development of writing dispositions had arisen, in part, from working with first-year (FY) writers over several semesters, during which time I eventually realized that I had to foreground and attend to what students believed they had

DOI: https://doi.org/10.37514/PRA-B.2020.0308.2.06

"learned" about writing in their secondary English language arts classes in order to better meet their needs as FY college writers. I had discovered that my FY writers, through no fault of their own, had some understandings about writing (and themselves as writers) that had to be addressed, for they were not only inaccurate and misinformed, but also an obstacle to the development of proficiency with written language (and confidence about the ability to become proficient). My reconceptualization of my FYC course had also resulted from my interest in transfer, the "ability to extend what has been learned in one context to new contexts" (National Research Council 51). I was wondering what learning my students might transfer from my FYC course to other writing contexts, academic or otherwise. Finally, Elizabeth Wardle and Doug Downs' scholarship regarding writing about writing FYC courses had elicited my interest. Like Wardle and Downs, I perceived problems with the nature of and reason for the existence of "college writing" courses, understanding that "college writing" as a monolithic form doesn't actually exist, given the many forms that writing in college can take.

Ashley, then, would be participating in an ENGL 101 course that looked rather different from my previous 101 courses. I was excited by the prospect of promoting ways of thinking about writing in the course and offering the opportunity for students to examine and reflect on their writing experiences up to this time along with their understandings of themselves as writers.

What follows is a look at the concepts of transfer and dispositions and an overview of some of the assignments I used to help my FY writers develop writing disposition. Ashley's voice, along with that of a few of her FYC peers, is featured to demonstrate ways of thinking about writing that developed and that I hoped would transfer to other contexts to inform and assist with the writing expected in these different contexts.

Transfer

The enduring existence of FYC in colleges and universities may result from the belief that what students learn in FYC courses, such as rhetorical knowledge and skills, will assist them with the writing they do for other courses, i.e., provide a service of sorts. While the acquisition of rhetorical knowledge and skills is key to effective college, workplace, and public writing, implicit in the design of most FYC courses is the belief that students will transfer the knowledge and skills they have acquired to other academic contexts—that they will bring this knowledge and these skills to bear when they are writing a paper for a political science course or a response to an essay question for an introductory theater course, or that they will be able to integrate source material into a research paper for their psychology course. Yet, what is known about transfer, the ability to apply knowledge and skills learned in one setting to different contexts, suggests otherwise.

As noted earlier, transfer is the "ability to extend what has been learned in one context to new contexts" (National Research Council 51). Doug Brent points out that notions of transfer evolved over the past century, from the belief that transfer occurs only if the "source and target situation" are nearly identical to a belief that learners must have a good understanding of principles that underlie skills in order for transfer to occur (561). Researchers ultimately found fault with narrow conceptions of transfer, preferring to understand transfer as re-creation of new skills that are demanded by new situations, these new skills arising from earlier learning (563). Brent also shares that "[m]any studies of transfer reveal a disturbingly uneven pattern of results. Frequently, learning acquired in one context seemingly evaporates when the learner is asked to apply it in another, even when the contexts seem relatively similar" (562).

Carl Bereiter refers to a "widespread pessimism about transfer" owing to research indicating that learned intelligent behavior doesn't typically transfer, nor do specific strategies, such as problem-solving strategies (28). Bereiter also alludes to "conceptual understanding" and the importance of prior knowledge for learning, citing research that suggests that conceptual knowledge, especially put to use to develop further learning, does transfer. Finally, though, and particularly germane for my purposes here, is his notion of "transfer of dispositions"—that it may be more possible to transfer dispositions, a propensity to act in a certain way, rather than skills, noting that mindfulness and openness to learning can work to help one act intelligently in any context (30).

I suggest, then, that providing opportunities for students to develop dispositions about writing, in addition to knowledge and skills, may increase the likelihood of their ability to transfer what they learn in FYC to other contexts that will demand different types of writing. However, before discussing how instructors can promote the development of appropriate dispositions about writing in their courses, it will be helpful to have a fuller understanding of dispositions and how dispositions, knowledge, and skills are related.

Dispositions

A helpful generic definition for dispositions comes from Harvey Siegel: "a tendency, propensity, or inclination to behave or act in certain ways under certain circumstances" (208). In other words, dispositions are habits of mind that bring about the use of skills and the application of knowledge. For my purpose here, dispositions are ways of thinking about writing (and about oneself as writer) that can be the impetus for students to put their capabilities as writers to use; that is, dispositions help bring about appropriate behaviors—including behaviors related to writing.

How do dispositions, knowledge, and skills relate? Rhetorical knowledge implies what one has learned about writing. Skills imply mastery—the ability to put the learning to use. Dispositions are different from knowledge and skills, yet the three are not mutually exclusive, given that understandings of intelligence have evolved to include not only ability but also how ability begets action—a dispositional view of intelligence. In other words, intelligence is "cognitive capacity" but also the ability to use "emotions and other stimuli as cognitive cues" (Tishman 49). Dispositions include, then, an ability to apply knowledge but also the predisposition to do so that results from awareness that an opportunity is available to use the learning (Tishman et al. 2).

Having made the case that teaching FYC should include strategies to help students develop relevant dispositions about writing and having asserted that dispositions transfer more successfully than do knowledge and discrete skills, it is time to address the "how" of teaching writing dispositions in our FYC courses.

Developing Writing Dispositions in FYC

Referring to Bereiter's work, Brent notes that dispositions can be taught most effectively through "long-term immersion in contexts that nurture the desired disposition in complex ways" (563). Shari Tishman et al. characterize this immersion as "enculturation," which must take place in a "sustained cultural context" that includes the "full educational surround" (6). Furthermore, they state that for enculturation to occur, there must be "cultural exemplars, cultural interactions, and direct instruction in cultural knowledge and activities" (6). Finally, they contend that attending to the acquisition of skills only is not adequate to foster tendencies to apply these skills in different contexts (9).

Furthermore, this notion of enculturation, including course design and teaching, works to create a culture of thinking in the classroom that is informed by a sociocultural theory of literacy, a theory that posits that literacy is both socially and culturally situated (Perez 5), given that different disciplines within the academy operate as communities of disciplinary cultures with their own literacy practices. Thus, an environment of enculturation in an FYC course will include introducing and acclimating students to the behaviors, values, ways of communicating, and norms of the discipline of composition, encouraging the development of ways of thinking about composition along with attention to the acquisition of rhetorical knowledge and skills.

James Paul Gee's concept of "Discourses" is relevant here. Gee posits that to understand and appreciate language (and here we can include written language), we must always place it within its social context (2). Gee's "Discourses" ("big D Discourses") are comprised of behavior, interactions, ways of thinking, and systems of values along with ways of reading, writing, and communicating (3). Our FYC students, then, will be enculturated into the Discourse of writing and of FY composition; they will learn not only writing but also how to act and communicate like a writer. The Discourse of the FYC course includes writing and reading (like a writer), interacting (with instructors in conferences, with peers in peer response groups), and thinking about writing in ways that go beyond what they think when they enter the course—that writing is formulaic, one-size-fits-all, and "correct."

Next, I examine an FYC course as a sustained cultural context within which students can develop ways of thinking about writing through enculturation.

Teaching Writing Dispositions in the Sustained Cultural Context of FYC

Remember that Tishman et al. assert that within a sustained cultural context, enculturation results from the use of "cultural exemplars, cultural interactions, and direct instruction in cultural knowledge and activities" (6). So to encourage the development of dispositions about writing in the FYC course, instructors must share examples of dispositions, provide opportunity for interactions among students and between the instructor and students that use the dispositions, and directly teach the disposition.

In the following section, I illustrate how to teach dispositions that follow Tishman et al.'s recommendations, sharing strategies to promote enculturation and the development of dispositions about writing.

Getting to Know FY Writers

New learning involves transfer based on previous learning; thus, before I have students reflect on their beliefs about writing (their habits of mind concerning writing), I want to ascertain students' current understandings of writing. This information is important, also, because we FYC instructors, along with our colleagues in other departments, know little about our FY students. Our FY students come to us with a variety of experiences with writing, some of which resulted from the high-stakes testing environment of most public schools, where a great deal of effort is dedicated to preparing students to write on demand for standardized tests. Our students' perceptions about academic writing are thus often skewed by these efforts, so it is important for us to determine our students' previous learning and thinking about writing prior to any attempts to change that thinking and to provide opportunity to develop new understandings. Furthermore, as Kara Taczak, Liane Robertson, and Kathleen Blake Yancey note in this collection, this prior knowledge can affect, in sometimes adverse ways, what students attempt to transfer into FYC and other writing contexts. As I do, Taczak et al. advocate for affording opportunity for students to remember and articulate prior learning and experiences with writing to construct what they call a conceptual foundation that will later allow for a reframing of this learning to accommodate different writing demands.

The first piece of writing that Ashley's class did and subsequent FYC classes do is a response to the question: What do you expect to learn in ENGL 101? Their responses help me understand and categorize their dispositions about writing while yielding information that can inform subsequent teaching.

The responses to this question that Ashley's class gave indicated dispositions about writing that reflected a belief in the necessity for and importance of "correct writing," such as "I expect to be able to correct my own errors . . . ," "[learn] correct usage of grammar and mechanics," "create . . . grammatically correct papers," and "I would like to be able to write a perfect paper by the end of this course." Also evident was a concern with the development of "skills" and "techniques": "improve the skills we already have" and "learn techniques of writing." There were also references to writing five-paragraph essays; one student wrote about her frustration with having to "stick with five paragraph essays" and "time limits" (perhaps a reference to writing on demand).

These responses illustrate previous learning and writing dispositions, some of which may get in the way of what I hope my students will achieve. For example, a concern for correctness and a belief in "perfect" writing can thwart the process of writing; getting started with a piece can be challenging when a writer is worried about making mistakes. The perception of writing as merely a set of skills, likewise, can hinder the development of style and voice. And, certainly, writing only on demand in response to prompts often results in very limited and misinformed understandings about how writers organize pieces when they consider purpose and content and the needs of their readers.

But, nonetheless, before I provide an exemplar of a more productive writing disposition, it is important to both acknowledge this prior learning and ways of thinking about writing and to probe a bit to determine the genesis of the learning and dispositions. For instance, FY students' focus on the need for "correctness" or "structure" may be a result of preparing for writing on demand that often requires a five-paragraph pattern of organization, given that it is an expedient way to write to prompts on standardized tests. Thus, subsequent to my reading through students' responses to my question about their expectations, I initiate a discussion during which I share what I learned from their responses and invite them to talk a bit about high school writing instruction, prompting them to explain, say, a concern for correct writing or asking about the importance of grammatically correct writing. To facilitate this discussion, I share a list of their expectations, categorized to demonstrate the "big ideas" about writing that emerged. For example, one list of expectations derived from this first piece of writing was divided into expectations related to improving and developing skills, correctness, and looking to the future/one's profession.

After discussing their expectations and what they suggest about understandings of writing, it is helpful to discuss "good" writing and to ask students to identify features of "good writing." Not surprisingly, given the many expectations that relate to "good writing," "better writing," and "proper writing," correctness is mentioned along with "structure." I then share a piece of writing that provides opportunity to reconsider what "good" writing is—a piece that is less structured in the conventional sense of the term but is, nevertheless, indicative of effective writing. (I have had success using Alice Walker's "Father.") Here, then, I share an exemplar (my appreciation for the essay resulting from Walker's shuttling among past, present, and future, her judicious use of one-sentence paragraphs,[1] and the essay's contemplative

---

1. The use of these is especially surprising to my students, many of whom have been taught that paragraphs *must* have at least five sentences. They are often so taken

and reflective tone), after which I offer opportunity for discussion about "correct" writing, followed by direct instruction about "good" writing and the problematic nature of narrow perceptions of "good" writing. Simultaneously, I am sharing my own way of thinking about writing—that what counts as "correct" writing is culturally mediated, as writing is a social endeavor dependent upon the situation in which it is occurring. I also suggest that forcing writing into a predetermined pattern (at least in most cases) counters what we know about how people write and ignores the fact that a great deal of writing transcends form—that these "forms" are really genres that "are ways of being and acting in the world" (Dean 7).

Another activity gets students thinking about writing while it shows them that writing is ubiquitous in their lives. When FY students are invited to think about writing, they often default to academic writing, the school-sponsored writing that they have done. However, of course, they engage in a great deal of writing that is not school-sponsored, such as to-do lists, emails, texts, and workplace writing. An assignment completed early in the course, a record of writing over the course of a few days, helps students see how common writing is in their lives. Again, as with the previous assignment, the intent is to initiate a new disposition about writing and about themselves as writers. While sharing my own record of writing, I also offer my way of thinking about writing (that in my life it is just as useful and necessary as reading), after which further discussion is conducted that includes a minilesson about the different purposes that writing has (and can have) in our lives—pragmatic, functional, as a tool for learning. The lesson culminates with students reflecting in writing on what they learned about their own uses of writing and themselves as writers through keeping a record of their writing. A component of dispositions, reflection begins with hard thinking but also includes "thoughtful consideration of one's assumptions, values, and ramifications of one's thinking and actions" (Schussler 263), thus serving to help students better comprehend the "why" of their thinking and how this thinking may affect their writing in the future.

In summary, these beginning writing assignments help me discover my FY students' understandings and knowledge about writing as well as, by extension, their beliefs about writing—their dispositions. Because all new learning is based on transfer from previous learning, it is imperative to access previous learning and habits of mind before moving forward with attention to meeting FYC objectives and learning outcomes—which will include the development, I hope, of different ways of thinking about writing.

The Writer's Profile

This writing assignment presents students with the task of sharing their perceptions of themselves as writers. Prior to beginning work on this assignment, students

---

with the rhetorical effect of a one-sentence paragraph that they use them in their own pieces.

read a model writer's profile (written by a previous FY student), and we discuss content, tone, and organization as a means to begin (or augment) the development of rhetorical knowledge and skills. However, as with the previous assignments, I am interested in ascertaining dispositions.

For this assignment, I ask students to write an essay in which they describe themselves as writers; I provide some questions to generate content, but there is latitude with regard to what content to include. As with the assignments mentioned earlier, these profiles yield insights into dispositions about writing that can, if necessary, be addressed. Furthermore, as students have, by this time, read a few pieces about composing (Donald Murray's "All Writing is Autobiography" and Sondra Perl's "The Composing Processes of Unskilled College Writers"), they are beginning to question and critique their beliefs about writing and about themselves as writers. At the same time, the reading and discussion of these pieces have allowed for enculturation. We can discuss, for instance, how a research study is written and the form that it takes and compare it to Murray's "All Writing is Autobiography." This discussion can lead to the realization that the type of writing called for is culturally determined, leading to the notion of discourse and discourse community, concepts that are introduced later in the course, with opportunity to revisit the concept of genre and predetermined forms, such as the five-paragraph essay.

A look at Ashley's writer's profile will demonstrate what she was learning about herself as a writer and some of her ways of thinking about writing that are changing. In her piece, Ashley described her writing process and was able to make a distinction between revision and editing as a result of having read Perl's article: "I make sentence-by-sentence changes which are referred to as 'changes between drafts,' and not editing, according to Sondra Perl. . . . " Here, Ashley is describing how she writes a piece that she refers to as "the strict five paragraph format," what most of her high school writing consisted of. Later, she wrote:

> My previous years as a writer in high school and middle school
> have consisted of following the strict format of the five para-
> graph essay. No matter what the topic, I was always asked to
> prove my point in a highly structured set-up. The . . . format
> called for so many rules and restrictions including a minimal
> number of "to be" verbs, no personal pronouns, and zero con-
> tractions. This prohibited me from me being able to let my per-
> sonality show and like Donald Murray says . . . "I do not think
> that we should move away from personal or reflective narrative
> in composition courses, but closer to it. . . . " I completely agree
> with Murray. . . .

Ashley's writer's profile, as well as those of other FY students, includes writing dispositions—and reveals how those dispositions may be problematized by the culture of our FYC course. For instance, Ashley always had to "prove my point in a highly structured set-up." Two ways of thinking about writing are implicit in this statement: that writing is always thesis driven and that it follows a predetermined pattern of organization—a "set-up" that is "highly structured." Another student wrote in her writer's profile that she never thought about what kind of writer she is because "I never considered myself much of a 'writer.'" Like the basic writers Helen Sitler features in this collection and the multilingual writers that Brian Carpenter features, this FYC writer was predisposed to think of writing as only academic writing, as her profile referenced only school-sponsored writing. Thus, for her, as well as for many other FY writers, it was difficult to see herself as a writer until opportunities were provided to perceive intersections among academic and everyday language literacy practices.

My FYC course challenges these dispositions. I provide an exemplar (a different way to think about academic writing, that it is not always explicitly thesis driven and that form should follow function), followed by reading models of academic writing that challenge the current ways of thinking about writing and then some discussion during which students are invited to articulate a new way to think about academic writing. I also circle back to the record of writing that students generated to remind them that not all writing that they do is academic— that they do a great deal of writing that is not school-sponsored, as a majority of students write only about themselves as academic writers in these profiles.

Writing About Rules

Subsequent to the record of writing and the writer's profile and after students have begun to consider themselves as writers in a different way than previously (I hope), students complete a journal entry in which they identify and discuss a writing "rule" that they were taught that didn't make sense to them. This idea comes from Elizabeth Wardle and Doug Downs' *Writing About Writing: A College Reader,* in which the authors share with students what they call "misconceptions" about writing and discuss "constructs" about writing (4, 5).

Not surprisingly, my FYC students have been taught many "rules" about writing that, while they gamely tried to follow, did not make much sense to them. Many of these "rules" relate to what they usually call the "five paragraph format." A student wrote, "It seems insane to . . . minimize someone's writing into just five paragraphs," while also sharing that while "it's a structure to help, I . . . disagree when . . . teachers force their students to use it." Another student also referred to five-paragraph essays while including related rules: "Three writing rules that I always felt have been absurd were the five paragraph format due to PSSAs [Pennsylvania System of School Assessment], five to eight sentences per paragraph and the no 'I' rule." This student enumerated reasons for finding these rules "absurd" and referenced Murray's "All Writing is Autobiography" when finding fault with the no "I" rule: "Donald M. Murray has made me realize that all writing we do has pieces of us in it. Therefore, why can't we use . . . 'I' in some cases?"

Interestingly, several students cited the "no 'I'" rule. "Never use 'I' in a piece of writing unless the writing is an autobiography," a student wrote, then went on to comment, "I never . . . understood the reason I shouldn't include my personal thoughts and stories into my work. . . . I feel as though all writings should include the writer's voice. . . ." Another writing "rule" that students found perplexing concerned what they deemed to be unreasonable restrictions on their writing in addition to the aforementioned "no 'I'" rule. For instance, students noted that sentences should not begin with the words "and" or "but," and it is not acceptable to repeat certain words, such as adjectives, within a piece of writing; also, contractions were never to be used. Unreasonable directives were shared as well, one of the most common being that all paragraphs must have five sentences.

Ashley's journal entry about writing rules was particularly interesting because it contradicted, at least to some degree, what she had written in her writer's profile. For example, she stated that the "rules and techniques of each [type of writing] seemed to serve a purpose" and that the rules "seemed comprehensive and easy to understand." However, she did refer to rules for "papers that required a bibliography," writing that "I struggled to cite sources correctly and had trouble compiling an organized list of author's [sic] works in the proper format." She also expressed confusion about comma splices, sharing that she would receive lower grades on papers because of this type of error. And she went on to write that "[t]o be honest, the whole concept [comma splices] still doesn't quite register with me and continues to confuse me." Her journal entry ends by stating that she does not believe that any of the "rules of writing" are "senseless or unnecessary because they are what the English language is made up of and they define literacy vs. illiteracy."

While I was somewhat surprised by Ashley's journal entry because of what she had written in her writer's profile, I believed that additional writing, discussions about writing, and reading mentor texts and research and scholarship about composition would provide opportunity for Ashley to continue to rethink and revise understandings about writing (and writing "rules") and to develop ways of thinking about writing that would be helpful to her development as a writer.

It occurred to me, too, as I had been getting to know her better, that Ashley was experiencing a kind of tension or conflict about the "rules." Even though she didn't enjoy being confined to writing five-paragraph essays in high school and actually hoped to learn to produce different kinds of writing, it was clear that she had followed the "rules" because she wanted to excel in school. In "My Literacy Ladder," she wrote:

> My lack of patience and . . . need to take everything and anything to the next level by my own means is what led me to become such a climber. I climbed trees . . . fences, rocks, and countertops. I found it necessary to climb the social ladder, my way

into a multitude of extracurricular activities and elite athletic
teams, and even academically to win [my parents'] attention.

Referring to her interest in reading and sharing a recognition of the power of
words, she wrote about literacy as a "necessary tool for survival" and attributed to
her competence as a reader "power and advantages over other students."

At the point, then, at which Ashley wrote this journal entry, while she was
beginning to rethink writing and was reading and producing writing that was not
formulaic, she nonetheless still perceived rules of writing in a strict sense. Even
after the semester ended, she shared that she believed that this assignment [writ-
ing about rules] was not as "helpful" as some of the others, in part, because "some
people still don't . . . know all of the proper rules of writing."

While these journal entries gave students a chance to vent about writing
"rules," the responses also indicated that many students possessed solid understandings of "good" writing despite the rules and teaching that they found incom-
prehensible. As noted earlier, one student referred to the importance of "voice" in
writing, and another wrote in reference to the "no 'I'" rule: "Facts only hit home
when we have [sic] personality to them. In my opinion, people are more likely to
believe you when there is feeling behind what you're saying." Finally, one student
shared this understanding of good writing: "My idea of good writing is expressing yourself in a way that the reader is into what your [sic] saying but at the same
time you still get your point across."

The knowledge that I gained about students' present ways of thinking about
writing through their discussion of writing rules informed lessons that focused
on the development of rhetorical knowledge and skills and writing dispositions.
For example, I wanted students to reconsider writing "rules" as "guidelines." To
achieve this objective, I taught a lesson on punctuation as a rhetorical tool that
began with a discussion of the difference between "rules" and "guidelines." We
then proceeded to talk about the reason for punctuation and examined some
excerpts from texts in which writers use punctuation in ways that are unconven-
tional or that deviate from rules. I also gave students a concise guideline for using
commas, semicolons, colons, and end marks, although I also reminded them that
in some cases it would be okay (or rhetorically effective) to ignore these guidelines. This lesson serves to help students develop rhetorical knowledge and skills
and encourages them to rethink writing "rules"—and fosters a new way to think
about writing, including "correct" writing.

Writing About Discourse Communities

Finally, my students write about a discourse community in which they participate. As with the journal entry about writing rules that cause confusion, this
assignment comes from *Writing About Writing: A College Reader*. After I introduce the concept of discourse community to my students, I ask them to create a

diagram that illustrates the discourse communities in which they participate and any connections that exist among them. (A helpful resource for introducing discourse community is "Does Coming to College Mean Becoming Someone New?" by Kevin Davis in *The Subject is Writing* 2nd edition, edited by Wendy Bishop.) I also share a diagram of the discourse communities in which I participate. Then students are asked to choose one discourse community and to write an essay in which they explain how the group qualifies as a discourse community. Because discourse communities include different ways of using oral and written language, this piece of writing helps students understand and think about writing from another angle—a social context—and thus they add to their previous learning about "academic writing," that what counts as acceptable academic writing is contingent on the discipline or field in which one is writing.

These assignments and the lessons that derive from them work to promote ways of thinking about writing that, as Bereiter maintains, may transfer to other contexts in which writing is used. Also, students are simultaneously acquiring rhetorical knowledge and skills through writing, reading, responding to peers' writing, and conferencing. While I am focusing on the development of dispositions, it is important to remember that dispositions, knowledge, and skills are closely related and that the "intelligence" about writing that students are developing is dispositional intelligence.

Now for some evidence that students acquired writing dispositions in my FYC course.

What Writing Dispositions Do Students Learn?

Having asked students at the end of the semester what they learned in ENGL 101, I can provide some evidence of their having learned dispositions about writing. Some responses to this question related to thinking about themselves as writers: "I can write a good piece," "I know I'm capable of good writing," and "Anyone can be a writer." I would argue that if students do, indeed, perceive themselves as writers, then this represents the acquisition of a key disposition—that we all can be writers, that the ability to write proficiently and effectively is not limited to only those who possess unusual skills and talents.

Acknowledging that they see themselves as writers, students often referred to learning about their own writing processes: "I know now that my writing will improve if I just let my thoughts flow on the first draft," "Writing, for me, is a process and not something than can be done in a short period of time," and "Writing takes time." Another student noted the idiosyncratic nature of writing processes: "I learned the way I write and my thought process can be different than other people's." Finally, responses reflected a disposition about writing that demonstrated an understanding of the many forms that writing can take and that there is no one right way to write: "Writing is a wide range of methods, not just the 5-paragraph format."

Ashley, with whom I remained in contact and who collaborated with me on a department colloquium session on FYC, shared her thoughts about what she learned in FYC in an email. With regard to the record of writing that she kept for a few days, she remarked that she had never realized how much writing she did until she kept track of it. Writing that she came to understand the importance of being able to write clearly on a day-to-day basis, she added, "Writing is power." She also referred to the discourse community assignment:

> I found myself thinking about the discourse communities dis-
> cussion/assignment . . . and how valuable it was for me . . . be-
> cause . . . as I've gone further into concentrating on Industrial
> Organization Psychology and have been getting into the groove
> of some of the business courses I'm enrolled in this semester,
> I've found that it's `. . . key to knowing the kinds of discourse
> . . . that is [sic] apart [sic] of that community. . . . I've realized
> that it's quite difficult to communicate with others who are
> well-seasoned in the area. Knowing the type of vocabulary for,
> say, my Business Technology Education course or my Econom-
> ics course, allows for an efficient and easy transfer of ideas and
> information.

Ashley also told me that writing about a discourse community in which she participated "changed my perspective on writing forever." She went on to say that our FYC course "helped me to see that there are so many different ways of writ-ing" and that it is "imperative that we first year writers heading into classes geared directly toward our . . . majors understand what type of writing is required in order to succeed . . . as members of our professional discourse communities."

Although I have evidence that my FY students did acquire productive writing dispositions, I am uncertain to what degree these dispositions transferred, if at all. However, Ashley's chapter in this collection will illustrate how dispositions about writing played out for her beyond our FYC course.

Conclusion

As stated earlier, the existence of FYC courses in our colleges and universities suggests a belief that what students learn in FYC will be useful to them when they write for other courses or for the workplace, yet research on transfer calls this "service" into question. I argue here, though, that attending to the development of writing dispositions in our FYC courses is a "service" that we can and should provide. As noted earlier, these dispositions, ways of thinking and propensities to act in certain ways, are more likely to transfer, rather than specific rhetorical skills. Ways of thinking about writing, however, combined with familiarity and mastery of rhetorical skills demanded by different writing contexts, will enable students to successfully write beyond FYC.

Works Cited

Bereiter, Carl. "A Dispositional View of Transfer." *Teaching for Transfer: Fostering Generalization in Learning*, edited by Anne McKeough et al., Lawrence Erlbaum Associates, Publishers, 1995, pp. 21–34.

Brent, Doug. "Crossing Boundaries: Co-Op Students Relearning to Write." *College Composition and Communication*, vol. 63, no. 4, 2012, pp. 558–92.

Davis, Kevin. "Does Coming to College Mean Becoming Someone New?" *The Subject is Writing*. 2nd ed., edited by Wendy Bishop, Heinemann, 1999, pp. 99–104.

Dean, Deborah. *Genre Theory: Teaching, Writing, and Being*. National Council of Teachers of English, 2008.

Gee, James Paul. *Social Linguistics and Literacy*. 4th ed., Routledge, 2012.

Murray, Donald M. "All Writing is Autobiography. *College Composition and Communication*, vol. 42, No. 1, 1991, pp. 66–74.

National Research Council. *How People Learn: Brain, Mind, Experience, and School*. National Academy Press, 2000.

Perez, Bertha, ed. *Sociocultural Contexts of Language and Literacy*. 2nd ed., Lawrence Erlbaum Associates, Publishers, 2004.

Perl, Sondra. "The Composing Processes of Unskilled College Writers." *Research in the Teaching of English*, vol. 13, No. 4, 1979, pp. 317–36.

Schussler, Deborah L. "Defining Dispositions: Wading Through Murky Waters." *The Teacher Educator*, vol. 41, No. 4, 2006, pp. 251–68.

Siegel, Harvey. "What (Good) are Thinking Dispositions?" *Educational Theory*, vol. 49, no. 2, 1999, pp. 207–21.

Sitler, Helen Collins Sitler. (this collection.) "Becoming a Person Who Writes."

Taczak, Kara, et al. (this collection). "A Framework for Transfer: Students' Development of a 'Theory of Writing.'"

Tishman, Shari. "Why Teach Habits of Mind?" *Discovering and Exploring Habits of Mind*, edited by Arthur L. Costa and Bena Kallick, Association for Supervision and Curriculum Development, 2000, pp. 41–52.

Tishman, Shari, et al. "Teaching Thinking Dispositions: From Transmission to Enculturation." *Theory into Practice*, vol. 32, 1993, pp. 147–53.

Walker, Alice. "Father." *Living by the Word*, Harcourt, Brace, Jovanovich, 1987, pp. 9–17.

Wardle, Elizabeth, and Doug Downs. *Writing About Writing: A College Reader*. 2nd ed., Bedford/St. Martin's, 2014.

Questions for Reflection and Discussion After Chapter 6

1. Chapter 6 emphasizes the value of getting to know our students and their current understandings of writing early in an FYC course. What writing or discussion activities do you currently employ to learn who students are as writers when they come into your course?
2. Jo-Anne mentions several texts that her FYC students read as models for their writing and as sources of knowledge for conversations about writ-

ing. What texts about writing have been most inspiring or instructional to your students in the past? What model texts beyond those she mentions might you have your students read as they prepare to write about their own writing beliefs or histories?

Writing Activity After Chapter 6

Make a list of all the writing "rules" you have learned, intuited, or adopted over the years for the writing you do. Consider rules for all types of writing, such as writing emails, memos, or social media posts in addition to any traditional academic writing you do. Which of these rules have you chosen to follow? Which have you broken, and with what results? How might sharing stories of your own rule-following or rule-breaking as a writer in the classroom benefit your students?

Further Reading

Dufour, Monique, and Jennifer Ahern-Dodson. "Good Writers Always Follow My Rules." *Bad Ideas About Writing*, edited by Cheryl E. Ball and Drew M. Loewe, West Virginia U, 2017, pp. 121–25. https://textbooks.lib.wvu.edu/badideas/bad ideasaboutwriting-book.pdf.

Parker, Kimberly N. "Response: Never Use 'I.'" Bad Ideas About Writing, edited by Cheryl E. Ball and Drew M. Loewe, West Virginia U, 2017, pp. 134–38. https://textbooks.lib.wvu.edu/badideas/badideasaboutwriting-book.pdf.

Rodríguez, Rodrigo Joseph. "Leave Yourself Out of Your Writing." Bad Ideas About Writing, edited by Cheryl E. Ball and Drew M. Loewe, West Virginia U, 2017, pp. 131–33. https://textbooks.lib.wvu.edu/badideas/badideasaboutwriting-book.pdf.

Chapter 7. Linguistic Socialization: More Than "regular talk," "paraphrase and stuff"

Brian D. Carpenter
INDIANA UNIVERSITY OF PENNSYLVANIA

Reflect Before Reading

Imagine you meet someone who has never set foot on a college campus, is years removed from their secondary education, and has never heard the term "academic writing." They ask, "What is academic writing?" How would you reply? How would you explain what readers of academic writing value?

~ ~ ~

"I feel like a research paper is more academic than the others because you have to paraphrase and stuff."

—*Marie*

"Do you remember like that first day when you had us write like the words we talk, because in my paper I said 'balling' when I talked about basketball, and I didn't know how to translate that to like regular talk like for playing basketball because it just sounds weird to me. . . . "

—*Charles*

Hopping into the way back machine, we set the dial to stop at 1978 and spy on my dining room table a little blue grammar book—my tenth grade grammar class book, which was a compendium of exceptions and rules. Maybe my attraction to working with novice writers stems from that little blue book. I let the book drive me to distraction, and angst. Now, as a professional, I hold the book tightly to remind me of how not to think about grammar and writing. Writing, particularly a basic writing course, needs to explicitly mark valued choices for particular contexts. Students need to manipulate and deconstruct the language and genres of collegiate writing in order to succeed. This manipulation and deconstruction are important for the success of all students, but particularly for multilingual students (see Achugar and Carpenter; Carpenter et al.; Gibbons; Schleppegrell).

DOI: https://doi.org/10.37514/PRA-B.2020.0308.2.07

This chapter, much like Ashley Ritter's chapter in this collection, hopes to shed light on what it means to be literate and to belong to a particular discourse community, in this case, a basic writing community. My little blue book would ruin this community, as the book demanded tests on rules, structures, and conventions. This community needs access and the tools to begin changing their life chances, not grades on comma usage.

The community in question here resided in a decrepit building and had as two of its members Charles and Marie. Both have Puerto Rican backgrounds to add to their United States urban experience. Marie is comfortable communicating in Spanish or English. Charles understands a lot of Spanish, but prefers to respond in English. Both would loathe the little blue book. In spring 2015, all three of us would be part of a community that tried to be explicit about valued choices in collegiate writing. All three of us would engage in reflection on this course. None of us, though, would pick up the little blue book during our journey.

For Charles and Marie, and two other students, Santiago and Janie, who we will meet shortly, one of their first dedicated attempts to enter the academic writing community in the university came in the spring of 2014 during my English 100 Basic Writing class. According to the course description in Indiana University of Pennsylvania's undergraduate catalog, in ENGL 100, "The student develops the basic English skills necessary for clear and effective communication" (*Undergraduate*). The syllabus of record for this course states that clear and effective communication is for both oral and written skills.

The syllabus states that Basic Writing is designed to "Develop coherence, unity, fluency, and stylistic control [of students'] written language—through shorter written assignments as well as by drafting, revising, and polishing several extended pieces of writing" as a way to develop "skills requisite for academic success." In other words, the class is designed to aid novices as they begin participating in the academic discourse community of the university. As Roz Ivanič notes, entry into this community, even for monolingual university students, can evoke feelings of strangeness.

This class and this group of students were charged with learning about academic discourse where the work "is not just a site of entry but a social, cognitive, and rhetorical process and an accomplishment, [but also], a form of enculturation, social practice, positioning, representation and stance-taking" (Duff 170). In short, my students were asked to adopt the practices and stance taking valued in academic writing, so they could assume the mantle of "college writer," or in other words, the identity of a writer in the university. Reflecting Ken Hyland's notion of identity, identity here is viewed as a social and collective enterprise created in and around interactions and text creation within the institutional practice of and performance in Basic Writing. As Len Unsworth points out, in addition to helping students develop as writers, an explicit connection to academic discourse allows students to expand on a linguistic repertoire valued in the academic discourse community.

Access to academic language and discourse and creation of this writerly identity are necessary for students if they want to participate in schooling and may even allow them to "challenge or support current institutions and social forms as they come to understand how language functions to establish and maintain social practices to articulate different ideological positions" (Schleppegrell 163). In other words, developing access to and revealing formations of academic discourse may not just allow students to succeed in schooling, but may also allow students a site of potential challenge and change to their very position within these worlds.

I begin this chapter by defining linguistic socialization and describing how my Basic Writing course serves as one entry point for the process of linguistic socialization. The chapter continues with an introduction to four focal students and includes excerpts of their writing work from the class, an explanation of class work, and finally data from interviews with these students as evidence for their processes of linguistic socialization. I show that a focus on schooling-valued language choices as a tool to develop academic literacy and as an explicit part of teaching and curriculum helps equip students, particularly multilinguals, with an expanded linguistic repertoire that is needed to succeed in schooling culture and in academic discourse communities.[1]

Linguistic Socialization

For the work I share in this chapter, I use Patricia Duff's definition of linguistic socialization that recognizes language and interactions around language as the central process through which socialization, or enculturation into the community of academic discourse, occurs. As M.A.K. Halliday notes, language is viewed as a social semiotic that allows one to view learning language, learning about language, and learning through language as a simultaneous endeavor. Thus, as both Basil Bernstein and Lev Vygotsky contend, at the center of linguistic socialization is work with language and its cultural practices focused on interactions with more proficient peers or authorities in creating culturally situated and valued oral or written text.

Frances Christie asserts that linguistic socialization puts language and interaction at the forefront of learning to override the assumptions that students enter university with the requisite skills necessary to succeed, while Caroline Coffin and Jim Donohue contend that simply teaching students about language is sufficient to engender success in higher education settings. Linguistic socialization, then, allows learning language, learning about language, and learning through language to situate appropriate language choices as inherent in revealing "worldviews, ideologies, values and identities of community members" (Duff 3).

---

1. For additional scholarship that suggests the importance of teaching valued language choices to promote the development of academic literacy, see Achugar and Carpenter; Carpenter et al.; Duff, Schleppegrell.

Briefly, my Basic Writing course, which was the site of the linguistic social-ization that I examine in this chapter, is based on the premise that expanding the linguistic repertoire of learners allows them to create academic texts and to make new meanings of and about their world, thus helping them develop novel ways of seeing, thinking, and enacting within the higher education community. Basic Writing is housed in the College of Humanities and Social Sciences and thus values academic texts, which are seen as being primarily about persuasion where writers "[make] choices to gain support, express collegiality and resolve difficul-ties in ways which fit the community's assumptions, methods, and knowledge" (Hyland 5). The course consistently orients learning to not only the immediate environment of Basic Writing but also to the wider community of the university, be it criminology or communication media (two popular majors for the students in the course), and to the other worlds of jobs and life. The course situates and gives prominent value to the creation of written texts, and thus students must en-act an identity as a college writer who can acquire "college success" as the course is designed to do. Not only are the students asked to enter into a contract to im-prove their college readiness, but they are also asked to develop an understanding of how college writers behave and what valued discourse choices college writers make when asked to produce written texts in the university.

Four Basic Writing Students

The four Basic Writing students whose processes of linguistic socialization I ex-amine in this chapter were first-year students in their second semester, 18 to 19 years old, and enrolled in an ENGL 100 course I led during spring 2014. Three of the students, Charles, Marie, and Santiago, identified with their Puerto Rican heritage, and two of these students, Marie and Santiago, considered themselves bilingual in Spanish and English. Charles noted that his mother was from Puerto Rico but that he only spoke household Spanish with his *abuela*. The fourth stu-dent, Janie, was a monolingual English speaker.

About My Course

The course assignments concerned readings and interactions with Winifred Gal-lagher's *The Power of Place*. This book is loosely about "the relationship between people and places" (7) and the power our place has on our physical, emotional, and psychological well-being. While not an academic textbook, it still relies heav-ily on the incorporation of other people's ideas and work to substantiate Galla-gher's claims about the power of place. It was an accessible reading about a topic my students could relate to, as they had all just relocated and changed places in physical, emotional, and psychological ways.

Linguistic socialization for students begins the moment they enter a class-room, but for us in English 100, the first explicit concept related to linguistic socialization we focused on in class was cohesion. The concept of cohesion I use in this chapter is rooted in Halliday's concept, which is concerned with the textual metafunction where "creating relevance to the context" is its main function (36). Cohesion, in short, allows the writer to construct discourse and make explicit the relationship across clauses independent of grammatical structure and is essential for successful academic writing. Stephen Witte and Lester Faigley find, for example, through an analysis of 90 first-year essays, that higher-rated essays are "more dense in cohesion than low-rated essays" (195). Carmel Cloran explains that cohesion is tied to thematic progression and uses František Daneš' "simple," "continuous," and "derived" patterns to show thematic progression (387). In short, simple cohesion is when the topic/comment or theme/rheme is built in. In this pattern, the rheme/comment becomes the theme/topic for the following sentence and builds meaning in a highly connected fashion. The "continuous" pattern is when theme/topic remains consistent but the rheme/comment is different and usually expanding or building meaning into the theme. "Derived" refers to the instance of picking up aspects of the theme, for example, a synonym or a date within a range, as a way of continuing to build cohesion.

As an English education professor and someone who works with pre-service and in-service English teachers, I find many English teachers use these ideas stated earlier, but wrap their meaning into the term "flow" as a way to describe cohesion. In fact, Martha Kolln explains, "the topic of cohesion is about the connection of sentences to one another, to the 'flow' of a text, to the ways in which a paragraph of separate sentences becomes a unified whole" (26).

Next, I highlight two students' work on cohesion, as cohesion, as a distinct and purposeful focus of the class, is a concept integral to students' linguistic socialization in the process of creating valued written texts for the university. Cohesion, as a valued concept in writing, becomes a material representation of the act of linguistic socialization. Socialization is not just an oral process but is demonstrated in texts and course materials that students generate for class.

This writing occurred prior to the fourth class meeting, where the previous three had been about syllabus introduction, university systems at their disposal (e.g., the writing center), and about two classes working on meaning from the introduction to Gallagher's book. The following two excerpts come from papers by Marie and Santiago,[2] the two self-identified bilingual students, and were written and posted in Desire2Learn (D2L), an online learning platform, prior to the fifth class meeting.

Figures 7.1 and 7.2 show the first two paragraphs from the students' writing and were selected to help show cohesiveness in writing. The analyses that follow focus on choices these students made to create cohesive links in service of creating coherent texts.

---

2. All names are pseudonyms.

```
1   In life most people have experienced a change that has impacted them
2   some sort of way. Some experiences can even turn out to be life-changing
3   experiences. I have experienced an environmental change that has made
4   be become the person I am today.
5               ... After living in Florida till the age of five, I moved to Puerto
6   Rico for 2 ½ years. These environmental changes did not create much of
7   an impact on me. I still lived across the beach and remained speaking
8   Spanish, my first language. The weather and culture was also no different
9   among each other and what I was already familiar with.
```

Figure 7.1. Excerpt from Marie's early-semester writing.

Marie's excerpt begins by using repetition as a cohesive device to talk about "change" and "experiences" (lines 1 & 2), which led to "an environmental change" (3). She then moves to writing about herself at the beginning of the second paragraph (5 & 6), and in the interest of space, I have included only the last sentence of this narration. The cohesiveness of her writing breaks down a bit as she moves from "I moved to Puerto Rico for 2 1/2 years" (5 & 6) to the referent "these environmental changes" (6). This breakdown, I believe, occurs because earlier we read a focus on duration and her age, as well as a change of location, and thus to label both of those factors "environmental changes" creates a repetition that is not wholly accurate. Her repetition of "environmental changes" in line 6 is expanded on in lines 7, 8, and 9. Marie's choices resemble the "continuous" or "block" type of cohesion attributed to Daneš earlier.

```
1   When I first got to Puerto Rico the air was fresh and I was still upset that I
2   had to leave my friends, so I wasn't really social at first. Seeing my family
3   provided me comfort and sleeping at night without hearing any kind of
4   disruptive noises from the outside helped me relax. Though the positive
5   change ends there. I started developing allergies, which was never an issue
6   for me. My mom, who is a nurse, told me that the reason being was
7   because of the climate change. Then at school my spanish wasn't so good
8   so the students mocked me and told me to stop speaking english because
9   this wasn't America
```

Figure 7.2. Excerpt from Santiago's early-semester writing.

Santiago heads the majority of his initial clauses with the theme "I" (1 & 2) and uses the rhemes to expand what he was thinking or doing. "Seeing my family" as the theme for his second sentence allows him to expand on why he was "still upset" (1). The familiar connection takes on the role of "positive change" (4 & 5) and gets expanded by the next sentence with the theme of "I" (5). However, a bit of a disruption with the choice of the theme "my mom" (6) breaks from "I" and thus makes this less cohesive than the previous examples. And, it struck me as more oral in its construction than written, as the references (i.e., from allergies to mom to nurse) seem to rely heavily on the reader/listener to make the connections ex post facto versus having the lexical and grammatical choices making clear the relations across the text.

Ruqaiya Hasan notes that working with students and reflecting on the valued idea of cohesion is part of the process of linguistic socialization (see "Ways," "What"). The examples in figures 7.1 and 7.2 help to demonstrate Marie's and Santiago's current understandings, or current developmental levels, of how to use cohesion and serve as evidence for their understanding of the concept of cohesion. For Vygotsky and others, it is at this level where teachers must begin the process of concept development. These examples from the students help us, students and teacher, to begin the process of developing a mutually shared understanding of the concept of cohesion and allow us to be explicit about the concept's place in our developing sense of valued academic terms. Without this initial instance and assessment, teachers can only focus on prescribed components of a curriculum, but for linguistic socialization to be successful, we must start with students' initial understanding of the concepts upon which we will focus.

In figures 7.1 and 7.2, the student voices heard in the excerpts from their writing lead us to the next section on class work and to the work done on cohesion. and choices writers can make to create more cohesive texts with the thought in mind and clearly marked in class that the more cohesive texts are the more likely they are to be coherent, as Witte and Faigley argue.

Additional Coursework

The work presented in the following examples is part of what was done with the whole class and recorded in notes after the class. This is by no means meant to represent the only work done on the concept of cohesion, but this was work presented to and worked on by the entire class during a class meeting. The first example came after the first essay had come in and occurred during the seventh class meeting. The following is an example I generated to exemplify one way writers can create cohesion in their texts:

> Directions: Here are two claims with examples. Underline the words that help connect the sentences. For example, in the sentences, I like pizza. It is good. I would underline "pizza" and "it" as they represent the connection across the two sentences.
>
> I like <u>pizza</u>. <u>It</u> is good.

The goal of this work was for the students to see that connecting sentences can be purposeful, and we used paragraphs A and B shown in Figure 7.3, which were student postings to a homework assignment in D2L, to expand the discussion of the ways writers can connect ideas across sentences.

During the discussion of the first paragraph, students brought up that "I" (1) connects the first and second sentence, but that the reference of "that deployment" (1) was hard to follow because the writer had not provided an earlier use or marking of "deployment." The class decided that the "it" (4) in the final sentence was from the phrase "from being in" (2) because "I" was implicit in who was "being in," and thus appropriate when used before "really opened my eyes" (3). Reference, then, is missing in one connection with "that deployment," yet somewhat appropriate for the final "it" reference. Further, the students noted the lexical repetition from the first to the second sentence with the choice of "I" as being a positive choice for this writer.

Example A
1   I gained a lot of good life experience. After that deployment I had a lot of
2   world cultures from being in so many different countries, from European to the
3   Middle Eastern countries. It really opened my eyes and I look at the world in a
4   better way with some of those countries knowing how good we have it here at
5   home in America.

Example B
1   There was a major change in diversity from my small town compared to the
2   large student population at SU. For example, in my small town the ratio is
3   close to 97% white 1% African American 1% Hispanic, and 1% Asian.
4   Throughout the week you would see someone of a different ethnicity than
5   yourself maybe once. At SU I have someone of a different gender sitting next
6   to me in every single class. Different ethnicities on each side nonetheless. The
7   ethnic backgrounds are on a much broader spectrum to that of my hometown.

Figure 7.3. Two example student paragraphs.

For paragraph B, the class came to the conclusion that the writer was trying to achieve cohesion by using expansion with "for example" (2) where the writer first introduces the "diversity" (1) of her high school, and then her current situation in her university setting, SU (2). There is also lexical repetition where "diversity" gets encoded as "different ethnicity" (4 & 6), "different gender" (5) and "ethnic backgrounds" (7) as the writer finishes this paragraph.

In all, these examples demonstrated the three areas we focused on in the class: reference, expansion/elaboration, and lexical repetition.

Learning through Language

These activities and classroom discourse highlight Halliday's idea about learning language, learning about language, and learning through language as a simultaneous endeavor. My students were discussing language choices and were negotiating meaning with not only peers but also with the teacher. This discourse allows the students to become socialized into not only the concept of cohesion but also to the very idea that discourse choices are, in fact, choices. Both Hasan and Duff point out that this engagement in productive talk about and with language valued in this discourse community is important for learners and classrooms in order to develop an expanded linguistic repertoire and thus participate in acts of linguistic socialization.

Similar discourse surrounding valued academic choices occurred when discussing the final essay for the course. These excerpts come from week 14 of the

15-week semester and are derived from an assignment that asked the students to summarize Gallagher's ideas from a chapter of their choosing. This assignment was designed to present the students with an opportunity to practice a valued concept in English, summary,[3] and to provide the students with a glimpse into the writing demands of the next course in the series, Composition I, ENGL 101.

By this moment in the semester, students had completed weekly writing in D2L, had completed two essays with rough draft and final draft components, and had done the two in-class activities focused explicitly on cohesion provided earlier. Classroom discourse and peer interactions had occurred on the concepts of summary and cohesion. This socialization into the valued choices involved in summary and the continuing talk about cohesion continued the students' work on and development of academic discourse. These examples are from a prompt designed to elicit summary, a type of academic writing that students would be expected to produce across the university curriculum.

Final Essay Examples

The excerpts in figures 7.4 and 7.5 are exactly as they were turned in by the students, as were the previous student writings. The cohesive devices deployed in these summaries resemble the types the students used in the early examples, though, I will argue, there are some differences in the choices they have made.

1 In chapter 3, North versus South, she elaborated how climate shapes our
2 behavior to a certain extent. At first a professor taught that people from
3 southern regional climates ("sun people") had a more of a communal and
4 collective culture. While on the other hand people from northern regional
5 climates ("icy people") originated a society of dominance, destruction and
6 death believing the difference in climate shaped them become that (52).
7 This controversy later goes on into how climate doesn't only influence
8 ones performance, but how your body responds to it. She informs no
9 matter where you are from you have the ability to adapt to a new
10 environment. For example, Eskimo, black or white, when in extreme cold
11 temperatures everyone is going to freeze equally. The Eskimo is just not
12 going to be affected much due to their few physiological adaptations to
13 the cold. The newcomer will only develop increased circulation after 6
14 weeks (55-56). This behavioral modification is triggered from settings in
15 which humans come into contact with.

Figure 7.4. Excerpt from Marie's final essay.[4]

To start, Marie uses her entire paragraph as an analysis or an expansion of her initial sentence to show how Gallagher "elaborated how climate shapes our behavior" (1 & 2). Marie does this by first using expansion as her first theme in

3. For more about summary as a valued concept in academic writing, see Brown, Campione, and Barclay; Brown, Campione, and Day; and Kintsch and van Dijk.
4. No changes have been made to grammar, punctuation, or content.

the second sentence by choosing "At first" (2) as another way to mark "for ex-ample." Marie continues to elaborate on this subject with "while" (4) and then encodes both of the ideas in sentences two and three in the reference and en-coding of the ideas as "this controversy" (7) to help her support her initial claim about "how climate shapes our behavior." The theme of the fifth sentence breaks the cohesiveness of this paragraph by using the pronoun "she" (8) as a reference to Gallagher, which is problematic, as between the initial Gallagher reference in sentence one we are presented with "professor," which could in fact be the "she" the writer is referencing. But this assumption is dispelled as we read forward to see how Marie continues elaborating on what the readers were inform[ed] (8) of with the "for example" (10) as the theme for the sentence following. This is fol-lowed by the theme of "Eskimo" (11) as a lexical repetition from the "for example" sentence. This repetition pattern is repeated, as "the newcomer" (13) theme is a repeated marking of "black or white" (10) as not native to Eskimo climes and thus are newcomers, who like "Eskimos" undergo "behavior modification" (14) which is the last repetitive cohesive moment, but one which I believe is a bit of a misreading from "physiological adaptations" (12). The type of expansion and elaboration (e.g., "at first" and "for example") and referencing with nominaliza-tions "controversy" (7) and "modifications" (14) Marie is demonstrating here are not as pronounced in her first writing sample.

```
1    Gallagher mentions a mother and infant emotional bond before
2    differentiation. She brings up several points that supports that emotion has
3    a structure on environment by talking about the mother/infant bond. She
4    talks about a biologist whom took infants with a naturally aggressive
5    strain in mice, and placed them with a foster mother that was easygoing,
6    which they grew up to be nice (119). This provides information on the
7    bond between infant and mother can structure the emotion of the infant.
8    The aggressive mice have the instinctual of being aggressive but were
9    raised to be nice habitually. She also uses another example of grandparent
10   monkeys being placed with younger male monkeys and the grandparents
11   started to put on weight, grow hair back and the male's sperm count went
12   up (119). This shows that grandparent monkeys had an instinctual
13   emotional reaction to the younger monkeys which caused the grandparents
14   to have a different emotional structure. However, Gallagher also talks not
15   just about structure but emotional addictions.
```

Figure 7.5. Excerpt from Janie's final essay.

Similarly, Janie uses reference as her main cohesive choice in her final writing. "Gallagher" (1) starts the paragraph and then is the theme for the majority of the remaining sentences (2, 4, and 9). Janie also uses themes of reference pronouns (e.g., "this provides" (6) and "this shows" (12)) as markers to coalesce the previ-ous information and then uses rhemes (e.g., "provides" (6) and "shows" (12)) to elaborate on Gallagher's ideas. The final "however" (14) theme is used as a way to connect the current paragraph with the preceding paragraph and expand on Gal-lagher's ideas. Janie's choices in this example are similar to her choices in the first example, in that she had control of cohesive choices throughout these examples and indeed throughout the semester.

Both examples show first-year composition students demonstrating changes in choices involving cohesion and also show production of the concept of summary discussed and framed in classroom discourse. The choices they made while creating these texts, and their texts as representative of their burgeoning academic voices, are linked to and demonstrate understanding of valued academic discourse. The options they exercised as writers indicate their growing linguistic repertoire, a repertoire that will provide them pathways to enter the university discourse community.

What Charles, Janie, Marie, and Santiago Had to Say

The following fall I spoke with Charles, Janie, Marie, and Santiago about their experiences in my Basic Writing class. Each interview lasted about 20 minutes and covered ground that ranged across the class, outside into the university, and into their personal lives. What I share in what follows are those parts of the interviews that touched on these students as writers and as writers and learners in my Basic Writing course. These data indicate these students' ideas about who they are as writers and how the experience we had in the spring might have affected them as writers in the university.

Marie shared she felt "scared" coming into the class and she "didn't feel like a good writer." But now when it comes to academic writing, she knows she has to "paraphrase and stuff . . . because I know I have to do it [and] we have to have facts to support our stuff and it's expected." For the Basic Writing course, she felt like we had "to do a persuasive paper, and things like that" and when asked how the genre of persuasive writing differs from other genres she stated, "like the structure and word choice" are different. And when asked about how cohesion works, she recalled it is "that flow thing and where you're not jumping around . . . that you write your stuff so it flows, like you don't want to write like an irrelevant sentence that's not going to make sense and stuff."

When Janie was asked about the class, she was positive and exclaimed, "I approach every class like I'm here to learn something and I'm going to learn something." When asked what she took away from the class, she mentioned how she is able to work on not repeating herself so much and that her vocabulary had improved to the point "like even my father has noticed how my language has changed and he makes fun of me." As for cohesion, she stated how prior to the class, she had been taught about it one way but now even at the writing center "when I am working with students, particularly 100 [level] students, I think about how they are connecting their sentences together" where they can "use similar words to connect sentences together . . . like they might have 'water' in one sentence and then 'H2O' in the next."

Similar to Janie's reference to her father, Charles mentioned how his understanding and use of language have changed. He referenced the first time we spoke in class about "talk language" and how this type of language is different from written language:

> Do you remember like that first day when you had us write like the words we talk, because in my paper I said "ballin'" when I talked about basketball, and I didn't know how to translate that to like regular talk like for playing basketball because it just sounds weird to me, so that kinda helped out too . . . and I can't remember what it's called the concepts of it (R—one of the things I talked about was the difference between everyday—) [Charles] yeah, that's it, I just kept saying regular talk but yeah everyday language but I knew it was something like that.

When asked about what he took away from the Basic Writing course, he recalled how the class talked about "academic language like when we talked about saying like 'talk' but instead like use 'states' and stuff like that . . . oh yeah and like cohesion with like the sentence structure and where it's like no run on sentences." Asked to follow up on cohesion, Charles said the following:

> It's like you start with a topic and you stay on topic like for example, "I went to the funeral" and you can't just jump and then say like "I went to the funeral—period" and then like "we got something to eat." Like you just can't say that and then say, "the funeral was sad" like you just can't jump like that you got to like stay on topic instead saying that "I went to the funeral. It was sad and I felt terrible" or something like that you have to stay on topic.

Here, Charles references the idea of cohesion where themes can be linked across sentences or where cohesion allows the writer a chance to begin expanding a topic as in his example of how he felt at the funeral.

Santiago's view of his coursework mirrors Janie's, and when asked what it meant to be in Basic Writing, he was pragmatic and said:

> I mean I look at college and I'm paying tuition so I want to take advantage of every opportunity so I was like "okay, let's see what this class has to offer" [and] this is how I deal with every class. Like I want to publish some books, so I was like "alright let's do this" . . . either way I like to see what new ideas it could bring and it had like new ideas for me to think about, it gave me some new ideas, and like was like you gave us this research part and I was like okay, like I knew I wasn't good at this part but I was like "okay let's do it" and then our first peer review came in and I was like "well, at least these people are honest" which I love, then you responded, and at the end of the day I was like "okay, I can see where I can improve and get better."

Santiago's recollection here shows a student with a positive attitude toward writing, as he wants to publish in the future. He also demonstrates how integral community was to his development during the class, suggesting the role the class community takes in the linguistic socialization that occurs during these writing classes.

He also commented about how the course makes connections across the curriculum. When asked to remember a concept, which came out of our summary work from the class, he said, "The big thing was the paraphrasing, that is a big thing, like I use that in my psych class . . . like we have to use paraphrasing and quoting." Santiago referenced aspects of the Basic Writing course that he now finds useful for other aspects of his university experience. In short, he is mapping one set of ideas and concepts, paraphrasing and quoting, and demonstrating how this knowledge is useful for a novel context in the university. As Coffin and Donohue point out, this type of knowledge building is important for students' success at the tertiary level.

During their interviews, students used terms such as "paraphrase," "topic," "everyday language," and "cohesion" to articulate their understanding of the course. These word choices resulted from interactions with the concepts and in their production in writing. Their use of these words also indicates that they connect discourse choices to the course and that they see the value of some of these concepts beyond Basic Writing as they meet other writing demands within the university.

Some Final Thoughts

These three areas of focus share student voices in text and oral interviews to demonstrate how these students changed their writing choices across time, and how, upon reflection, they recalled experiences in a writing course. Discourse, both written and spoken, gives us a picture of how the process of linguistic socialization affects students across time. Coffin and Donohue are clear in saying "[t]eaching and learning . . . hinge on developing the capacity of students and teachers to harness the meaning-making resources of language efficiently and effectively in relation to purpose and context and to expand their language and meaning-making repertoires as necessary" (2). This learning and expansion of meaning-making repertoires are in line with the university's goal that students develop skills that will ensure academic success. Furthermore, the development of these skills allows students to assume what James Paul Gee calls "the mantle" of basic writer, and by doing so, they will have what Duff refers to as the space and time to become enculturated into the community of academic discourse. This enculturation, or socialization, is evident as students begin to map concepts like cohesion, paraphrasing, or quoting from their Basic Writing course on to novel contexts, such as the writing center or a psychology class. Research (Achugar and Carpenter; Schleppegrell) asserts that, for multilingual students, this explicit focus on meaning-making resources such as those mentioned earlier is critical to their success.

One aspect of my students' linguistic socialization was the concept of cohesion, and for Janie and Santiago's writing, a focus on expansion, a component of cohesion, was a focal point. Marie and Charles similarly tried on how to elaborate and expand on an author's point of view. Not all incidents of meaning-making were clear, as we see in the tries at the pronoun repetition of "this," where a process or idea had not been clearly marked and thus was not able to be represented by the "this" pronoun. But changes in cohesive choices occurred in these students' writing. They moved from a series of personal descriptions, where breakdowns in cohesion occur more frequently, to a more academically valued writing, where interruptions occur in the service of expansion or reference, but largely hold up in the face of focusing on an author's ideas and clearly trying to persuade the reader of the writer's focus, a feature of successful academic writing as identified by Hyland.

The syllabus of record for English 100 notes that "drafting, revising, and polishing" writing are important to the students' development as writers. This directive could be amended to acknowledge the important role classroom discourse plays when working on the development of concepts needed to "develop coherence, unity, [and] fluency." Hasan states that the process of linguistic socialization during which talk and production are tied together allows the learner to not only orally negotiate meaning about the concepts of valued writing like cohesion, but also practice the concept and ultimately reflect on the concept, as students participate in the entire process of learning to create valued academic texts (see "Ways," "What"). As stated earlier, according to Schleppegrell; Achugar and Carpenter; and Christie, this explicit focus on language and choices is empowering to all students, but particularly multilingual students and basic writers as they engage in meaning-making in schooling.

My students were assigned the label of "basic writer" by the institution, but within what Gee calls an institutional identity and a discourse identity are individual traits recognized in their talk about how they view themselves. Janie was there "to learn something," and "work with students." And Santiago wants to "publish books" and Charles and Marie displayed talk about differences in "talk language" and written language. These identities, as Gee notes, "interrelate in complex and important ways" (101). For these students, this interrelation occurred under the guise of "basic writers," and we can see them developing along the continuum of academic writing. Their capacity to speak about differences in "talk language" and verb choice (e.g., "talks" and "states"), and their connections to new subjects (e.g., psych) and new environs (e.g., the writing center) mark aspects of the linguistic socialization process. My students took up concepts and terms and began orienting them outward and towards their continuing journey in the university.

Works Cited

Achugar, Mariana, and Brian D. Carpenter. "Tracking Movement Toward Academic Language in Multilingual Classrooms." *Journal of English for Academic Purposes*, vol. 14, 2014, pp. 60–71.
Bernstein, Basil. *Pedagogy, Symbolic Control and Identity: Theory, Research, Critique.* Taylor and Francis, 1996.

Brown, Ann L., Joseph C. Campione, and Craig R. Barclay. "Training Self-Checking Routines for Estimating Test Readiness." *Child Development*, vol. 50, 1979, pp. 501–12.

Brown, Ann L., Joseph C. Campione, and Jeanne C. Day. "Learning to Learn: On Training Students to Learn from Texts." *Educational Researcher*, vol. 10, 1981, pp. 14–24.

Carpenter, Brian, et al. "Working with Documents to Develop Disciplinary Literacy in the Multilingual Classroom." *The History Teacher*, vol. 48, no. 1, 2014, pp. 1–12.

Charles. Interview. Conducted by Brian Carpenter, 12 Nov. 2014.

Christie, Frances. *Language Education Throughout the School Years: A Functional Perspective.* Wiley-Blackwell, 2012.

Cloran, Carmel. "Defining and Relating Text Segments: Subject and Theme in Discourse." *On Subject and Theme: A Discourse Functional Perspective,* edited by Ruqaiya Hasan and Peter H. Fries, John Benjamins, 1995, pp. 361–403.

Coffin, Caroline, and Jim Donohue. "Language, Teaching, and Learning: General Orientations." *Language Learning*, vol. 64, supp. 1, 2014, pp. 1–10.

Duff, Patricia A. "Language Socialization into Academic Discourses." *Annual Review of Applied Lingusitics*, vol. 30, 2010, pp. 169–83.

Gallagher, Winifred. *The Power of Place: How Our Surroundings Shape Our Thoughts, Emotions, and Actions.* Harper Perennial, 2007.

Gee, James Paul. "Identity as an Analytic Lens for Research." *Review of Research in Education*, vol. 25, 2000–2001, pp. 99–125.

Gibbons, Pauline. *English Learners, Academic Literacy, and Thinking: Learning in the Challenge Zone.* Heinemann, 2009.

Halliday, M. A. K. *An Introduction to Functional Grammar.* Edward Arnold, 1994.

Hasan, Ruqaiya. "Ways of Saying: Ways of Meaning." *Ways of Saying: Ways of Meaning. Selected Papers of Ruqaiya Hasan,* edited by Carmel Cloran, David Butt, and Geoffrey Williams, Cassell, 2015, pp. 191–242.

Hasan, Ruqaiya. "What Kind of Resource is Language?" *Ways of Saying: Ways of Meaning. Selected Papers of Ruqaiya Hasan,* edited by Carmel Cloran, David Butt, and Geoffrey Williams, Cassell, 2015, pp. 13–36.

Hyland, Ken. "Genre, Discipline and Identity." *Journal of English for Academic Purposes*, vol. 20, 2015, pp. 1–12.

Ivanič, Roz. *Writing and Identity: The Discursal Construction of Identity in Academic Writing.* John Benjamins Publishing Company, 1998.

Janie. Interview. Conducted by Brian Carpenter, 12 Nov. 2014.

Kintsch, Walter, and Teun A. van Dijk. "Toward a Model of Text Comprehension and Production." *Psychological Review*, vol. 85, no. 5, 1978, pp. 363–94.

Kolln, Martha J. *Rhetorical Grammar: Grammatical Choices, Rhetorical Effects.* 4th ed., Longman, 2002.

Marie. Interview. Conducted by Brian Carpenter, 19 Nov. 2014.

Reder, Steve, and Erica Davila. "Context and Literacy Practices." *Annual Review of Applied Linguistics*, vol. 25, 2005, pp. 170–87.

Ritter, Ashley. (this collection). "A Transition."

Santiago. Interview. Conducted by Brian Carpenter, 12 Nov. 2014.

Schleppegrell, Mary. *The Language of Schooling: A Functional Linguistic Perspective.* Erlbaum, 2004.

Undergraduate Catalog 2018–19. Indiana University of Pennsylvania, www.iup.edu/registrar/catalog.

Unsworth, Len. "Developing Critical Understanding of the Specialised Language of School Science and History Texts: A Functional Grammatical Perspective." *Journal of Adolescent and Adult Literacy*, vol. 42, no. 7, 1999, pp. 508–21.

Vygotsky, Lev. *Thought and Language*. MIT, 1986.

Witte, Stephen, and Lester Faigley. "Coherence, Cohesion, and Writing Quality." *College Composition and Communication*, vol. 32, no. 2, 1981, pp. 189–204.

Questions for Discussion and Reflection After Chapter 7

1. Brian's chapter begins with an anecdote of a "little blue book" about grammar, and he describes his pedagogy as actively resisting the type of learning contained in that book. If you had to choose an artifact that, in metaphorical terms, your pedagogy either actively embraces or actively resists, what would that artifact be? Again in metaphorical terms, how is community in your FYC courses built in response to or in resistance of that artifact?

2. Chapter 7 introduces us to multilingual students, two of whom identify as bilingual. In what ways are students' multilingual abilities recognized in your FYC course? What opportunities might you create for students to draw on these abilities in their speaking and writing?

Writing Activity After Chapter 7

Choose a writing concept valued within academic discourse and design an activity that leads students to "zoom in" on their use of this concept in their own writing. What model or mentor texts would students read to see the concept in action? What texts of their own from FYC would they "zoom in" on to find evidence of or the need for revision in the area of the concept? What tips would you give students for employing this concept in their writing?

Further Reading

Bird, Barbara. "A Basic Writing Course Design to Promote Writer Identity: Three Analyses of Student Papers." *Journal of Basic Writing*, vol. 32, no. 1, 2013, pp. 62–95.

Duff, Patricia A. "Language Socialization into Academic Discourses." *Annual Review of Applied Lingusitics*, vol. 30, 2010, pp. 169–83.

Fernsten, Linda A., and Mary Reda. "Helping Students Meet the Challenges of Academic Writing." *Teaching in Higher Education*, vol. 16, no. 2, 2011, pp. 171–82.

Part 3. Promoting Student Agency in FYC

In Part 3, authors describe the potential we have in FYC to give students agency over their own writing education. Angela Clark-Oates, Michelle Stuckey, Melissa Williamson, and Duane Roen discuss how practicing metacognition allows students in an online FYC course to engage effectively in writing for academic and professional purposes.

Kara Taczak, Liane Robertson, and Kathleen Blake Yancey explore how students completing a theory of writing assignment within FYC courses using the Teaching for Transfer curriculum gain the language and confidence to describe their own writing abilities.

Finally, Ashley Ritter writes about her own FYC experiences and describes how she has carried the writerly agency she gained in FYC through a bachelor's degree and into graduate school and her career.

Extras

- Listen to a podcast conversation among authors Kara Taczak and Kathleen Blake Yancey and editors Jo-Anne Kerr and Ann Amicucci for ideas on how to implement a Teaching for Transfer curriculum in FYC: ⌾ Listen to the Podcast[1]

---

1. The videos and podcasts referred to on this page are available on the WAC Clearinghouse at https://wac.colostate.edu/books/practice/stories/.

Chapter 8. Design Into: Reflection as a Tool for Growth

Angela Clark-Oates
CALIFORNIA STATE UNIVERSITY, SACRAMENTO

Michelle Stuckey
ARIZONA STATE UNIVERSITY

Melissa Williamson
GREAT BAY COMMUNITY COLLEGE

Duane Roen
ARIZONA STATE UNIVERSITY

Reflect Before Reading

Think about students you have had in the past who are non-traditionally aged, who work in contexts off campus, or both. In what ways does your FYC course prompt students to think about the writing they have done in their lives or the writing they do on the job? In what ways does your course ask students to make connections between the classroom and their non-academic writing lives?

~ ~ ~

In *The Things They Carried*, Tim O'Brien ruminates on the difference between story-truth and happening-truth, writing, "What stories can do, I guess, is make things present" (180). In his words, storymaking is a form. In our words, it's a method for inventing oneself. It's an intentional practice that allows the story-maker to transfer events from the past to the present to construct knowledge and understanding. Similarly, Maxine Greene in *Releasing the Imagination* writes about the impact of recalling, reflecting, and becoming present to our past experiences: "I find the very effort to shape the materials of lived experience into narrative to be a source of meaning making" (75). In both these texts, the authors are examining the inextricable link between the practice of reflection and imagination. Greene writes, "Meanings derived from previous experiences often find their way through the gateway of imagination (as Dewey saw it) to interact with present-day experience. When aspects of the present are infused by materials originating in the past, there is always a re-viewing of the past, even as the new experience (enriched now) comes to consciousness" (76). In the writing classroom, then, tethering the practice of reflection to imagination has the potential

DOI: https://doi.org/10.37514/PRA-B.2020.0308.2.08

to encourage us, as faculty and administrators, to recall, rethink, and reimagine how and why the practice of reflection is the linchpin for assessment models.[1]

In *Principles for the Postsecondary Teaching of Writing*, first drafted in 1989 and most recently revised and approved in March 2015, the leading professional organizations in writing studies assert that sound writing instruction includes "opportunities for reflection and fostering the development of metacognitive abilities that are critical for writing development. It also includes explicit attention to interactions between metacognitive awareness and writing activity" (Conference). Bolstered by the field's research and scholarship on metacognition and student reflection in the writing classroom since at least the early 1990s, like many other writing programs, we, as administrators in the Writers' Studio, a fully online first-year composition program in the College of Integrative Arts and Sciences at Arizona State University (ASU), design curriculum to engage students in constructing multimodal texts, using a portfolio model of assessment that privileges the students' practices of reflection. Equally influential in our assessment model and our development of methods for scaffolding the development of students' reflective practices is the *Framework for Success in Postsecondary Writing*. When the National Council of Teachers of English (NCTE), the National Writing Project (NWP), and the Council of Writing Program Administrators (CWPA) collaboratively crafted the *Framework for Success in Postsecondary Writing*, the task force focused on eight habits of mind: curiosity, openness, engagement, creativity, persistence, responsibility, flexibility, and metacognition (Council, *Framework* 1). In the Writers' Studio, we introduce these habits of mind to the students early in the semester because we believe it helps shape how they articulate *what* they imagine their writing knowledge to be, providing more in-depth and insightful moments in their reflections because these habits of mind become a sort of prism for re-seeing and understanding their writing knowledge in the present. Moreover, this reflection is then crafted in a language that is not solely written in English-ese but in a language that is transferrable to what Duane Roen et al. call the four arenas of life—the academic, professional, civic, and personal; but as Kathleen Blake Yancey notes, Moreover, this reflection is then crafted in a language that is not solely written in English-ese but in a language that is transferable to what Duane Roen et al. call the four arenas of life—the academic, professional, civic, and personal. Although we introduce all eight habits to our students and discuss their importance, Kathleen Blake Yancey notes that metacognition—"the ability to reflect on one's own thinking as well as on the individual and cultural processes used to structure knowledge"—may be the most universally useful tool for students, particularly when developing a practice of reflection tied to outcomes-based self-assessment, knowledge making that they can "carry into life outside of and beyond educa-

---

1. The title of this chapter reflects Kathleen Blake Yancey's differentiation between reflection that is "expected from the student instead of designed into the curriculum" ("The Social" 189).

tional settings" ("Reflection and Electronic" 1). Hence, when students are given opportunities to flex and grow their metacognitive practices with a method for re-imagining the past in the present, they are more likely to transfer their learning in first-year composition to other courses and other arenas of their life, making critical and informed decisions about what they communicate, how they communicate, and to whom they communicate based on an intentional analysis of the rhetorical situation. In this way, they also have more opportunities to develop and articulate a rhetorical stance through the practice of reflection.

Working from this premise, in this chapter, we demonstrate the importance of designing curriculum that allows students to develop and grow their metacognitive practices through intentional and systematic reflection. This kind of reflection, we assert, allows students to more fully understand the rhetorical stances that they take in the course and to consider ways to imagine those stances differently in other academic, personal, professional, and civic contexts. As we hinted in the chapter opening, we situate our discussion of this practice of reflection in the Writers' Studio, illustrating how to develop curriculum that will scaffold student learning toward meaningful reflective practice. We draw on the reflective writing of eight students across ENG 101 (the first composition course in our required two course, two-semester sequence) and ENG 105 (the advanced one semester, first-year composition course): Karen, Sarah, Gina, Jennifer, Cathy, Ryan, Mandy, and Susan, all of whom are non-traditional students returning to college after a significant break. Finally, we advocate for constructing a learning space that engages students in the processes of reflective practice, values the habit of metacognition, and promotes the development of this habit over time within authentic rhetorical contexts, all of which echo Yancey's notion of "design in" ("The Social" 189). In what follows, we begin by looking at some theoretical considerations of reflection before demonstrating how we have designed curriculum to support students as they develop a practice of reflection in some of our online courses.

Conceptualizing a Practice of Reflection

Throughout his career, John Dewey did much to promote the importance of reflection, defining reflective thinking as "[a]ctive, persistent, and careful consideration of any belief or supposed form of knowledge in light of the grounds that support it and the further conclusions to which it tends" (9). Further, Dewey notes that reflection "impels" inquiry (7), which, in turn, enhances learning. Dewey also notes that reflecting on past activities leads to a "look into the future, a forecast, an anticipation, or a prediction" (117). That is, making predictions about the future based on past experiences helps prepare learners for the future. Dewey provides several examples of this, including the physician who makes a diagnosis and then uses past experience to make "a prognosis, a forecast, or the probable future course of the disease" (117). In the research that we discuss here, we see echoes of Dewey's foundational concepts. Therefore, when writing teachers encourage students to compare their learning to the learning outcomes of the course, teachers emphasize the importance of metacognition. Emphasizing reflection in this way encourages students to be more deliberate, thoughtful, and effective communicators.

In this way, reflection in the writing classroom also has the potential to foster the transfer of knowledge and practices from one context to another, "generalizability," as Yancey, Liane Robertson, and Kara Taczak prefer to put it in *Writing Across Contexts: Transfer, Composition, and Sites of Writing* (6). These scholars point to their experiences with asking "students to tell us in their own words what they have learned about writing, how they understand writing, and how they write now" (3). Further, Yancey et al. ask students to articulate how they are able to "recontexualize [writing] for new situations" (3). These questions are integral to the practice of reflection in the writing classroom. Without the ability to imagine how the students might apply their writing knowledge and practices in contexts outside the writing classroom, the value of writing instruction and writing knowledge diminishes. As Yancey et al. find in their extensive research, successful students "tend to theorize in ways that not only show us connections across writing sites, but also how the process functions for them" (135–36). With that finding in mind, they recommend that teachers can teach for transfer more effectively if they design courses that, among other things, "build in metacognition" (139). Similarly, Elizabeth Wardle uses the apt term "repurposing" to describe students' abilities to apply writing knowledge and practices across a range of contexts. In courses that focus on honing and developing students' use of rhetorical knowledge while also providing meaningful opportunities for application, students become more proficient at using writing to act as agents in the world.

In an effort to promote reflection, Patrick Sullivan, in *A New Writing Classroom: Listening, Motivation, and Habits of Mind*, asks secondary and postsecondary writing teachers to reconsider how their writing curricula and pedagogy can focus more on reflective writing and emphasize the value of listening to peers' perspectives to allow for an opportunity for the writer to see their text through a lens informed by different sociocultural experiences. This would encourage students to participate in "an active, generative, constructive process that positions readers, writers, and thinkers in an open, collaborative, and dialogical orientation toward the world and others" (3). Sullivan's assertion, which explicitly connects listening and reflective practice, echoes a sociocultural theory of learning, a theory that defines learning as a process mediated by tools and experienced with others. As Lev Vygotksy notes, learning happens in a "zone of proximal development" constructed with and by more capable peers. These peers can aid in learning because they help to form a "distance between the actual developmental level as determined by independent problem solving and the level of potential development as determined through problem solving under adult guidance or in collaboration with more capable peers" (86). In this case, the concept of "more capable peers" is not necessarily constant. Hanna, for example, may be a more capable peer at one moment in a discussion, and her classmate Ryan could be a more capable peer when the discussion turns a few minutes later. Among other things, peers can encourage greater reflection because they offer perspectives that may exist outside the experience of a student. Sullivan also asserts that, in addition to fostering dialogic interactions to promote reflection, such courses should place reflective writing assignments at the center of the curriculum (181) to encourage "an openness to others and to new ideas and a willingness to acknowledge complexity and uncertainty" (3). Further, teachers need to "make listening, empathy, and reflection the primary skills we value in our classrooms" (181). Being open to others' perspectives is a useful habit of mind in writing courses and in life more generally.

Despite foundational research in the field of rhetoric and composition and the field of education that demonstrates how integral a reflective practice is to student learning, many writing teachers experience uncertainty when attempting to design a curriculum focused on developing a reflective practice with students. To address this uncertainty, many writing programs and writing teachers use the *WPA Outcomes Statement for First-Year Composition* (3.0) as foundational to a curricular design that supports students as they construct a reflective practice. With the *WPA Outcomes Statement*, in particular, learning consists of four areas: (1) rhetorical knowledge, (2) critical thinking, reading, and composing, (3) processes, and (4) knowledge of conventions (Council, *WPA*). By providing students with a language for discussing their learning in relation to these four areas, teachers encourage students to think forward to future writing tasks.

Once students have a language for discussing their learning, they must be given a variety of opportunities to do so. Yancey offers an extensive analysis of reflection in *Reflection in the Writing Classroom*. Building on Donald Schön's concept of "reflection-on-action" in *Educating the Reflective Practitioner: Toward a New Design for Teaching and Learning in the Professions* (passim), Yancey focuses on three kinds of reflection: reflection-in-action, constructive reflection, and reflection-in-presentation. Reflection-in-action is "the process of reviewing and projecting and revising, which takes place within the composing event." Constructive reflection is "the process of developing a cumulative multi-selved, multi-voiced identity, which takes place between and among composing events." Reflection-in-presentation is "the process of articulating the relationships between and among the multiple variables of writing and the writer in a specific context for a specific audience" (*Reflection* 200). This range of reflective practices can enrich students' experiences in writing courses, allow for knowledge transfer across contexts, and support the potential to develop (intentionally) a rhetorical stance in civic, personal, and professional spaces.

Designing a Practice of Reflection

To enrich students' experiences in our courses, the faculty in the Writers' Studio have designed a curriculum to foster the practice of reflection we discuss in the previous section. Like other FYC programs at ASU, the Writers' Studio offers students the option of completing their FYC requirement either through a two-course, two-semester sequence or through an advanced, one-semester course. Students have the option of 7.5-week or 15-week iterations of the courses. In these courses, students are required to complete two projects consisting of essay, multimodal, and reflection components, with the reflection component consisting of consistent engagement with the WPA outcomes and the *Framework for Success* habits of mind in conjunction with the completion of various assignments.

The Writers' Studio's curriculum design promotes an active, learner-centered approach to teaching and learning writing, where faculty support students to develop and articulate a rhetorical stance in their writing through rigorous and recursive participation in the process of writing. Reflection is a core component of the course, and we emphasize the centrality of metacognitive practices from the beginning in a number of ways. For example, in English 101, the first course in our two-course sequence, the first written assignment is essentially a metacognitive activity that encourages students to reflect on their knowledge and experiences with writing in academic as well as personal and professional contexts. After reading Chapter 1, "Writing Goals and Objectives for College and for Life," of their textbook, *The McGraw-Hill Guide: Writing for College, Writing for Life* (Roen et al.), the students consider their past experience with writing in relation to the WPA outcomes previously discussed. They then compose a discussion board post in which they share with their classmates, instructors, and writing fellows (advanced undergraduate and graduate students who respond to students' drafts) their perceived strengths and weaknesses, using the language of the *WPA Outcomes Statement*. In the following example, Gina, a Starbucks employee who has returned to school after many years, clearly discusses how "dissecting," or reflecting, on her past writing through the lens of the WPA outcomes has helped her understand how she is already engaging in the rhetorical strategies we emphasize in Writers' Studio and how she can strengthen her writing practices:

> I have discovered a writing strength that I have is Rhetorical Knowledge, as most of my writing mainly consists of work emails. When sending my emails I have to consider my audience, I have to make sure I am getting my message across to my reader in a way that makes sense, without creating anger or frustrations. I have to be mindful of my email tone and verbiage to make sure I do not cause ill feelings. I also create many different types of documents for work, mostly visual tools for my team so they are aware of up-to-date information.
>
> After reviewing the WPA Outcome Statement for this class, I feel I have a long way to go in order to be a well-rounded writer. My first goal for this class would be to focus on developing my writing process. I feel this is a crucial part as to what holds me back from creating the documents I envision in my head. My second

goal, since I have not been in an English class for a very long time, I am VERY rusty in my knowledge of conventions. I know it's like riding a bike so I am confident as the weeks progress this will no longer be one of my goals. I would like to also develop my skills using critical thinking, reading, and composing.

This passage also illustrates the value of giving students a language in which to talk about their writing, a language that we argue is transferable to other contexts, while also bringing them into the larger conversation around what it means to cultivate writing practices. Beginning our courses by giving students opportunities to reflect on past experiences, current practices, and goals for future development, we attempt to foreground for students the value of metacognition and prepare them for the course-long engagement with reflection on their own composing in the context of the course learning outcomes.

In English 102, the second course in our two-course sequence, and English 105, the advanced one-semester FYC course, the instructors ask students to watch a video of students, staff, and faculty discussing rhetoric and then define rhetoric and explain how rhetoric influences participation in their daily lives. Much like the opening reflective assignment in English 101, this assignment allows students to draw on their prior knowledge to orient themselves to the learning outcomes by building from what they already know and how they already communicate differently depending on the context, the audience, and the purpose. In asking students to recall and reflect on their prior knowledge about writing and rhetoric, we are showing them that when encountering new learning in any context, they should begin with identifying what they already know about the topic, idea, or concept. Then, we ask them to evaluate these experiences against the course content and through writing and revising in the present. As a result, students are more likely to re-see these prior learning memories and construct new knowledge, such that they begin to theorize their own knowledge, imagining new possibilities for their writing practice. Once the students can reflect on their own practice, they have the language for constructing a theory of writing from their experiences inside and outside the classroom. After participating in this activity, Sarah, a registered nurse who had recently moved to Phoenix to pursue a Bachelor of Science in nursing at ASU, writes in our spring 2015 ENG 105 course,

> Before this video, I did not really understand the word rhetoric in a literary sense. I now realize that I use a rhetoric approach almost every day as a registered nurse. All too often, RN's [sic] are responsible for communicating and sometimes persuading patients to complete tasks or follow physicians [sic] orders they might not agree with initially. For example: administering medications like insulin in a timely manner, performing physical therapy exercises to strengthen their joints, and schedule yearly physical examinations to preventively screen for diseases and disorders.

In this example, Sarah connects her new conceptual understanding of rhetoric to her practice as a nurse and, in doing so, constructs a theory of writing: rhetorical knowledge is used in everyday practice. Therefore, in both the ENG 101 assignment that asks students to assess their strengths and weaknesses and the ENG 105 assignment that asks students to articulate prior knowledge of key terms, instructors pair students' writing processes with their metacognitive practices to, as Yancey et al. describe, "aid in the understanding of writing as theory and practice" and use "reflection as a tool for learning, thinking, and writing in the course and beyond" (57). Drawing further on Yancey's "The Social Life of Reflection: Notes Toward an ePortfolio-Based Model of Reflection," we have structured our course in such a way that reflection is "designed into" the class rather than "expected from" students. For example, students reflect on their composing as they engage in it. Further, the course portfolio assignment provides a semester-long opportunity for students to hone their reflective practices.

Reflection is cultivated from the beginning of the course, and it is also built into the assignment description for both major multimodal projects. In the project assignment overviews, students are asked to review the self-assessment questions in a specific chapter of their textbook as a guide for framing their reflections. These reflections are given significant weight in the rubric used to assess both projects. After completing both projects and reflecting on how the process impacted their learning, students are asked to revisit their reflections, re-reading for patterns and themes to synthesize the meaning of their learning. All of the reflections throughout the course are archived in a digital portfolio, through Digication (an electronic portfolio system), and through the curation of this digital portfolio, students grow a practice of reflection to support their learning and their writing by collecting and referencing artifacts such as drafts, written feedback, and dialogue with peers, writing fellows, and faculty.

This digital portfolio assignment is aligned with both assessment scholarship (see Hamp-Lyons and Condon; Huot; White) in the field of rhetoric and composition and best practices put forth by the Conference on College Composition and Communication. This research supports our decision to place reflection at the center of our curriculum and assessment approach, which engages students in reflecting *toward* the learning outcomes of the course, addressing authentic audiences in a digital space, and designing and organizing artifacts and reflections digitally by honing their knowledge of both genre conventions and diverse media. To support their reflective practices, in addition to archiving their writing process artifacts and engaging in structured (and required) reflection assignments, students must also make claims about their learning, substantiating those claims with evidence from discussion board dialogues, peer-to-peer feedback, writing fellow interactions, readings, invention work, drafts, and even from writing composed outside of the class in professional, personal, and civic arenas. We also ask students to engage with one another's reflections throughout the course, teaching them to listen to their peers, prior to submitting their final drafts. This is a method for bringing into focus what Yancey calls "the social life of reflection" and serves as a way for us as writing teachers to witness students "enact the curriculum" by "bridging process and practice" ("The Social" 191–92). The digital portfolios are then submitted at the end of the semester with "reflection as their centerpiece" ("Reflection and Electronic" 5).

To support students in sustaining a cumulative reflective practice through the course-long digital portfolio assignment, we also designed weekly reflection assignments with specific guiding questions generated from the week's course material. In the assignment guidelines, we highlight the connection between the *WPA Outcomes Statement* and the eight habits of mind stated in the *Framework for Success in Postsecondary Writing* by asking students to reflect each week on how one of the eight habits of mind is fostered through specific learning experiences and composing practices highlighted in the *WPA Outcomes Statement*.[2] For instance, an early guideline focused on the habit of curiosity as students were completing invention work and choosing their subject for their first writing project. To aid in their understanding that writers and researchers pursue opportunities that engage their curiosity, we asked students to consider how curiosity impacted their choice of interview subject for a profile piece. Mandy, a Starbucks employee who is returning to college after a 17-year hiatus, reflects on how curiosity factored into her invention work and helped her sustain her research throughout the project as follows:

> My first project was fueled by my curiosity. I genuinely wanted to know the story of my subject, and it helped drive the brainstorming process. . . . As I conducted the interview, my curiosity led me to dig deeper into researching some of the history of the time through the New York Times historical database—where many questions were answered, and even more arose.

Our courses also include a great deal of collaboration with others on discussion boards and through peer review activities; therefore, in one weekly prompt, we ask students to consider how they were open to new ideas and perspectives, engaged with their peer and their peers' topics, and persisted in their writing practices after these interactions. Many students enter our courses with little to no experience infusing collaboration into their composing practices. In their reflections, students discuss the challenges of participating in online discussions and working with peers remotely. Ryan, a returning college student with a 15-year career in information systems management who is studying global logistics, reflects on how responsibility factored into his collaboration with classmates as follows:

---

2. The *Framework for Success in Postsecondary Writing* states, "Because this Framework is concerned primarily with foundations for college-level, credit-bearing writing courses, it is based on outcomes included in the CWPA Outcomes Statement for First-Year Composition" (Council, *Framework* 2–3).

> Concretely this week I took responsibility to try to make the
> team activity happen as a Google Hangout online. It was [a]
> difficult experience. I initially tried to arrange a time through
> a quick survey of possible times, but during that process I re-
> ceived feedback that I was not considering enough time slots.
> . . . So I returned and created another survey dividing the re-
> maining days into chunks, and then used the top two time slots
> to have additional votes on a particular time. At that point I felt
> good about the process . . . but only one person showed. We
> continued with the assignment and I tried again, though for the
> second meeting it was only the original two people plus one
> additional. I probably should have started the process earlier. I
> did have to incorporate ideas from others in the rescheduling.
> . . . A more responsible approach overall would have been to
> 1) Start the process of planning much sooner, 2) Talk up front
> about general preferences and 3) work to accommodate those
> with particular difficulties joining something at a similar time
> to others. While I took responsibility, I did not take responsibil-
> ity in a responsible way, really I was just reacting to the fact that
> no one else had stepped up.

Thus, these reflections suggest that by intentionally offering students opportunities to make connections between the habits of mind, the WPA outcomes,
and the specific activities they perform in the course, students develop an understanding of themselves as active participants in their own learning. These multiple avenues for engaging in reflective activity habituate students to metacognition
as a core habit of mind for synthesizing learning.

Growing a Practice of Reflection

To further explore the theoretical underpinnings we describe earlier in this chapter, we will also discuss examples from student portfolios in relation to Yancey's
three modes of reflective practice previously discussed: reflection-in-action, constructive reflection, and reflection in presentation (*Reflection* 200). Specifically,
we have found that peers play a central role in enabling students to practice reflection-in-action, as engaging in collaborative, social writing practices such as
peer review emphasizes the centrality of review, reconceptualization, and revision. The constructive reflection students engage in "between and among composing events" (Yancey, *Reflection* 200) enables students to document their learning
in such a way as to explore their relationship to their own learning and their own
identity as writers. Finally, we discuss the way multimodal projects support reflection-in-presentation, such that students are encouraged to reflect on how they
adapt their inquiry to multiple contexts and multiple audiences.

First, we sequence activities so students can construct an active reflective practice throughout the course by promoting the importance of peer-supported learning in the writing and reflecting process. As we mentioned earlier, students interact with peers in a number of ways: through discussion board assignments in which they are required both to post and respond to peers, in writing team activities in English 101 in which students collectively discuss and offer feedback on rhetorical decisions they have made for each major project, and, of course, through peer review. These activities allow opportunities for students to engage in "reflection-in-action, the process of reviewing and projecting and revising, which takes place in a composing event" (Yancey, *Reflection* 200)—that is, reflection "as an accompaniment to any given text (and all of its instantiations)" (Yancey, "The Social" 189–90). Through these interactions, students not only receive feedback on their work but also respond to that feedback. Peers propose alternative perspectives to fellow writers to enable those writers to achieve some metacognitive distance from their own patterns of thinking that influence their rhetorical decisions.

In her portfolio reflections, Jennifer, a business sustainability student, emphasizes how important peer review was for her learning in the course. Jennifer is a returning student with a previous degree in art; she also owns her own sewing business. In Jennifer's reflections, she consistently foregrounds the way in which collaborating with others on her writing enabled her to engage in reflection-in-action through the multiple opportunities for receiving feedback, reviewing her work, and revising. Early in English 101, before engaging in the peer review process, students are asked to reflect on past experiences with peer review and discuss any concerns or apprehensions they might have. In response to this activity, Jennifer writes,

> I think that sometimes when receiving feedback on work that you've invested a considerable amount of time, heart, and possibly tears in, it's hard at first to open your mind to receive the feedback. Peer feedback is so essential because it's a fresh perspective, a new way of thinking. I think that it will be challenging at first to be open in receiving feedback, to look at my piece through the eyes of someone else. I am just going to keep in mind that the benefit of receiving this feedback and applying/considering the ideas of my peers will lead me to create a richer piece of work. I may be able to approach certain topics in ways I hadn't thought of. I was going to the Art Institute the last time I was reviewed by my peers. We were having a portfolio review in my fashion illustration class. I remember feeling very guarded about the feedback I received. The importance of peer review was not explained to me then. I just took it as criticism, instead of ideas as to how I could make my work better. Looking back I

wish I would have understood that it takes a team of people to produce meaningful work.

Jennifer's initial reflection on the peer review process reveals an emerging understanding of the value of collaboration for students to re-imagine their writing and ultimately to support students in crafting more "meaningful" works. Especially compelling is her discussion of her portfolio review in a previous institution. Jennifer notes that because she did not fully understand the importance of peer review, she did not fully benefit from the process—she was not open to it as an opportunity for learning and growth. As Taczak, Robertson, and Yancey suggest in their piece in this volume, both prior knowledge and experience, as well as the development of a strong conceptual framework, play important roles in students' ability to develop writing knowledge and practice. Simply providing opportunities to collaborate with peers is not enough. More than merely offering moments for collaboration, faculty should design and sequence activities that scaffold students' learning *toward* robust collaboration, enabling students to develop an understanding of the concept or strategy, then to put into practice the concept or strategy, and finally to reflect on the experience with others.

After participating in these structured peer review activities, Jennifer reflected by comparing her experiences from the past with her experiences in the present, explaining how she enacted the habit of mind of openness to imagine the possibility that her experience with peer review in the present, in our course, did not have to be determined by her experiences in the past, and this re-imagining was significant to her growth as a writer:

> Being open to other's [sic] feedback and perspectives is an area I feel I have grown in. I dealt well with ambiguity by recognizing that I obviously do not have all the answers. After receiving my peer's feedback I would generally read the notes then let the comments simmer in my head for the rest of the day. It was necessary for me to step back from my work and read it objectively. . . . My writing would have stayed stagnant, with little to no progression, had I not opened up my mind and been transparent about my writing style.

Moreover, her reflection indicates an awareness of both the difficulty and value of attaining some distance from her own ways of thinking, both about and within her own writing. Ultimately, in discussing how she engaged with the collaborative and social aspects of the writing process in the course, Jennifer concludes, "Without the feedback from others it would have been difficult to see my piece objectively and revise appropriately. The changes I made directly correlate to my collaborations, without them my writing would not have progressed." She clearly perceives the growth—the "progression" in her writing—that has occurred as a result of "reflection-in-action" through collaborative writing opportunities within the course.

Cathy, a Spanish literature student and self-described "second-time college student, returning after a 30-year hiatus," also emphasizes the value of collaboration for generating moments of reflection-in-action. In her reflections, she discusses how collaborating with peers enabled her to reconsider the rhetorical choices she made in a multimodal composition piece:

> I was appreciative of the extra set of eyes on my paper, and always approached their peer reviews with an open mind. . . . Of course, there were times that I experimented with suggestions and chose to disregard them because of what I felt were valid reasons. I learned that, in the end, it is my responsibility for the quality of the paper. However, I always appreciated the opportunity to really examine every suggestion and choose my own path of action.

Like Jennifer, Cathy emphasizes the importance of remaining open to peer feedback. In responding to questions and comments from peers, this openness enabled her to "experiment" with alternative ideas. Her reflection enables us to glimpse a moment of reflection-in-action, as she contemplates and reconceptualizes her reasoning for her rhetorical decisions. She was able to view her work with fresh eyes, which she asserts was instrumental in improving the design of her project. In a later reflection, Cathy remarks on the valuable lessons learned in the class from participating in peer review: "Peer review has probably been the most beneficial aspect of this entire class. I understand now why so much time is dedicated to this process, and I'm sure the lessons of peer review will serve me in every writing assignment I encounter throughout my time at ASU." Cathy notes that these lessons will help her in subsequent writing assignments. She recognizes the value her peers' suggestions had on her project as well as the larger value of peer review as a practice. Ultimately, these examples suggest the significance of "reflection-in-action" to students' growth and development as writers.

Second, the course-long digital portfolio assignment asks students to construct reflections regularly as they complete a variety of assignments and participate in various peer-to-peer and peer-to-teacher interactions. This ongoing reflection is designed to scaffold students' learning toward constructing a sustainable, reflective practice. Like the reflections they craft at the end of each major project, these more systematic reflections are also housed in their digital portfolio, but the purpose of these smaller, reflective assignments is to afford students an opportunity to approximate what Yancey refers to as "constructive reflection, the process of developing a cumulative, multi-selved, multi-voiced identity, which takes place between and among composing events" ("The Social" 189). That is, we emphasize to students that the digital portfolio is *cumulative*; it is not simply an assignment to be compiled at the end of the semester or at the end of a more substantial written project. By requiring students to engage in an ongoing reflective process, we aim to habituate them to employing metacognitive practices they can transfer to other learning and composing situations beyond our classes.

Student digital portfolios speak to students' awareness of the value of cumulative reflection for developing these metacognitive skills. For instance, Jennifer discusses her perception of the impact this reflective process had on her development as a writer in more general terms: "I view the result as an academic capsule of my time in English 101. If the portfolio was not a requirement I would not have reflected on my writing to the extent that I have and probably would not have progressed by learning from my opportunities as a writer." Her reflection indicates a clear understanding of the value of constructive reflection in enabling her to archive her learning such that she can review, reconsider, and build on her learning beyond our course.

Cathy also offers a specific illustration of how reflecting on an ongoing basis throughout the course enabled her to document changes in her attitude about the writing process, specifically peer review:

> After re-reading about my previous experience with and impression of peer review, I can clearly see that I have changed dramatically in this aspect over the course of the semester. I stated that peer review was the most difficult aspect of English 101 that I had experienced up to that point. I no longer feel that way. In the beginning, I was very uncomfortable offering advice to other students. After all, I am in English 101, too! I am by no means an expert, and disliked being put in a position of judgment. As I grew to understand that my role as a peer reviewer was to offer to the writer my perspective as only a reader and not an expert writer, I began to feel much more relaxed with this process. . . . I also grew very comfortable with receiving advice from my peers.

She notes that her feelings about giving and receiving peer feedback changed as her understanding of the process changed. Cathy became more "relaxed" with this process once she understood she could give feedback as a reader rather than as an expert. This reflection reveals the value of building a conceptual framework for students for strengthening their writing practices. In re-reading and responding to her previous reflections on the process of peer review, this student in effect witnessed her own learning and growth as a writer during the course and could articulate the shifts in her perception of herself as a student-writer.

Ryan also engages with the value of constructive reflection in his digital portfolio. He playfully yet earnestly considers the way that the reiterative, reflective nature of the course allowed him to more deliberately evaluate, reorient, and ultimately strengthen his rhetorical practices:

> Well, this is almost unbearably Meta, isn't it? A reflections piece written about reflecting on one's own thinking? But if anything, this process has been the core habit of the course. By reflecting

> on my own thinking, I have learned to also reflect on the think-
> ing of others. . . . In both major projects a significant shift in my
> focus and thinking occurred once the project had already start-
> ed. For project one the project shifted from a story of education
> to a story of racism and perseverance, and for project two the
> story shifted from one of food and diet in Egypt to one of labor
> taken for granted and feminism. Neither of these shifts would
> have occurred without the reflection that the writing process in
> the class encouraged.

The emphasis in this course on cumulative reflection allows students to construct a much more sustainable reflective practice because they begin to document and revisit previous work, beyond essay drafts, to reflect on how they can
improve in all of the literacy practices they cultivate in this course.

Ryan also reflected on using technology to document his research methods
for a project that required he interview someone for a profile piece, as follows:

> I also found that certain pieces of research caused me to reflect
> on my own thinking. Listening carefully to the first interview
> I conducted with James I realized that there were many times
> when quite unconsciously I interrupted James to steer his re-
> sponse to a question in a particular way. . . . I used this self-
> reflection to try to change my approach in the second two inter-
> views, to allow James to tell his own story.

Documenting his work in such a way enabled this student, as he notes, to
improve his practices and ultimately evaluate his "own thinking" by becoming
present to his past practices and experiences. Thus, this type of constructive
reflection allows students to record their views on writing, their understandings of their own writing processes, and their sense of identity as writers, both
witnessing and archiving their learning—these small shifts—throughout the
course.

Third, drawing from the core principle of the textbook we use, *The McGraw-
Hill Guide: Writing for College, Writing for Life* (Roen et al.), we encourage students to include evidence for their reflections from writing in all arenas of their
lives: academic, professional, civic, and personal. We also ask students to compose multimodally in such a way as to support their understanding of the need
for flexibility and creativity when communicating similar information to different audiences, in different genres, and across different media. This supports Yancey's concept of "reflection-in-presentation" (*Reflection* 200), which, we feel, has
the effect of impelling students to inquiry such that they might reflect on how
to best utilize their rhetorical knowledge in a particular writing context and for
a specific audience, thinking carefully about how those decisions impact their
multiple drafts. For instance, Mandy connects the flexibility she has developed in

the personal and professional areas of her life with the development of flexibility in her writing practices throughout the course:

> With my job and my home life I have learned to live a consistently flexible lifestyle. I have never had as much exposure to flexibility in writing before this course. Really analyzing the audience you are trying to reach and constructing a tone for your message are things I have subconsiously [sic] done personally, but never through a written work. When writing for my first project I was trying to reach a more informal audience than I was during my second project, and with my second projects [sic] multimodal paper I was trying to reach the same audience, but give them a different feel. In addition to these projects, peer reviews, emails, groupme [sic] chats, and general peer correspondence required even more flexibility with communication. I learned that what you are trying to communicate can be received in a much richer way when you tailor your delivery to a more specific audience and situation as necessary.

In effect, she is noting that the class gave her a conceptual framework for understanding and more deliberately implementing a practice she "subconsciously" engaged in. This deliberate focus on audience, Mandy states, enriched her writing.

Mandy also reflects on how the course enhanced her creativity (a habit of mind from the *Framework for Success*). She discusses how the practices she developed in multimodal composition have enhanced the composing she does in her professional life. Specifically, as part of her multimodal project, she created a Prezi:

> I started out creating a Tumblr blog, but learned about Prezi through a Blackboard discussion and was intrigued! . . . I was asked to make a quick ASU presentation at a large Starbucks operational meeting and I made another Prezi to use as a visual aid. I thought it would be more impactful to my audience to present this way because we are rapidly becoming a more tech savvy company and I wanted to show them an example of the things we are taught at ASU that can be used in our work. . . . I credit this course for the success of that presentation, it was the consideration of my audience and the exposure to communicating in multimodal formats that allowed it to resonate the way it did.

Mandy notes that her consideration of her audience in relation to the media she chooses is an important outcome of the learning she has done in the course. This, we suggest, is an example of Yancey's reflection-in-presentation, which in effect enables this student to generalize her learning in this class to other rhetorical situations.

Susan, an art history major returning to college after a 20-year hiatus, also draws from writing she does in her professional life. She reflects on the way in which she integrates her own ideas with those of others while considering the needs of her audience, as follows:

> As part of my daily job description, I collect information from different sources within our school and publish this information on our Middle School website on a page called "This Week in the Middle School." Each Friday, the Principal, Assistant Principal and I collaborate to update this page. . . . I am responsible for writing most of the announcements for the page. We have to integrate all our own ideas as well as information from different sources. It is important we create a useful page for our parents and students.

Students have also reflected on how the rhetorical choices they make in certain projects will impact their families. In the following example, Karen, a self-described full-time student, stay-at-home mom, and part-time personal chef, articulates the connection between the audience, medium, and purpose of her project and how these rhetorical decisions were directly linked to the personal rationale for making an audio recording for her children of the first Christmas she spent with her husband and his family:

> Not only was this a project for my composition course, but I also created something my children can listen to when they are older. . . . My first instinct was to create something specifically for my children to enjoy when they are in their teens. . . . I feel my rhetorical understanding of the needs of this project based on my audience was pretty solid. Strangers listening to this recording (my chosen medium) will not gain as much from the way I share my experience because I left out many details that would be redundant to my kids. However, part of knowing one's audience is understanding what they already know in addition to what they don't. . . . I tried to wear the hat of a storyteller, like my Grandpa, but following my script felt forced and too constructed. I think next time I want to tackle a project with a "story" genre and a recorded medium, I think I will construct a loose storyboard.

This student is reflecting on her learning in the classroom using language from the *WPA Outcomes Statement*, but she is also predicting—using this same language—how she might extend this learning in ways that will allow her to continue this tradition for her family in the future in a much more personal arena. All of these examples, these student voices, illustrate why the digital portfolio capstone project is vital to reaching the larger goal of enabling students to use this reflective knowledge to enhance their writing and composing in other classes and in other areas of their lives.

Transferring a Practice of Reflection

Our experience with the course suggests that students are developing habits of reflection that they can apply not only in other writing courses but also in courses across the curriculum and in their professional lives. As discussed by Taczak et al. in this collection, when a student is constructed as an agent through reflection and theory building, "they are better able to make sense of how their prior knowledge and experiences *with* writing, as well as their knowledge *about* writing, can be used to transfer successfully." But just as we ask our students to continue to generate new knowledge about writing, we too, as teacher-scholars, should continue to design, reflect on, and revise our curriculum, so we can continue to offer substantial opportunities for students to enact agency to build a practice of reflection that will transfer to these other contexts, allowing them to "deliberate about their levels of engagement, their knowledge, desires and skills, and their concerns with outcomes and expectations, to make learning choices within the structures in place"(Ryan 7). Put simply, our overarching goal is to ensure our students can use reflection as a tool for writing, reading, and learning more effectively in a variety of contexts. Further, we hope that they will take this sustainable reflective practice with them as they perform a wide range of tasks in the world—not only in the academic arena but also in the professional, civic, and personal arenas.

Greene argues that recalling literacy experiences can inspire "the reflection that may enable us to create a narrative and to start understanding imagination in our lives" (76). We assert that recalling literacy events can also ignite this type of reflection. In light of our experiences, we call on other faculty to build into their courses more opportunities for students to engage in metacognition through a reflective practice. The more students hone their reflective practices, we are convinced, the more they will understand what and how they are learning, as well as how they can apply their learning in other contexts. Like Greene, they will be able to identify patterns across these contexts while expanding their understanding of these contexts, "to imagine being something more" (86).

Works Cited

Conference on College Composition and Communication. *Principles for the Postsecondary Teaching of Writing.* Mar. 2015, https://cccc.ncte.org/cccc/resources/positions/postsecondarywriting.

Council of Writing Program Administrators. *WPA Outcomes Statement for First-Year Composition (3.0).* 17 July 2014, http://wpacouncil.org/aws/CWPA/pt/sd/news_article/243055/_PARENT/layout_details/false.

Council of Writing Program Administrators, National Council of Writing Program Administrators, and National Writing Project. *Framework for Success in Postsecondary Writing.* Jan. 2011, http://wpacouncil.org/aws/CWPA/pt/sd/news_article/242845/_PARENT/layout_details/false.

Dewey, John. *How We Think: A Restatement of the Relation of Reflective Thinking to the Educative Process.* D.C. Heath, 1933.

Digication. https://www.digication.com.

Greene, Maxine. *Releasing the Imagination: Essays on Education, the Arts, and Social Change.* Jossey-Bass Publishers, 1995.

Hamp-Lyons, Liz, and William Condon. *Assessing the Portfolio: Principles for Practice, Theory and Research.* Hampton, 2000.

Huot, Brian. *(Re)Articulating Writing Assessment for Teaching and Learning.* Utah State UP, 2002.

O'Brien, Tim. *The Things They Carried.* Broadway, 1998.

Roen, Duane, et al. *The McGraw-Hill Guide: Writing for College, Writing for Life.* 3rd ed., McGraw-Hill, 2013.

Ryan, Mary. "Introduction: Reflective and Reflexive Approaches in Higher Education: A Warrant for Lifelong Learning?" *Teaching Reflective Learning in Higher Education: A Systematic Approach Using Pedagogic Patterns,* edited by Mary Elizabeth Ryan, Springer International, 2015, pp. 3–15.

Schön, Donald A. *Educating the Reflective Practitioner: Toward a New Design for Teaching and Learning in the Professions.* Jossey-Bass, 1991.

Sullivan, Patrick. *A New Writing Classroom: Listening, Motivation, and Habits of Mind.* Utah State UP, 2014.

Taczak, Kara, et al. (this collection). "A Framework for Transfer: Students' Development of a 'Theory of Writing.'"

Vygotsky, Lev S. *Mind in Society: The Development of Higher Psychological Processes.* Edited by Michael Cole et al., Harvard UP, 1978.

Wardle, Elizabeth. "Creative Repurposing for Expansive Learning: Considering 'Problem-Exploring' and 'Answer-Getting' Dispositions in Individuals and Fields." *Composition Forum,* vol. 26, 2013, http://compositionforum.com/issue/26/creative-repurposing.php.

White, Edward M. "The Scoring of Writing Portfolios: Phase 2." *College Composition and Communication,* vol. 56, no. 6, 2004, pp. 581–600.

Yancey, Kathleen Blake. "Reflection and Electronic Portfolios: Inventing the Self and Reinventing the University." *Electronic Portfolios 2.0: Emergent Research on Implementation and Impact,* edited by Darren Cambridge et al., Stylus, 2009, pp. 5–16.

———. *Reflection in the Writing Classroom.* Utah State UP, 1998.

———. "The Social Life of Reflection: Notes Toward an ePortfolio-Based Model of Reflection." *Teaching Reflective Learning in Higher Education: A Systematic Approach Using Pedagogic Patterns,* edited by Mary Elizabeth Ryan, Springer International, 2015, pp. 189–202.

Yancey, Kathleen Blake, et al. *Writing Across Contexts: Transfer, Composition, and Sites of Writing.* Utah State UP, 2014.

Questions for Discussion and Reflection After Chapter 8

1. The pedagogy described in Chapter 8 rests on Kathleen Blake Yancey's premise that reflection and opportunities for metacognition should be an integral part of course design, not an occasional, tacked-on course component ("The Social" 189). What do you see as the distinguishing characteristics of reflection that is "designed into" curriculum? How might you rethink your FYC course to design reflection into its curriculum?

2. Chapter 8 shares stories of students who have intertwined their FYC learning with workplace writing tasks in meaningful ways. How can your FYC course connect with students' professional and workplace contexts outside of school when those contexts vary widely?

Writing Activity After Chapter 8

Think of a current or former student whose FYC work you know well. For each of the eight habits of mind discussed in the *Framework* (curiosity, openness, engagement, creativity, persistence, responsibility, flexibility, metacognition), write one sentence about the degree to which this student did or didn't engage with the habit of mind (see *Framework* 4–5 for examples of how writers can engage with each habit). Write a few sentences about how you can use this student's example to talk with other students about engaging with the habits of mind.

Next, repeat this process by thinking about your own work in the current term or a recent term in which you taught FYC. Write about the degree to which you engaged with each habit of mind and the results of this engagement.

Further Reading

Driscoll, Dana Lynn, and Jennifer Wells. "Beyond Knowledge and Skills: Writing Transfer and the Role of Student Dispositions." *Composition Forum*, vol. 26, 2012, http://compositionforum.com/issue/26/beyond-knowledge-skills.php.

Kastner, Stacy. "Introducing the Composition Student to the Writer He or She Already Is." *The CEA Forum*, vol. 39, no. 1, 2010, pp. 24–33.

Lindenman, Heather, et al. "Revision and Reflection: A Study of (Dis)Connections Between Writing Knowledge and Writing Practice." *College Composition and Communication*, vol. 69, no. 4, 2018, pp. 581–611.

Chapter 9. A Framework for Transfer: Students' Development of a "Theory of Writing"

Kara Taczak
UNIVERSITY OF DENVER

Liane Robertson
WILLIAM PATERSON UNIVERSITY OF NEW JERSEY

Kathleen Blake Yancey
FLORIDA STATE UNIVERSITY

Reflect Before Reading

Before reading this chapter, consider your FYC course and these questions: What is your present understanding of transfer and its relevance for your work as a teacher of FYC? What activities and assignments do you include that you believe will help students write successfully in different contexts, academic and otherwise? How do you determine what knowledge and understandings about writing your FYC students have at the start of the course?

~ ~ ~

"Writing, in general, is when a person composes some sort of coherent text, on paper and/or physically copying it down, that express thoughts and ideas that are to be shared with some sort of audience. . . . "

—Margaret, first year writing student

Transfer of knowledge about and practice in writing continues to prompt discussion in the field of composition studies, as we explore how the goal of assisting students with the transfer of writing knowledge and practice might be most effectively realized. Defined basically as the repurposing of knowledge and practice from one writing context to another, "transfer" here most often refers to the writing knowledge and practice students bring with them into new contexts and the ways that they repurpose both for new writing tasks. However, while this is a useful, quick definition, transfer, as both scholars and instructors can attest, is much more complex, as is the research focusing on it. Moreover, because transfer occurs in context, it's difficult to achieve generalizability in transfer research, though writing studies scholars are trying—as we demonstrate here.

If transfer is an important goal of writing courses, then we would be wise to consider the research on transfer demonstrating that teaching for transfer is possible: research has documented how a curriculum designed to foster transfer can be successful in helping students repurpose what they learn in such a classroom for new contexts (see Beaufort; Wardle; Yancey et al.).[1] More specifically, if one goal of first-year writing courses and programs is to help students take up the knowledge and practices they learn in writing courses and transfer them to writing situations within and outside of college, we should look both at the content taught within the first-year writing classroom and at related factors influencing student learning in that classroom.

We know from such research on prior knowledge and its effect on college writers that students bring into college a range of knowledge, beliefs, attitudes, practices, dispositions, experiences, and values about writing (see Driscoll and Wells; Reiff and Bawarshi; Robertson et al.). Cultivated over years of writing in and out of school, students' prior knowledge and experiences with writing, positive and negative, have shaped these writers as they enter college. Likewise, we know from transfer research that such prior knowledge can both help and hinder students as they attempt to transfer what they know into first-year composition (FYC) and other collegiate writing situations (see Yancey et al.). Another factor accounting for students' writing experience in college is an absence of prior knowledge (see Robertson et al.), which can include students' limited conceptual schemas they might use to frame new writing situations. Developing such a framework is one goal of our curricular design for transfer, which we call Teaching for Transfer (TFT), which includes three interlocking features: key terms, systematic reflective activity (including readings, activities, and assignments), and a culminating "Theory of Writing" project in which students articulate their understanding of writing. In other words, in the TFT curriculum, students are asked to develop a theoretical approach to writing by drawing on both prior and new knowledge and practices. In addition, in developing writing knowledge and practice, students find the Theory of Writing instrumental; in combining cognitive and reflective practices, the Theory of Writing assignment, and the activities leading up to it, relies on the type of mindful abstraction[2] necessary for transfer. Students who engaged successfully in developing their Theory of Writing were

---

1. For more on the various positions and perspectives about transfer in writing studies, see *Writing Across Contexts: Transfer, Composition, and Sites of Writing*, especially Chapter Two (Yancey et al.).

2. As stated by Daniel Perkins and Gavriel Salomon, mindful abstraction encourages high road transfer and occurs when the learner is able to *abstract* information from one context of learning and *mindfully* searches for connections in another context (7).

able to see themselves differently as writers—as writers who adapted to writing situations by calling upon the conceptual framework of writing knowledge and practices they understood as appropriate in that situation and which they knew they could utilize regardless of whether or not the situation was new.

In our discussion of the Teaching for Transfer curricular model throughout this chapter, we focus in particular on the Theory of Writing, a curricular feature that has helped our research subjects—both previously and currently—transition from understanding writing as a universal practice to understanding writing as a contextualized practice keyed to each situation. Through detailing the experiences of three participants, two first-year students from a private liberal arts university in the West and one first-year student from a public university in the Northeast, as they enter FYC, complete the Teaching for Transfer curriculum, and write in other classes, we illustrate how students' development of the Theory of Writing helps them both frame new writing situations and compose in them.[3] To do this, we begin with a brief overview of the Teaching for Transfer curriculum and a background of the study to help contextualize the Theory of Writing assignment and its effects.

The TFT Curriculum: A Set of Key Terms, a Reflective Framework, and a Theory of Writing

The Teaching for Transfer curriculum reported in *Writing Across Contexts: Transfer, Composition, and Sites of Writing* (Yancey et al.) has now been used on multiple campuses, two of which we focus on here.[4] As identified earlier, the TFT model includes three integrated features: (1) a set of key terms for writing concepts, (2) an intentional reflective framework that is both systematic and reiterative, and (3) students' development of a Theory of Writing as a recursive, cognitive, and reflective assignment. The culminating Theory of Writing assignment requires students, after a quarter- or semester-long reflective process of several iterations, to define their writing knowledge and practice as developed in the TFT course, its ultimate aim being to support students in creating a conceptual frame for bridging the writing in FYC and the writing in other sites. As an assignment, the Theory of Writing engages students in a set of practices tapping into both their prior and emerging writing knowledge as they continue generating an understanding of their own writing practices. The specific attention to reflection in the TFT model, especially the Theory of Writing assignment, often changes the way students understand composing, in part because they are asked to take up their knowledge and practices in new situations within the course.

---

3. There are two institutions involved in this research, one public and one private; our findings are not school-specific, an important observation given the school's differing populations.

4. For more on the TFT curricular model as adapted to new contexts, see http://writingacrosscontexts.blogspot.com/.

Since the field's turn toward process over product more than 30 years ago, writing classes have focused on process as a kind of content, one that the research suggests is necessary but insufficient on its own to help students transfer. In the TFT curriculum, by way of contrast, students engage in an intentional reflective framework asking them, concurrently, to *think*—consider, reflect, theorize, mentally map—and *act*—compose, revise, edit—to address a writing task, as opposed to thinking and acting separately. More specifically, students are asked to *recall, reframe,* and *relocate*. As detailed in what follows, students begin the course by *recalling* their prior knowledge and experiences they bring into FYC, which provides a conceptual foundation. Next, in different reflective activities and assignments, students are asked to *reframe* their prior knowledge and experience to meet the writing situation presented by each assignment in the course. In asking students to reframe a writing situation based on both prior knowledge and experience and current knowledge and experience, we want students to put the two in conversation with one another in order to build their conceptual foundation. Lastly, writers can then *relocate* the knowledge and practices gained from the current writing situation to other writing situations; in other words, they can see opportunities to use what they now know. Learning acquired and articulated through the reflective activities and assignments helps students not only read across assignments, but also read across subjects, genres, and process(es). In sum, this reflective sequence—*recall, reframe,* and *relocate*—has students theorizing about both their past and current knowledge and practices in meaningful ways that promote transfer.[5]

Students develop their Theory of Writing in response to scaffolded prompts encouraging them to forward their thinking about and understanding of writing. The Theory of Writing, for which they mindfully abstract their own knowledge about writing, helps students develop as writers and as agents of their own learning (see Yancey, *Reflection*). With that agency, they are better able to make sense of how their prior knowledge and experiences *with* writing, as well as their knowledge *about* writing, can be used to transfer successfully. As we outline in what follows, the Theory of Writing becomes the framework students utilize to transfer writing knowledge and practice into concurrent writing situations and forward into future writing contexts.

The Theory of Writing can be particularly advantageous in helping students overcome barriers to progress in writing that might be created by the prior knowledge they bring to college (see Cleary; Driscoll and Wells; Reiff and Bawarshi; Yancey et al.). Given that writing involves both theory and practice, we can assume that knowledge about writing goes beyond what is involved in just the "doing" of writing to include thinking about writing conceptually, a point made

---

5. See also Taczak's threshold concept, "Reflection is Critical in the Development of Writers," in Linda Adler-Kassner and Elizabeth Wardle's edited collection *Naming What We Know*.

in signature pedagogies, an educational reform effort emphasizing the idea that helping students *think like*—for example, like a chemist, a sociologist, or in this case, a writer—is fundamental to helping students develop into that identity (see Gurung et al.). Moreover, addressing writing more specifically, Linda Adler-Kassner and Elizabeth Wardle argue that "writing is a subject of study and an activity" (15), and it is this idea of writing as both knowledge and practice—concept and process—that the TFT curricular model, and the Theory of Writing assignment specifically, aims to help students understand. The conceptual knowledge *about* and practice *in* writing, using their conceptual model (Theory of Writing), helps students *think like* the writers they are becoming in FYC and the writers they need to be in the contexts beyond it.

Background of the Study

For the purposes of this chapter, we provide participant excerpts from interviews and writing samples from two IRB-approved research studies conducted at two different sites.[6] The first is a private, selective doctoral degree-granting institution in the West classified as a "research university with high research activity" with 11,500 students, 5,000 of whom are undergraduates. The university encourages an interdisciplinary approach to intellectual work and supports students' majoring in more than one area, and the first-year writing courses (a two-quarter sequence is required of all students) are housed in an independent, award-winning writing program. The second institution is an Hispanic-serving, public comprehensive suburban university in the Northeast, with an undergraduate enrollment of approximately 10,000 and a graduate enrollment of approximately 1,500 students, who are largely of working class background and are mostly first-generation students. This institution features a wide range of majors, has a high transfer-in rate from local community colleges, and features a writing program with a one-semester course requirement in composition.

For the purpose of this chapter, we base our observations on the experiences of three students from these two institutions, focusing primarily on interviews and on Theory of Writing assignments. The participants were interviewed as they moved from first-year composition to new writing contexts, specifically other college courses in various disciplines in which writing was required. Like the earlier students we studied, the participants discussed in this chapter also

---

6. As we continue to conduct research featuring the TFT curriculum, we constantly re-evaluate to consider potential adaptations given different institutions, different student populations, and different writing program goals; we also refine the model based on our past findings. As noted previously, our initial study (described in detail in *Writing Across Contexts*) included several findings that centered on students' prior knowledge, and from these findings we aim to tap into students' prior knowledge as they learn in our TFT-model FYC course.

demonstrated—through their Theory of Writing assignments—an uptake of key terms, which they use in framing an approach to new writing contexts.

The Theory of Writing: A Reiterative Sequence of Moves

In order to promote students' Theory of Writing, reflective activities and assignments are built around the four major course assignments, which means that at any given moment students are reflecting on one or more of the key terms, the course readings, and the major writing assignments. Because the Theory of Writing is developed and re-developed through a series of reflective activities and assignments, students are able to articulate what they've learned about writing and about themselves as writers, as well as identify where they can repurpose this learning. The Theory of Writing assignment thus provides a space for students *to make sense of* their writing—the knowledge and practice—in ways they have not been asked to do before.

During the first week of the TFT course, for example, students are asked to complete a reflective assignment asking them to explore their prior understanding and attitudes about writing, ways they define writing, and ways they identify as writers. The purpose of this first reflection is two-fold: (1) to have students articulate their understanding of what writing is and (2) to have students articulate their sense of their own writing. In response to this reflective assignment, for example, Margaret, a participant from the private institution in the West, defines writing capaciously:

> Writing, in general, is when a person composes some sort of coherent text, on paper and/or physically copying it down, that express thoughts and ideas that are to be shared with some sort of audience. . . . How good or bad writing is [is] based on the opinion of the reader; personally any writing that has the ability to hold me captive simply from the voice and language used is good to me. I see myself as a pretty good writer that has enough knowledge to write in several genres but I am by no means an expert in any of them. My key terms are Voice, Effective, Thoughts, Opinions, Interesting, Language, and Syntax.

Margaret's understanding of writing is fairly sophisticated for a first-year college writer. She understands writing as a material practice, and she theorizes writing as more than mere authorial "express[ion]," instead asserting that writing is to be "shared" with an audience and that the "opinion of the reader" will speak to writing's quality. Margaret herself identifies as a reader, commenting that "any writing . . . has the ability to hold me captive simply from the voice and language," and she also identifies herself as "a pretty good writer . . . but . . . by no means an expert." As important, in outlining her sense of writing and herself as a writer, Margaret uses the vocabulary of writing: "writer," "audience," and "genre." Among our participants, Margaret's response indicates an understanding about writing, and a vocabulary for writing, that is unusual for first-year students so early in the TFT course. At the same time, as Margaret herself asserts, she is a novice, someone who is not an expert. As Nancy Sommers and Laura Saltz argue, students who accept their status as novices have a greater opportunity to learn how to write as college composers, and as we will see, Margaret's acceptance of herself as a novice helps her as she develops her knowledge about and her Theory of Writing.

A second reflective activity involves the introduction of some new key terms: students read both theoretical texts on key terms (such as Lloyd Bitzer's "The Rhetorical Situation" and Kerry Dirk's "Navigating Genres") and texts that exemplify the key terms (such as the way audience is invoked in Martin Luther King, Jr.'s "Letter from a Birmingham Jail"). Their next step is theorizing for themselves through reflecting on the key terms, which allows them to begin developing a Theory of Writing. More specifically, students are asked to compose a reflective essay that organizes their response into three areas: a discussion of the key terms they value at this point in the course, a discussion of how they identify as a writer at this point, and a very brief statement of their emerging individual Theory of Writing. This reflection is designed to be reiterative and intentional, as students build on and return to the previous week's reflection.

The reflective framework of the TFT course creates a recursive process by which students begin to theorize about writing, often in ways they haven't experienced before, and which encourages thinking about their approach to writing every time they start to write. In the early iterations of the reflective assignments in the course, however, student reflections are more reporting than theorizing, as Scott, our participant from a public institution in the Northeast, demonstrates. In responding to instructions to (1) discuss what you value about writing—your writing, writing that you read, or just writing in general and (2) identify the key terms about writing you think are important for writers to understand, Scott indicates no awareness of the course key terms (only two—genre and audience—have been discussed at this point) and articulates a limited understanding of research writing, based principally on high school courses:

> My key terms are editing, layering, and evidence. My writing is better when there is evidence to explain what I'm writing about, and when I can use layering to add more information that might be important to tell. These both make my writing more full and factual. And then editing, because writing and editing go hand in hand to make any writing better you have to edit it a few times. Another of my terms is persistence. I have to be persistent to make sure the other terms are happening.

Scott's focus here includes attention to qualities of writing and to a strategy of layering that he finds helpful. Better writing, Scott says, includes evidence because it "explain[s] what I'm writing about," and the strategy of layering—"to add more information that might be important to tell"—can help provide more information; combined, evidence and layering make the writing "more full and factual," qualities that Scott values. Likewise, "better" writing is edited writing, Scott believes. Not least, creating such writing—informed, evidential, and edited—requires persistence on Scott's part. These terms, based on Scott's prior composing experiences, don't match the course key terms, of course, but rather articulate Scott's understanding of writing, which is located in specific qualities, in one strategy for achieving them, and in a required behavioral pattern.

As the term moves forward, students in the TFT course develop more sophisticated reflection about aspects of their writing, moving from relying heavily on prior knowledge to integrating both earlier and new knowledge developed in the course. Again, Scott's example illustrates his thinking about his own writing during a later iteration of the Theory of Writing assignment. In the sixth week of the 15-week semester, Scott was asked to look back at his previous iterations of his Theory of Writing to consider what he thought he knew about writing on those previous occasions and what he thinks he knows currently:

> I think my key terms are changing because I looked back at my [previous reflection outlined earlier] and I don't know why I used all those. Those things are important but I don't know if they are key terms for me. I think maybe evidence is key if you're always doing research I guess. But now I think my terms are audience, purpose, and genre. And I guess perseverance is still a good one. But audience, purpose and genre work together, because you need the genre that fits your audience and the purpose and all of them need each other to work right. As a writer I need to have those things figured out so my writing will do its job. So my Theory of Writing now is more about knowing who your audience is and what genre they need from you, if you're the writer, and why you are writing to them or what need are you filling? These are the things you have to know as a writer. . . . I can still edit or whatever, but fixing my mistakes doesn't matter really if my audience gets the wrong kind of writing from me.

Here, Scott identifies the three key terms of "audience," "purpose," and "genre" as "things figured out so my writing will do its job." Writing, he says, is more than composing an argument, although "maybe evidence is key if you're always doing research." But writing for Scott is now more than research, less tied to the genre of argument: it's "more about knowing who your audience is and what genre they need from you, if you're the writer, and why you are writing to them or what need are you filling." As important, just as he revised his sense of writing to expand beyond argument, Scott also revises his view of editing so that the writing itself comes first: "I can still edit or whatever, but fixing my mistakes doesn't matter really if my audience gets the wrong kind of writing from me."

Final Theory of Writing: Students' Framework for Transfer

While students' Theory of Writing continually evolves throughout the entire course, it culminates in the course's final major assignment: a Theory of Writing that is also a reflection-in-presentation (see Yancey, *Reflection*) students develop by reflecting on the entire semester, in which they *recall, reframe,* and *relocate* key terms as a means of writing themselves into other writing situations (Taczak 78). The reflection-in-presentation assignment specifically asks students to identify the key terms they believe are most important to writing in order to theorize as to why they chose these key terms and to use the key terms in explaining how they understand writing. The reflection-in-presentation assignment asks that students consider the following:[7]

1. Define your Theory of Writing.
2. What was your Theory of Writing coming into this course? How has your Theory of Writing evolved with each piece of writing?
3. How have you already used your Theory of Writing in this course and/or other writing contexts?
4. How might your Theory of Writing transfer to other writing situations, both inside the classroom and outside the classroom?

Asking students to articulate their final iteration of Theory of Writing (in the course) engages them in thinking about the ways in which they make knowledge about writing, the ways in which they practice writing, and the ways in which writing impacts who they are as writers. As Yancey's work has also shown, reflective practices like the culminating reflection-in-presentation, and the reflective activities leading to it, allow students to make assessments about their writing, help them make sense of their writing practices, and over a period of time, support them in becoming a writer who "invents, repeatedly and recursively, a composing self" (Yancey, *Reflection* 168, 187, 200).

Margaret's final Theory of Writing shows us what a culminating Theory of Writing looks like: here it continues to emphasize the role of genre and audience, but the key expression of rhetorical situation anchors a more complex understanding:

> So what makes writing good? Writing is much more than forming sentences using the grammatical and punctual structures we were taught as children, it's more than just the use of language to communicate an idea or thought. My Theory of Writing is that

---

7. The final Theory of Writing assignment—the reflection-in-presentation—involves several class periods, reading of a chapter on transfer from *How People Learn* (Bransford et al.) and an excerpt from Yancey's *Reflection in the Writing Classroom*, and a good deal of process work involving drafting, self-analysis, peer review, and revision.

writing is an action; the act of reflecting in the past and looking
into the future in order to strategically respond to a rhetorical
situation. It is a process of transferring knowledge and creating
new ideas in response to the situation. Writing should meet basic requirements, such as being grammatically correct as well
as fit into a specific genre in which the author intrigues and influences the audience through their language, tone, and use of
facts and opinion.

Like Scott, Margaret is interested in quality, in "what makes writing good," her
view that it's "more than forming sentences using the grammatical and punctual
structures we were taught as children, [and] it's more than just the use of language
to communicate an idea or thought." What that "more" is, Margaret identifies, is
writing as action. Unintentionally echoing Kenneth Burke, Margaret defines writing as "an action" and observes that it requires a kind of reflection: "the act of
reflecting in the past and looking into the future in order to strategically respond
to a rhetorical situation." In doing this, Margaret says, a writer can both transfer
"knowledge and creat[e] new ideas in response to the situation." The situation, in
other words, becomes the governing key concept in Margaret's theory. In sum, in
her Theory of Writing, Margaret demonstrates development of her writing knowledge through her theorizing and using the key terms to create a conceptual frame.

Theory (Reflect) and Practice (Reflect); Repeat

In order for students to develop their Theory of Writing so that it functions as a
frame for facilitating transfer, the theory needs to be conceptual and practical.
Practice is based on the understanding that the students are developing as writers, and the theory informs their practice. Therefore, as noted previously, the TFT
curricular model engages students in reading both theoretical pieces about the
key rhetorical concepts and examples of key terms in action. These readings—
which focus on and exemplify the TFT model's key writing concepts—are an-
alyzed in class instruction and discussion, then reflected upon through writing
about the conceptual content and about what students think about that content.
This curricular model works best when students are constantly engaging in directed, intentional reflection throughout the process, which prompts them to begin to make connections across what they are learning and what they are actually
doing. A guiding assumption for this work is that students are novices who, like
the participants Sommers and Saltz studied, can write their way *into* expertise rather than *from* a position of expertise. Alena, another student from the private university in the West, illustrates this by writing her way into expertise in her science
classes. In this section, then, we provide an analysis of Alena's experience over the
span of a year, first as she began the TFT writing course and then as she moved
into organic chemistry courses.

Alena's first reflection in the TFT course theorizes about writing as focused on organization as a strategy, which her key terms suggest:

> Writing is a form of communication. But I believe that it is a way to turn actual thoughts into a more organized form of communication. Sometimes I feel that communication is incomplete of your own thought process. A lot of times it is so hard to form words to what you are processing in your mind. But the best way to organize and present your thoughts is usually writing. . . . This all depends on what I have to write and how it is related to me. These are the key terms . . . flow, convincing, organized, detailed, emotionally engaging, complete, personal, and a presented counter-argument.

Alena here identifies writing with organization, a word (and its roots) repeated three times in this short passage: organization is her grounding concept. She also associates writing with a means of expression because without it, it can be "hard to form words to what you are processing in your mind." Writing is also personal for Alena in another way: central to her writing is "how it is related to me." And her list of eight key terms, in its juxtapositional listing of values (e.g., "detailed") and strategies or textual chunks (e.g., "counter-argument") characterizes a somewhat disjointed conception of writing.

In her first interview of the research study, conducted midway through the term, she responds to a prompt asking what she believes is good writing: "[I believe that good writing is] putting down your thoughts in words in order to communicate with someone or persuade them. . . . [An author] I think that puts a lot of outside things into her books like knowledge and really connects things well [with an audience] is Jodi Picoult." Later in the same interview, she responds to whether or not, based on her definition of good writing, she is herself a good writer: "I think it depends on what I'm writing because if it's something that I don't have a lot of knowledge about or I don't want to write about it then I'm not going to put enough effort in, but if it's something I want to write about or know a lot about, I do better." Alena's initial understanding about writing and herself as a writer is connected to authorship: to Picoult as a best-selling author that Alena admires for her writing, and to herself as the author of her own writing. When discussing her writing, Alena qualifies the context in which she is writing as having a lot to do with how "good" her writing will be, or how much effort she puts in, and although she doesn't use the term "context," Alena does recognize that there are different situations for writing. In discussing her example of Picoult, however, Alena says that a writer should connect with an audience, even if she says so in the context of discussing a commercially successful author. At the point of this interview, the term "audience" had been discussed in the TFT course, so it's possible that Alena is mirroring that discussion in her interview or suggesting it because she thinks it is the "correct" response. But Alena also recognizes that writers in general must consider the impact of their writing on those for whom it is intended, and she indicates a belief that, for her, "expert" writing is based on whether or not there is effort behind it and whether or not she has knowledge about the subject. Alena also has an analytical approach to writing, attempting to partition writing into various objectives and connections, even if she doesn't articulate more specifically what those objectives or connections are.

As Alena continued in the course and as the research study progressed, she reported that at the beginning of the course she was uncertain of what she was learning and was resistant to approaching writing in new ways, especially since she had been successful in her previous academic writing emphasizing research, personal writing, and cultural analysis. She expressed a discomfort, in particular, with the idea of a Theory of Writing: "while I was in class I freaked out about some of the writing assignments because it was the first time I ever had to approach writing in that way [by theorizing about it]. Now I looked back on it . . . it just seems like a different way to write now that I have been exposed to it." Because students are asked to theorize in ways that are unfamiliar to them, they do tend to "freak out" or resist. Theorizing about writing often seems counterintuitive to them: writing is something they are used to doing, but not something they are used to thinking about, at least in the ways required in the TFT course. The reiterative reflective framework of the TFT model, however, requiring that students revisit both writing practices and writing knowledge, can help reduce such resistance. In her final reflection-in-presentation/Theory of Writing drawing on her understanding of key terms, Alena continues to emphasize analysis, but now includes it inside the rhetorical situation:

> I am a very analytical writer. This has developed my theory and also allows for me to have identity as a writer. All writing starts with a rhetorical situation. When writing I always like to establish a good knowledge base by using my own ideas, but also looking at other ideas and sources that can contribute to my writing. In doing so, I can also find a way to set up my paper and organize all of the thoughts that I would like to include. . . . I would have thought that writing in English and writing up a chemistry lab report were two completely different things. Now that I have established who I am as a writer and also how to write I know that I can apply my writing methods to all pieces. I will always identify with being analytical and know how to apply that across all subjects and ways of writing.

Alena hasn't abandoned the idea of organization, which she values in writing, but she uses that previous thinking within the context of new knowledge about rhetorical situation, which she also values: "all writing starts with a rhetorical situation." Here she also articulates that writing is not only about the writer expressing oneself, but also about the elements of the rhetorical situation a writer must consider, which expands her earlier, less sophisticated position that writers like Picoult are successful because they connect with an audience or that good writing is related to effort. She sees the rhetorical situation as foundational to writing across contexts—as she indicates by registering her surprise at the similarities between writing for English and writing for chemistry when viewed through the lens of rhetorical situation. Likewise, in this developing Theory of Writing, she indicates a growing acceptance of theorizing, which she initially resisted. Finally, she indicates a level of expertise (see Bransford et al.; Robertson et al.; Sommers and Saltz) when she identifies patterns across different writing situations in discussing the analysis required in English class and in chemistry lab reports. She concludes that her Theory of Writing centers on "address[ing] a rhetorical situation in an organized manner and specific genre through logos, pathos, and ethos to achieve my purpose of writing."

As Alena explains in her exit survey ten weeks after the completion of the TFT course, the most important thing she learned in the TFT course is her Theory of Writing:

> I think the Theory of Writing . . . because I understand why I'm writing and how to do it. But it also helps me with something like my lab reports because it helps me set up the purpose and once you get to the higher levels [in science classes] it's hard to always understand what's expected or what goes into . . . so for example what's expected in organizing chemistry lab reports. But after learning the key terms and identifying and understanding them, I can fit those to the writing pieces in [both] biology and chemistry. And even apply my theory . . . I can develop and understand my writing in many situations.

Moreover, as she explains in an interview one year later, she puts her theory into practice in writing her lab reports for Organic Chemistry:

> For lab reports, it's kind of habitual now. I usually focus on . . . the introduction, and what I need to tell the reader, and then the materials and the methods is a quick summary, and for the discussion, which is the bulk of it, I usually look over sources and the prior knowledge that I have on it. So, I look at the purpose, first, then the information being able to pull as sources are something important for me, and then answering the question. I always think, too, about my audience.

She explains that it was learning the key terms (from the TFT course) and developing her Theory of Writing that enabled her to understand how to successfully write her lab reports, explaining, "I think with lab reports [the Theory of Writing] helps me because it helps me to direct my writing more. . . . I know why I'm writing and I also have the resources to give me the information that's needed to answer the question and I know I have to have it make sense for the audience. . . ." Later in the interview, she stated that the Theory of Writing "made me be able to focus why I'm writing and how I'm writing better and also give me a reason to write instead of just kind of blabbing on about stuff." Alena thus suggests, through her interview a year after taking the TFT course, that she relies on her Theory of Writing, specifically for her Organic Chemistry lab reports, to help her understand *how* to approach the assignment: *I also have the resources to give me the information that's needed to answer the question and I know I have to have it make sense for the audience.* She notes that this understanding began with the first reflective assignment, which made her stop and re-evaluate her prior experiences with writing: "it wasn't like an aha moment like I get it now, but it was a moment where I began to understand that writing could be done in a different way because I had never been asked to do a writing like that." In sum, after beginning FYC by "freak[ing]out," Alena found out that the TFT course, specifically the culminating Theory of Writing assignment, helped her develop her writing knowledge and practices for purposes of transfer.

The framework students develop in the Theory of Writing assignment—with its reiterative quality and its requirement that they think about *why* they are writing, not just *what* and *how* they are writing—continues to evolve as they grow as writers and learners. Often in new contexts during the TFT course and after completing it, when the required assignments of the Theory of Writing are finalized, students, including the participants in this study, find themselves continuing to theorize and learn on their own when encountering new writing contexts. They use their Theory of Writing as the conceptual frame to analyze new situations and plan approaches to them, not merely applying what they know to a given situation, but re-envisioning the situation within the frame of their Theory of Writing, as we see in Scott's account:

> Now I always think about my Theory of Writing, of what is going to be important for every assignment I have to write. Everyone reads it in class and they just look for the minimum pages we have to have or the kind of essay it says, like if it's a research essay or whatever. But I read the assignment and think about it as a mixture of my audience, even if it's just the professor for this, the genre I need to use, the context that the writing happens in, and the purpose, which is the easy part. The purpose is usually right there in the instructions, because the professor tells you what you're writing for. But I think about it anyway because what if there's more to it than just the professor telling you what to write and why. Or who you write it for. It should be bigger than that. Ever since [the TFT] class I use my Theory of Writing everywhere. I had to do this artist statement and that was hard for everyone but I just thought of my Theory of Writ-

> ing and put all those parts together to figure out what to write.
> I mean I had to work on it a lot but the bones of it were always
> there because I knew about my audience and purpose and the
> genre a little bit. It made it easier for sure.

Scott demonstrates in this excerpt that he has developed an approach to writing in context based on his Theory of Writing. He understands that his Theory of Writing is a framework guiding an approach, depending on the context for which he is writing. He thinks about the audience for the assignment in analyzing what the assignment requires, but he thinks beyond the requirements of the assignment since "It should be bigger than that." To accomplish this, he analyzes the writing needs of a situation to identify genre, audience, context, and purpose. In doing so, he demonstrates a strong use of a conceptual frame for approaching writing in new contexts.

Conclusion: Reaction into Action

Students' initial reactions to creating a Theory of Writing, those of students in general and of the three participants here, are what we might imagine, and they take two forms. In one, students are simply surprised that there could be such a thing as a Theory of Writing, especially given that they have not previously encountered any explicit theory about writing. In the second, students believe that they cannot create such a theory, in part because they don't yet understand how to theorize about writing, and in part because they sense that they don't qualify as writers who can create a Theory of Writing. However, by the conclusion of the course, many students in the TFT course can both create a Theory of Writing and put it into action, to varying degrees, as demonstrated by our participants. Through understanding writing as a process of moving from a reaction to a considered action, students can shift from relying *only* on their previous underdeveloped approaches to writing to drawing on prior and new knowledge and practices in a conceptual, intentional, and recursive process, one that we outline here in steps but that in practice tends to be recursive, which offers several benefits. First, using their Theory of Writing as a frame for taking up each new composing task, students interpret the situation based on their prior and new knowledge and practices, drawing on what they know or have experienced to identify the writing situation they're in and what might be similar to other situations. Second, students assess the situation, also drawing on what they know to determine what is required or called for in this writing situation and what they might have experienced that is like it. Third, students consider how they might approach the situation by drawing upon their Theory of Writing to develop a "solution" to the problem the writing situation is presenting. And fourth, they *repurpose* their Theory of Writing successfully to the new context by extracting the knowledge and practices they know are appropriate for the situation, based on the identification, assessment, and consideration of the previous three moves, and *repurpose* them to compose the written artifact most appropriate for the situation. These moves are recursive in nature. Through recursive reflection, and by repurposing the conceptual framework they have developed, writers can continue to develop or adapt as they meet each new writing situation.

More than 20 years ago, Ann Berthoff argued that "in reflecting, we can change, we can transform, we can envisage" (751); our intent is that through the Teaching for Transfer curricular model, students "change . . . transform . . . [and] envisage" their writing knowledge and practice through the creation of their Theory of Writing. Our participants Margaret, Scott, and Alena show us how they did, in fact, change and transform in their practice as writers and in envisioning their future as writers. The Theory of Writing provides students with the intellectual space to do exactly that, as Margaret explains:

> The reason I signed up for this class was basically to meet my credit requirements, maintain a good GPA. . . . I had no expectations to learn anything new about writing, I just assumed that we would read some articles and write a few papers to show the university that we were proficient in college level writing. I was wrong. We learned more about good writing this quarter than I learned in my entire high school career. . . . My Theory of Writing can be applied to other writing situations because I have to use all of its components in any writing process I go through. I must think about the rhetorical situation I am responding to, the genre I am writing in, what information I want to include, and the language I use whether I am composing a paper for another class, texting a friend, or writing an email to a future employer.

In sum, the TFT curriculum's Theory of Writing provides students with a conceptual frame that assists them as they develop as writers and as they adapt their knowledge and practice to the writing situations in their future.

Works Cited

Adler-Kassner, Linda, and Elizabeth Wardle, editors. *Naming What We Know: Threshold Concepts in Writing Studies.* Utah State UP, 2015.

Beaufort, Anne. *College Writing and Beyond: A New Framework for University Writing Instruction.* Utah State UP, 2007.

Berthoff, Ann E. "Is Teaching Still Possible? Writing, Meaning, and Higher Order Reasoning." *College English,* vol. 46, no. 8, 1984, pp. 743–55.

Bitzer, Lloyd. "The Rhetorical Situation." *Philosophy and Rhetoric,* vol. 1, 1968, pp. 1–14.

Bransford, John D., et al., editors. *How People Learn: Brain, Mind, Experience, and School.* Expanded ed., National Academies Press, 2000.

Burke, Kenneth. *Language as Symbolic Action: Essays on Life, Literature, and Method.* U of California P, 1968.

Cleary, Michelle Navarre. "Flowing and Freestyling: Learning from Adult Students About Process Knowledge Transfer." *College Composition and Communication,* vol. 64, no. 4, 2013, pp. 661–87.

Dirk, Kerry. "Navigating Genres." *Writing Spaces,* vol. 1, 2010, pp. 249–62, http://writingspaces.org/sites/default/files/dirk--navigating-genres.pdf.

Driscoll, Dana Lynn, and Jennifer Wells. "Beyond Knowledge and Skills: Writing Transfer and the Role of Student Dispositions." *Composition Forum,* vol. 26, 2012, http://compositionforum.com/issue/26/beyond-knowledge-skills.php.

Gurung, Regan A. R., et al., editors. *Exploring Signature Pedagogies: Approaches to Teaching Disciplinary Habits of Mind.* Stylus, 2008.

King, Martin Luther, Jr. *Letter from a Birmingham Jail.* American Friends Service Committee, 1963.

Perkins, Daniel, and Gavriel Salomon. "Transfer of Learning." *International Encyclopedia of Education,* 2nd ed., Pergamon, 1992, pp. 2–13.

Reiff, Mary Jo, and Anis Bawarshi. "Tracing Discursive Resources: How Students Use Prior Genre Knowledge to Negotiate New Writing Contexts in First-Year Composition." *Written Communication,* vol. 28, no. 3, 2011, pp. 312–37.

Robertson, Liane, et al. "Notes Toward a Theory of Prior Knowledge and its Role in College Composers' Transfer of Knowledge and Practice." *Composition Forum,* vol. 26, 2012, http://compositionforum.com/issue/26/prior-knowledge-transfer.php.

Sommers, Nancy, and Laura Saltz. "The Novice as Expert: Writing the Freshman Year." *College Composition and Communication,* vol. 56, 2004, pp. 124–49.

Taczak, Kara. "Reflection is Critical in the Development of Writers." *Naming What We Know: Threshold Concepts in Writing Studies,* edited by Linda Adler-Kassner and Elizabeth Wardle, Utah State UP, 2015, pp. 78–83.

Wardle, Elizabeth. "Understanding 'Transfer' from FYC: Preliminary Results of a Longitudinal Study." *WPA: Writing Program Administration,* vol. 31, no. 1–2, 2007, pp. 65–85.

Yancey, Kathleen Blake. *Reflection in the Writing Classroom.* Utah State UP, 1998.

———. *Writing Across Contexts.* Blogspot, 2015, http://writingacrosscontexts.blogspot.com/.

Yancey, Kathleen Blake, et al. *Writing Across Contexts: Transfer, Composition, and Sites of Writing.* Utah State UP, 2014.

Questions for Reflection and Discussion After Chapter 9

1. The authors contend that the theory of writing that students create enables them to see themselves differently as writers and, as a result, they are better able to adapt their writing for different situations and contexts. What assignments are you currently using in your FYC course that work to help students re-see themselves as writers? Or what assignments might you use to allow students to see themselves differently as writers?

2. Kara, Liane, and Kathleen note that FYC courses should accommodate writing both as an activity and as an object of study. Identify a text that you could use in your FYC course to promote students' understanding of some aspect of writing. What would students learn from reading this text? How might this learning be of benefit to them?

Writing Activity After Chapter 9

Create your own theory of writing and explain how you might use your theory of writing in your FYC course. For example, what learning might result from sharing your theory of writing with your FYC students? In what ways could your theory of writing inform your pedagogy?

Further Reading

National Research Council. *How People Learn: Brain, Mind, Experience, and School.* National Academy Press, 2000.

Taczak, Kara, and Liane Robertson. "Reiterative Reflection in the Twenty-First Century Writing Classroom: An Integrated Approach to Teaching for Transfer." *A Rhetoric of Reflection*, edited by Kathleen Blake Yancey, Utah State UP, 2016, pp. 42–63.

Yancey, Kathleen Blake, et al. "Writing Across College: Key Terms and Multiple Contexts as Factors Promoting Students' Transfer of Writing Knowledge and Practice." *The WAC Journal*, Fall 2018, pp. 44–66.

Chapter 10. A Transition

Ashley M. Ritter
West Chester University

Reflect Before Reading

What do you know about your FYC students' experiences with writing in elementary and secondary school? Have you ever noticed that your students' previous writing experiences and what they "understand" about writing interfere with what you are attempting to teach them about writing? What assignments, if any, do you have your students complete that help them understand writing (and themselves as writers) differently?

~ ~ ~

Every morning, right around 8:15 a.m., I walk briskly along a long, curved stone path to a pair of tall, large glass doors on a 210,000-square-foot building where approximately 1,500 people scurry about from conference room to conference room, coffee corner to coffee corner, and printing station to printing station. Following suit, I too make like the busy worker bee that I am and head to my second-floor cubicle space in one of several global Human Resources departments of the world's largest inter-enterprise software company.

Currently, I work as an HR Business Partner (HRBP) associate, supporting numerous senior-level HR Business Partners in the North American region of my company responsible for the various corporate functions of the organization. To succeed in this position, I have to have a solid knowledge foundation for many concepts, especially workplace motivation, employee engagement, leader-member exchange, team member exchange, change management, and executive coaching—all of which I've come to grasp as a result of my current work on a master's degree in Industrial-Organizational Psychology (IOP). A real mouthful of a title, right?

Chances are, you've probably never heard of this field. Furthermore, I bet you're wondering how one ultimately ends up in this area of psychology. For me, it's not too long or mysterious of a story. Intrigued by the intricacies and oddities of the people I encountered over the course of my first eighteen years on this spinning playground we call Earth, I decided to attend a mid-sized public university in the middle of western Pennsylvania to receive my bachelor's degree in psychology. As a psychology major, I was introduced to dozens of appealing topics on the science of human behavior; however, only one made sense to pursue in terms of real world applicability. In other words, there was only one branch of

DOI: https://doi.org/10.37514/PRA-B.2020.0308.2.10

psychology where I could apply the concepts I learned and eventually pay off my ever-increasing student debt.

As an HRBP associate and Master's I/O student, I spend a fairly significant portion of my time researching, debating, and discussing ideas related to performance appraisal, leadership development, job descriptions, training programs, statistical analyses, organizational development, and so on. But the majority of my time is allocated to writing. Whether it's a long email to a manager, a midterm exam, an executive summary, a presentation, a blog, or a term paper, I find myself fully engaged in writing on all of the topics mentioned earlier on a daily basis. Thus, it seems relatively fair to conclude that the ability to write is a pertinent and imperative skill one must master in order to be a successful, highly performing individual in not only the classroom but in the workplace as well. I could say that my ability to write effectively and well so frequently came only as a result of the four years of college and year and a half I've spent so far in grad school; however, that's not really the case. In fact, I've been writing from as far back as I can remember.

It was in the second grade that I wrote my very first book. As a classroom activity, each student was instructed to author and illustrate his or her own short story so that it could be published into a small, hardback keepsake. Before beginning the assignment, our teacher welcomed us to the basics of writing: that is, every piece must have some sort of a beginning, middle, and an end—the rest was up to us. Although my story was brief and my writing skills as a second grader were not quite up to par, I was still able to write authentically and creatively. I wasn't forced to comply with narrow guidelines, and I was free to communicate my imagination in a manner that I chose, within reason.

As I continued my way through elementary and secondary schooling, those relatively simple rules of writing evolved into something more complicated and restrictive. From sixth grade language arts classes and on, almost every English-class-related writing assignment required us to use a standard writing model—otherwise known as the five-paragraph essay.

Drilled into my head year after year, the process of writing five-paragraph essays consumed not only the ways by which I conceptualized writing, but it also prohibited cultivation of any other stylistic and organizational abilities. The five-paragraph theme essentially coerced my thoughts into a set-up that didn't allow much room for creativity. In fact, the "recipe" went something like this: introduction with a catchy attention-getter and concise three-part thesis statement, followed by three body paragraphs each with a topic sentence, thesis-supporting analyses with complementary quotations, transition sentences between paragraphs, and a conclusion that summed up the main points and restated the thesis. Besides its obvious restrictive nature, the five-paragraph theme had many additional limitations. First-person pronouns and a personal tone were unacceptable. Paragraphs could include no more than eight sentences, but no fewer than five, and the number of "to be" verbs was limited. The thesis statement had to be three-pronged—no more, no less—the goal being to convey some overall point with only three "strong" points to develop, or grade points were deducted from the overall evaluation of the paper. An example of such a set-up stands out clearly in my mind.

In eleventh grade, I was enrolled in an Honors English course that focused its curriculum on reading and writing about several of the American classics. For one assignment, I remember we were told to read Arthur Miller's famous play, *The Crucible,* and write a five-paragraph theme essay to support a given prompt. Following the assumed format, I concocted a three-page, double-spaced paper detailing three specific catalysts (mass hysteria, superstition, and revenge), that sent the Salem witch trials into a downward spiral for numerous women of the small Massachusetts community. First, I started with a catchy introduction about Russia's communist regime, which then bled into the history of Salem and a clearly-defined relevant thesis statement. This was followed by three individual paragraphs identifying the aforementioned catalysts, and then a short summary decorated with a final, memorable closing sentence.

About a week or so later, I received my grading rubric that included five major measures (introduction, body paragraphs, conclusion, and mechanics/format). Underneath each heading were various additional criteria including "thesis statement (No 'to be' verbs), body paragraphs have minimum four sentences/max eight sentences each, restated thesis in conclusion, interesting clincher sentence, no more than ten 'to be' verbs in the whole paper, no fragments, no run-ons or comma splices, no first or second person, and no slang/vague language or contractions." Pretty restricting, right? Students couldn't break or bend the rules. We weren't allowed to step outside of the box and take risks. And worst of all, while seven-some-odd years were spent nailing this structure down pat, the opportunity to become familiar with other styles and ways of writing that I would need to succeed not only in college-level writing, but for my career, was never offered.

As a result of the Pennsylvania System of School Assessment (PSSA), with its emphasis on AYP (Adequate Yearly Progress) and its standardized tests of writing, teachers in the state of Pennsylvania were forced to spend a disproportionate amount of time teaching the five-paragraph theme essay to ensure high scores on the PSSA writing tests. In turn, my classmates and I rarely wrote outside of this standardized type of writing, so other kinds of writing such as poetry, autobiography, play writing, and fiction fell by the wayside.

By the time I was ready to graduate from high school, I had become a master of the five-paragraph essay. I felt comfortable—maybe a little too comfortable— that I possessed all of the skills that would be necessary from there on out as a writer because to the best of my knowledge, being a good, competent writer just meant executing that genre. If I was able to force my thoughts into a structure that matched what I had been trained to do time and time again in every English class I'd come across since the beginning of middle school, I'd be set for life.

However, as my first semester of college-level English approached, and the professor for the class, Dr. Kerr, began emailing course materials over the summer, it became evident that I was mistaken about being well-prepared for writing in college. As I glanced over the syllabus stretched out across my laptop screen and read the course description, "a study of the field of composition," I panicked. Literacy? Social constructions? Discourse communities? This course sounded nothing like all the other English courses I'd encountered throughout the years, and I was deeply concerned that the writing skills I'd possessed would be no match for the work of the upcoming semester. I felt as though the minimal exposure I had to other writing forms outside of the five-paragraph theme and my lack of authenticity as a writer would put me at a disadvantage. However, throughout the semester, these new concepts and others became much clearer and proved extremely beneficial to my overall understandings of writing and to my identity as a writer.

The assignments for this first-year composition course were different than anything I'd done previously. For the very first one, we were asked to keep a log of all the times we used writing in our daily lives over the course of a week. Not realizing just how frequently this would be, I pushed the task off to the side with little regard. But, then, as I found out, we do indeed write a lot—evidently more than we think. Whether it's text messages, emails, papers, or lists, writing is a tool we utilize every day, and we take it for granted. This was just one of many assignments that spoke to the importance of writing and its significance in countless other aspects of life. This assignment showed me that even though I'm not a novelist or any other type of writing-related professional, I am still very much a writer whether I realize it or not, and I will be using writing for the rest of my life. This notion, or conceptualization of myself as a "24 hours a day, seven days a week" writer, is what gave me the confidence to know I can write any genre that comes my way.

About midway through the semester, we began to talk about literacy. When posed the question, "What does it mean to be literate?" I immediately thought of "possessing the skill to read and write." I mean, what else could literacy possible entail? As it turned out, the concept is much more complex. Being "literate" can mean "to be able to read and write," but it can also mean to "have an understanding of." Through a "Literacy Narrative" assignment, I was able to think about and process what literacy is and what it means to me. In my narrative, I wrote about how I first became literate in reading and what that ultimately symbolized. I came to recognize that literacy represented a sense of identity in the world and, with that, a source of power. In my literacy narrative, I wrote, "I noticed that the more words I knew, the more competent I was overall. This competence gave me power and advantages over other students. I sounded more knowledgeable and mature than the others. This sense of maturity, I felt, allowed me to be taken more seriously, and with that, I felt brave and confident to try new things, and eventually land success." To me, literacy not only reflected self-efficacy and knowledge, but it allowed one to be viewed as a well-respected member of society.

In addition to literacy, we talked about discourse communities. When our discussions surrounding this concept began, I had little familiarity with the term or the meaning behind it. To introduce "discourse communities," Dr. Kerr related a brief story. Having recently taken up an interest in jewelry beading, she joined a group of women who beaded together. New to the trade, Dr. Kerr had to understand the discourse, or language, being used to communicate understandings of beading that were specific to the group. This included the different types of beads and names of techniques. This story helped me to see that I, too, am a part of numerous discourse communities. For instance, at the time, I was an employee at a local pharmacy where I was responsible for tending to patients' calls and questions, counting quantities of medications to ensure that each prescription had the right number, finding and ordering medications, and knowing where products were located within the store. Being an employee there meant being a part of the pharmacy discourse community in which I was literate in the various brand and generic names of medications and the quantity types and knew what effects various medications could have and could communicate these effects to customers. Understanding the term "discourse community" helped me understand that in order to be a fully functioning member of any group, understanding the culture, the norms, and the language (including writing) of the community is absolutely imperative to how well one functions within said community.

In reflecting on all of the assignments and related course concepts from my first-year composition course, it became apparent that the ways in which I think about writing and myself as a writer are much more important than the rules or "typical" conventions of writing.

This course showed me that writing in a single, one-track way doesn't work. As I went further in my field of study and engaged in the nitty-gritty aspects of psychological research, I realized I couldn't apply the five-paragraph theme format to the kind of writing typically engaged in by my professional community. Rather, I needed to approach writing in a completely different manner and be literate in the concepts and discourse in my field. I had to be well-versed in American Psychological Association (APA) format, which required an understanding of how to write a 250-word abstract along with the necessary components of one, how to accurately cite sources and create a reference list for a thesis paper, and how to write in a concise, scientific manner using the correct table formatting and statistical symbols, among many other skills.

An example of this style of writing, along with its respective standard formatting, can be seen from a short excerpt from my undergraduate Honors Psychology thesis that examines gender differences in negotiation/interviewing capabilities:

> In contrast, the research presents only minimal flaws. The mean age of the participants/interviewees in both phase 1 ($\bar{x} = 21.23$) and phase 2 ($\bar{x} = 24.8$) are relatively young. Thus, their perceived feelings of job interview anxiety may actually be greater than, say, a sample with a mean age of 40, due to lack of exposure to interview situations which could artificially increase their anxiety significantly. A second drawback of this study was the

gender makeup of the interviewers in phase 2. Out of the 182 interviewers, 82%, or the majority, were male. Although less than
half (39.3%) of the job applicants in the phase 2 sample were
female, a predominately male interviewer sample may affect
interview anxiety among female applicants, and thus, gender
could be a confounding variable that would need more exploring (McCarthy and Goffin, 2004).

My first-year composition course prepared me for not only a successful career in the field of psychology and human resources, but also gave me the tools
necessary for digesting ideas and writing in ways unrelated to psychology overall. For instance, in a sociology course I took during my junior year of undergraduate school, we were required to write weekly journal posts relating to the
course material we had been assigned to read. I by no means knew exactly what
went into the standard journal post, let alone a well-written one. Not to mention the fact that I had been meticulously groomed to conduct all of my writing
pieces in a manner that was consistent with psychological writing, as I had been
three years deep in the Honors Psychology program and it was all I had come
to know. But fortunately, thanks to the first-year composition class I had taken
as a freshman, I held the skills and technique necessary to transition my writing
abilities and competently execute the journal posts. Here's a brief excerpt from
one I did on the difference between referring to someone as "survivor" or "vic-
tim" of sexual assault:

> As we briefly touched on in lecture, it's definitely interesting that
> we use these two words in our language to discuss the topic of
> rape. "Victim" and "survivor" clearly have very different mean-
> ings attached to them and they most certainly have an impact
> on the way that we refer to individuals who experienced sexual
> violence. I think it means that we have to be very careful when
> it comes to which ones we choose to use in conversation and
> in general. Personally, I almost feel like I can't use either of the
> words, but, it then becomes difficult to describe someone who
> underwent such an awful and traumatic experience and I don't
> want to discredit that.

As you can see, there's really no set of strict guidelines dictating what you
can and cannot write. No penalty against using first person, speaking without
colorful word choice, or including direct quotes or numbers to support every last
statement. In truth, I was really writing about what I personally felt on the subject
and conveying my thoughts in an honest, open manner to try to dissect the ideas
put in front of me. This is a much different style of writing than what is used in
the five-paragraph theme and even psychological writing. However, because I

was fully equipped with the right tools and understanding of how to transform my writing across all situations, this style was just as easily conquered as all the others I'd mastered before.

Not only did I learn how to convert my writing as a result of this first-year composition course, I began to imagine myself as a writer in a completely new and different way. I was no longer circumscribed by a strict format that required me to write one specific way, using one specific outline, and one specific set of rules. I was able to rediscover my voice and produce the kind of authenticity I had before I was molded into a five-paragraph-theme-making machine. I was able to think about choosing and assembling writing topics, organization, and the rules of grammar in a different way. I saw writing as not only meaningful for how often we use it but for how crucial it is to my literacy and competency within the various discourse communities I'll become a part of throughout life.

More importantly, the course allowed me to gain more strength and power as a writer. I became more versatile in the different styles of writing that were thrown at me throughout college because the first-year composition course equipped me with the right tools (understanding the study of composition, literacy, discourse communities) to do so. Because of that, I feel completely confident in my abilities as a writer and a professional and believe that I will always be able to make the transition to any style of writing put in front of me.

Questions for Reflection and Discussion After Chapter 10

1. What do you know about the standardized testing that your state department of education mandates for public school students? What subjects are tested? In what grades? When during the school year does the testing take place? How are scores reported and used? Is writing proficiency assessed? How?

2. What are some means by which you can have your students articulate what they know about writing and themselves as writers at the beginning of your FYC course? How might these assignments be used to encourage students to rethink their understandings and perhaps revise them as they continue in the course?

Writing Activity After Chapter 10

Write about a time when, as a learner, you had to rethink and revise an understanding that you had. Perhaps this experience occurred when you were an undergrad or later as a graduate student. How was this opportunity to revisit and rethink an understanding presented to you? What allowed you to revise your understanding? How did you feel as you engaged in this process?

Further Reading

Kohn, Alfie. *Schooling Beyond Measure and Other Unorthodox Essays about Education*. Heinemann, 2015.

Ohanian, Susan. *One Size Fits Few: The Folly of Educational Standards*. Heinemann, 1999.

Popham, James. *The Truth About Testing: An Educator's Call to Action*. Association for Supervision and Curriculum Development, 2001.

Ravitch, Diane. *The Death and Life of the Great American School System: How Testing and Choice are Undermining Education*. 3rd ed., Basic Books, 2016.

Afterword. What's Next?
Advocating for the Value of FYC

Jo-Anne Kerr

INDIANA UNIVERSITY OF PENNSYLVANIA

Ann N. Amicucci

UNIVERSITY OF COLORADO COLORADO SPRINGS

Taken together, the ten chapters included in this collection present a portrait of first-year composition as it exists in a variety of institutions and demonstrate first-year composition courses that function as spaces in which first-year writers construct writerly identities while simultaneously developing agency as writers. It is telling that while the pedagogies shared in each chapter differ, they are all grounded in current understandings of composition that have resulted from decades of careful and thoughtful research and scholarship by individuals who asked important questions about writing and teaching because they cared about their work and about the student writers whom they served.

Early teacher-researchers devised ways to uncover and demystify what writers do when they write, ushering in a paradigm shift in composition research—from a focus on product to a focus on process. Later, having recognized the shortcomings of early research studies using experimental design, researchers honed methodologies and turned to naturalistic research techniques to accommodate what had begun to become clear—that writing is both a cognitive and social endeavor—and one that is richly complex and not easily described or understood. They also tapped into other fields, including cultural anthropology, linguistics, and psychology, to augment their work. Ultimately, among other things, this scholarship encouraged a re-visioning of FYC, its function as a "service" course, and its role in the academy.

In retrospect, we can see these early composition theorists and researchers as advocates for the importance and value of writing—in its many forms and genres. Today, as we note in the introduction to this volume, it is more imperative than ever to advocate for FYC. With that in mind, we invite you (graduate students, teachers, teacher-scholars) to consider and identify ways to promote FYC and the work being done for and in service of students in this course.

To assist you with this task, we include here content that clearly makes the case for advocacy in light of the challenges to FYC that exist in the current climate. We follow this content with a list of prompts designed to promote thinking that can lead to advocacy. Finally, we include a brief list of specific suggestions for applying any relevant thoughts and ideas generated through engagement with the prompts.

DOI: https://doi.org/10.37514/PRA-B.2020.0308.3.2

The Need for Advocacy

Given the still-prominent public perception that FYC exists to inoculate students against writing errors (Downs 54) and the multiple opportunities available to students to skip FYC altogether (see Anson; Carter), it is not enough for FYC teachers to be FYC teachers alone. Rather, every stakeholder in FYC needs to play a part in pushing back against this public perception—in telling the story of why FYC is valuable in students' development as writers and their gaining agency in writing and of helping to advocate for the presence and resourcing of FYC courses and programs. In *The Activist WPA: Changing Stories About Writing and Writers*, Linda Adler-Kassner describes ways that writing program faculty and administrators can reframe composition's public perceptions by targeting communication at specific audiences. She writes,

> There will always be much that we want to change, of course, because there will always be people (and organizations) who de-cry students' preparations, or what's happening in classrooms, or other aspects of education that are important for us. But we can have some influence on how these discussions take place and how they are framed if we work strategically. We can think about where we have the most influence and the loudest voic-es—at our local levels. We can think about who we can reach out to, learn from, and enlist as allies. And with them, we can develop a communication plan that helps all of us shape and communicate messages about writers and writing to audiences who might just attend to those messages—and change the sto-ries that they tell. (163)

We invite you to pause on Adler-Kassner's word "influence" and to recognize that each of us, no matter whether we are new to the profession or have long been stakeholders within it, can have influence on the state of writing education broad-ly and on FYC in particular.

Taking Action

We encourage you to choose one (or more) of the following prompts to use as a catalyst for reflection and to generate some thoughts and ideas that can be used to help you choose how to advocate for FYC.

1. Identify one core belief that is essential to your FYC pedagogy. Why do you hold this belief? How might you make this core belief explicit for your students so that they better understand your course's workings and what they are asked to do as student-writers?

2. How might you encourage your FYC students to be advocates for FYC? As students, how can they help you clarify the role that FYC has in the academy and its value to FY students?
3. What is one question about FYC that you have found yourself thinking about? How might you go about attempting to answer this question? How might you share what you discover as a way to advocate for FYC?
4. Choose one chapter from this collection that is especially valuable to you as a composition teacher. Why is this chapter valuable to you? How does it (or can it) inform your pedagogy? Your advocacy?
5. In the introduction to this collection, we allude to Maxine Greene's idea of "wide-awakeness" and note that teachers committed to dialogic pedagogy must also practice this habit of mind to successfully resolve the conflict between what they are expected to teach in FYC and what they believe they should teach. Being wide-awake in the context of FYC means thinking about conditions and questioning forces that make it difficult to teach what ought to be taught. Think about the conditions of your FYC classes and identify any forces that work against your pedagogy. What are some ways to combat these forces and, in doing so, advocate for FYC best practice?

We recognize that readers may be tempted to see activist communication as the domain, or the responsibility, of administrators alone. Yet we encourage readers to consider the effects we can have in even small communicative acts in shaping how the public and our own institutions perceive FYC.

Here are some suggestions for doing so:

- At your institution: Talk with administrators about what you teach and how your FYC courses position students to be agents of their own learning and to be successful as college writers.
- In your local area: Talk with friends, neighbors, and parents of future college students about your and your institution's commitment to developing strong writers through FYC.
- In your state: Join faculty at other institutions in professional development work and broadcast this work to state legislators to emphasize the value of the education happening within FYC programs.

By considering your own orientations toward FYC and the possibilities you see for enacting change, we hope you will begin to see openings for advocating for FYC's continuation. In addition to considering the questions above, we hope you will return to the material that accompanies each chapter in this collection—Reflect Before Reading prompts, questions for discussion, and writing prompts—as well as to this collection's multimedia components, all of which may also inform and encourage your advocacy for FYC.

Works Cited

Adler-Kassner, Linda. *The Activist WPA: Changing Stories About Writing and Writers*. Utah State UP, 2008.

Anson, Chris M. "2013 CCCC Chair's Address: Climate Change." *College Composition and Communication*, vol. 65, no. 2, 2013, pp. 324–44.

Carter, Joyce Locke. "2016 CCCC Chair's Address: Making, Disrupting, Innovating." *College Composition and Communication*, vol. 68, no. 2, 2016, pp. 378–408.

Downs, Doug. "What is First-Year Composition?" *A Rhetoric for Writing Program Administrators*, edited by Rita Malenczyk, Parlor, 2013, pp. 50–63.

Greene, Maxine. "'Wide-Awakeness' and the Moral Life." *Exploring Education: An Introduction to the Foundations of Education*, edited by Alan R. Sadovnik et al., Routledge, 2018, pp. 218–24.

Contributors

Ann N. Amicucci is Assistant Professor of English and Director of First-Year Rhetoric and Writing at the University of Colorado Colorado Springs. Her recent work has appeared in *Computers & Composition* and *The CEA Forum*.

Brian D. Carpenter is Associate Professor of English at Indiana University of Pennsylvania. His articles have appeared in *Reading Research Quarterly, Linguistics and Education*, and *The History Teacher*.

Angela Clark-Oates is Assistant Professor of Composition and Rhetoric and writing program coordinator in the English department at California State University, Sacramento. Her research interests include writing program administration and faculty learning, feminist rhetorics and pedagogies, and multimodal literacy. Her scholarship has been published in the journals *Communication Design Quarterly* and *The Journal of Writing Assessment*. She has also published in the anthologies *The Framework for Success in Postsecondary Writing: Scholarship and Applications, A Fresh Approach to the Common Core State Standards in Research and Writing, Working with Faculty Writers*, and *Rhetorics of Names and Naming*.

Doug Downs is Associate Professor of Writing and Rhetoric at Montana State University, founder of its Writing major, and was Director of its Core Writing Program from 2013 to 2018. He served as Editor of *Young Scholars in Writing*, the national journal of undergraduate research in rhetoric and writing studies, from 2015 to 2020. Downs researches conceptions of writing, student reading, and writing pedagogy. With Elizabeth Wardle, he is co-author of the textbook *Writing about Writing* and a foundational 2007 *College Composition and Communication* article on Writing About Writing. He is a co-editor of *Next Steps: New Directions for / in Writing about Writing* (2019), and has published numerous chapters and articles on FYC, writing pedagogy, student reading practices, undergraduate research, and the disciplinarity of writing studies.

Howa Furrow is a part-time faculty member at Georgia Perimeter College. Her work has previously appeared in *Journal of Ethnographic & Qualitative Research*.

James Paul Gee is the Mary Lou Fulton Presidential Professor of Literacy Studies at Arizona State University. His most recent books include the 5th edition of *Sociolinguistics and Literacies, What Video Games Have to Teach Us About Learning and Literacy*, and *Situated Language and Learning*.

Jo-Anne Kerr is Professor Emerita at Indiana University of Pennsylvania, where she taught composition and English education courses. She has co-edited, with Linda Norris, *Thinking Like a Teacher: Preparing New Teachers for Today's Classrooms*.

Ashley M. Ritter is a senior Human Resources Business Partner at SAP. She holds a Master of Applied Industrial & Organizational Psychology degree and a Bachelor of Science in Psychology degree with a minor in Sociology.

Duane Roen is Professor of English at Arizona State University, where he currently serves as Dean of the College of Integrative Sciences and Arts and Vice Provost of ASU's Polytechnic campus. His most recent books include the 4th edition of *The McGraw-Hill Guide: Writing for College, Writing for Life*, co-authored with Greg Glau and Barry Maid, and *Contemporary Perspectives on Cognition and Writing*, co-edited with Patricia Portanova and Michael Rifenburg.

Liane Robertson is Associate Professor, Director of Writing Across the Curriculum, and Director of the University Core Curriculum at William Paterson University of New Jersey. She is co-author of the award-winning *Writing Across Contexts: Transfer, Composition, and Sites of Writing* (2014). Her most recent work on knowledge transfer appears in *College Composition and Communication* (2019), *The WAC Journal* (2018), *Composition, Rhetoric, and Disciplinarity* (2018), and *Understanding Writing Transfer: Implications for Transformative Student Learning in Higher Education* (2017).

Martha Wilson Schaffer is Associate Director of Composition at Case Western Reserve University, where she coordinates and teaches in the Foundational Writing Program. She has presented at the Conference on College Composition and Communication and the Feminisms and Rhetorics Conference, as well as the International Conference on Writing Analytics. Her current research projects include programmatic assessment of first-year writing learning outcomes and teaching and a study of how computer-enhanced textual analytics can help us to understand student reflective essays in electronic portfolios.

Helen Collins Sitler is Professor Emerita at Indiana University of Pennsylvania, where she taught composition and English Education courses. Her publications include "Writing Like a Good Girl," winner of the *English Journal* Edmund M. Hopkins award.

Michelle Stuckey is Writing Program Administrator for the Writers' Studio at Arizona State University, where her teaching and research focus on increasing equity, inclusion, and accessibility in post-secondary education, digital literacy, and community-based writing. Her work, co-authored with Zachary Waggoner and Ebru Erdem, appears in *Catalyst in Action: Case Studies in High Impact ePortfolio Practice*.

Kara Taczak is Teaching Associate Professor at the University of Denver, where she also directs Faculty Development and ePortfolio Initiatives. She is the current co-editor of *Composition Studies*, and her work has appeared in *College Composition and Communication*, *The WAC Journal*, *Composition Forum*, *Teaching English in a Two-Year College*, and *Across the Disciplines*. Her co-authored book, *Writing across Contexts: Writing, Transfer, and Sites of Writing* received the 2015 CCCC Research Impact Award and the 2016 CWPA Book Award.

Melissa Williamson is a writing professor at Great Bay Community College in Portsmouth, NH and University of Massachusetts, Lowell. She earned a Ph.D. in Curriculum and Instruction from Arizona State University. Her research focuses on first-year composition students' writing processes.

Kathleen Blake Yancey is Kellogg W. Hunt Professor of English and Distinguished Research Professor at Florida State University. Her most recent books include *Writing Across Contexts: Transfer, Composition, and Sites of Writing,* co-authored with Liane Robertson and Kara Taczak; *Assembling Composition,* co-edited with Stephen J. McElroy; the edited *A Rhetoric of Reflection;* and the edited *ePortfolio-as-Curriculum.*